Essays in the
History of Canadian Medicine

Essays in the
History of Canadian Medicine

edited by
Wendy Mitchinson and
Janice Dickin McGinnis

M&S

Canadian Cataloguing in Publication Data
Main entry under title:
Essays in the history of Canadian medicine

(The Canadian social history series)
Bibliography: p.
ISBN 0-7710-6063-7

1. Medicine – Canada – History. 2. Public health –
Canada – History. I. Mitchinson, Wendy. II.
McGinnis, Janice P. Dickin (Janice Patricia Dickin),
1947-   . III. Series.

R461.E87 1988   610′.971   C87-093721-9

Printed and bound in Canada

McClelland and Stewart
The Canadian Publishers
481 University Avenue
Toronto, Ontario
M5G 2E9

Contents

FOR REX AND DAVID

We would like to thank Associated Medical Services for its financial support of this project. We would also like to thank Cathy Paige and Gail Heideman for their valuable assistance.

Introduction

Social history has become an important field in Canadian history as a result of research done in the last decade or so. If at one time the history of the family, ethnic groups, women, the working class, childhood, and education were on the fringes of academic endeavour, this is no longer the case. Many of these fields even have their own journals and associations to promote them. Medical history can now be added to that list. In recent years, increasing numbers of historians have become interested in the field, and more and more theses are being written on medical topics. Both the Hannah Institute for the History of Medicine and the Social Sciences and Humanities Research Council, by providing funds for research, publications, and conferences on the history of Canadian medicine, have encouraged much of this activity. The Institute, moreover, supports chairs in the History of Medicine at several Ontario universities. Other educational institutions also have started offering courses on societal aspects of medicine, reflecting interest on the part of faculty and students alike. In addition, the field's vitality is attested to by the growth of the Canadian Society for the History of Medicine which, through the *Canadian Bulletin of Medical History* and its annual meetings at the Learned Societies, keeps its members abreast of new research. Regular conferences on the history of science, technology, and medicine in Canada have taken place and out of these has emerged *Scientia Canadensis: Journal of the History of Canadian Science, Technology and Medicine*. The essays in this volume are a reflection and outgrowth of all this activity.[1]

The new medical history which emerged has been fortunate in finding a solid foundation of research on which to base its studies. Like all professional groups, the medical profession has always taken an interest in its own development and a considerable literature has been compiled by physicians interested in researching their own antecedents. They have charted the increasing regard in which medical practice was held, the development of medical institutions, and the greater demand for and control of medical education by the profession itself. Indeed, it is these early writers who defined medical history. They brought to their study of history an orientation which emerged from medicine's classical heritage, the tradition in which they had been trained.

In the classical tradition there were two ideas concerning man's health: one, associated with the goddess Hygieia, that it could be achieved by a rational way of life; the other, personified by the god Asclepius, that it depended largely on the physician as healer of the sick. Both concepts are to be found in Hippocratic writers, and they have survived in medical thought and practice down to the present day. However, since the seventeenth century at least, the Asclepian approach has been dominant. Philosophically, it derived support from Descartes' concept of the living organism as a machine which might be taken apart and reassembled if its structure and function were understood; practically, it seemed to find confirmation in the work of Kepler and Harvey and in the success of the physical sciences in manipulating inanimate matter.[2]

Such a heritage led to an "engineering approach" to the body. The body was depicted as being invaded from without; it was the physician's responsibility to fight the invasion and the patient's to allow the physician to do so.[3] Not surprisingly, the medical historiography influenced by this tradition structured itself around the role of the individual practitioner. It also focused on the internal developments of medicine, emphasized the way in which medical discoveries were made, and, in general, stressed the scientific aspects of medicine. The tendency was to look at changes within medicine and to evaluate them by how much closer they brought us to the present state of medical practice. The historiography approved the direction medicine had taken. Until recently, historians left this approval unexplored. They were content to accept the medical profession's view of its own discipline, seeing medical history as a narrow and technical field, best left to those trained in it. Historians may have felt uncomfortable with the specialized nature of the language used in medicine and they were certainly unfamiliar with the kinds of sources available in the field. However, lack of commitment really reflected lack of interest. They did not see medical history as part of the mainstream of historical writing which, until the 1960s, emphasized political, economic, and national themes. The emergence of social history challenged that perspective.

The reason for social historians' interest in medicine is obvious. It is an area where the private and public worlds merge. Health lies at the centre of every person's life and as such is the common denominator among all people.[4] Social historians see health and efforts to maintain it through medicine as a reflection of culture. By the very nature of their discipline, they see society as an organic whole, every aspect of experience related and integral to all others. Health goes beyond the personal; it goes beyond the doctor/patient relationship. As Eliot Freidson argues in *The Profession of Medicine*, "the sick are tied up, not with other deviants to form a 'subculture' of the sick, but with a group of non-sick, his personal circle."[5] Looked at from the perspective of society in general, health also has repercussions on the economic and political systems. A people's health determines the number of workers a society can call upon and how much work can be demanded of them. As the high number of World War One recruits in poor health indicated, it even has the possibility of determining the fate of nations.[6] A study of medicine and its relationship to health opens new fields of enquiry to historians and can contribute significantly to historiographical debates which to date have taken place outside of the field of medical history. For example, in "The City of Wealth and Death: Urban Mortality in Montreal, 1821-1871," Jean-Claude Robert's argument that poor health predated industrialization and was tied not just to class but to ethnicity will illuminate the age-old discussion over the impact of industrialization. To the socio-economic variables which have dominated the debate will have to be added ethnicity in its cultural manifestations.

More importantly for our purposes, the issue of health broadens the perception of what medical history entails. Although many medical advances in therapeutics have been worthwhile, they have not been the only ingredients accounting for the relatively high standard of health current in today's industrial nations. Better nutrition and improved standards of living have saved more lives over the past two centuries than has any single medical discovery.[7] Perhaps that is the reason why many historians, such as Heather MacDougall in "Public Health and the 'Sanitary Idea' in Toronto, 1866-1890," are focusing increasingly on the development of the public health movement in this country. It was an area where the laity could become involved and it was an area which showed results. Medicine has always consisted of prevention and cure but by the nineteenth century the two aspects had become artificially separated. Prevention had become the domain of the public health officials who, although often physicians, were viewed by their peers as civil servants and by other civil servants as interlopers. Cure, the more dramatic and individualistic aspect of health care, was left in the hands of private physicians to whom accrued most of the power and prestige. In a culture which has traditionally prized individual advancement over group action, public health workers have, until recently, remained the unsung heroes of medical history.

The difference between recent medical history and that which preceded it is one of emphasis and orientation rather than of kind. New topics are added but traditional ones are not ignored. The older historiography inclined strongly to a biographical approach. The physician was central. Social historians, while acknowledging the importance of individuals, hold that the personalities of individuals are explored most usefully as vital ingredients in the process by which a society makes and carries out its decisions. Although emphasis is on the process, the biographical, political, and institutional approaches which dominated earlier medical historiography are maintained. It would be difficult to argue that Canadian health and medical policy cannot be dealt with, at least partially, within the realm of institutional history. The articles in this volume demonstrate the results of this marriage. For example, institutional history is touched on in the articles heavy with references to hospitals, asylums, clinics, and research laboratories. The realm of political history is also entered through discussions of the political manoeuvring involved in arriving at the current standards of health and medicine. But while the social history of medicine naturally builds on the historiography which preceded it, it looks at it from a different perspective. An excellent example of this is Michael Bliss's piece, "J. B. Collip: A Forgotten Member of the Insulin Team." He focuses on a very traditional topic, the discovery of a great medical achievement. However, in doing so, the traditional interpretation undergoes a metamorphosis. There was progress but it was not achieved by a genius working in isolation against the forces of adversity, nor was it accomplished according to the dictates of rational scientific research. The story was more exciting and complicated than that. Insulin was the result of team work, incorrect theories, and battling egos. This reality does not take away from the benefits and greatness of insulin but it does indicate that progress, if it comes, comes in a less than straightforward manner.

Through the tendency of social history to focus on non-elite groups, the patient has emerged as a central figure in recent research. The patient serves as the nexus between medicine and society and it is with the patient that the perception of illness originates. While patients are central figures in the dialectic of medicine, until recently they have remained faceless and passive.[8] This partially reflects the difficulty in obtaining patient records and information from the patient perspective. It also reflects the hesitancy of historians, archivists, and medical authorities to come to terms with the question of patient confidentiality.[9] Yet patients tend to be anything but passive in the history of medicine and new methods for collecting and processing historical data have allowed the patient's role to assume its rightful place in the historiography. Without the patient, a doctor cannot act, cannot intervene. It is the patient who determines if, when, and whom the doctor treats. It is the patient who determines whether he/she is healthy or not. This is important to stress, because we still do not have an adequate sense of what past society considered healthy. This may be influenced by medical expertise and by the profession's definition, but often it is the individual who decides whether to accept the patient's role or not. Once patients become the focus, the perspective of medical history shifts dramatically.

Although in most cases it is the individual who decides whether to seek out medical assistance, in others it is society which labels them sick (and therefore deviant). As a consequence, these individuals lose the right to determine their own "medical fate." This is what happened to persons perceived as a social threat, for example, those judged to be mentally ill as studied by Wendy Mitchinson in "Reasons for Committal to a Mid-Nineteenth-Century Ontario Insane Asylum: The Case of Toronto," or infected with contagious diseases, the group focused on by Janice Dickin McGinnis in her article "From Salvarsan to Penicillin: Medical Science and VD Control in Canada." Removal of choice also occurred for other groups. Feminist historians have argued that it was the success of the medical profession in defining pregnancy as a pathological state necessitating intervention that changed childbirth from a domestic occurrence attended to by laywomen to one dominated by medical professionals. In other words, the new medical treatment reflected and reinforced society's conviction that women were truly passive, even in giving life, the ultimate female prerogative. The work of these historians reveals how closely interwoven medical treatment and specific cultural attitudes are. Their conviction that medicine is not objective but rather is informed by such factors as cultural and sexual bias[10] has its counterpart in the historiography of medical treatment of the poor.[11] It is more convenient and attractive for those in control of a society to label its deviant members as "sick" and to concentrate on their "cure" than it is to disturb the organism of the society. In this spirit, prostitutes at the turn of the century were deemed feeble-minded, as were young girls who bore illegitimate children. Such anti-social acts could not be tolerated as normal and healthy in a society founded on succession of property through the male line. Social historians approach medical history with an eye to reconciling the various impressions a society has of its own well-being and therefore are not bound simply to a study of the "science" of medicine.

While recognizing the central position of patients, the social history of medicine does not ignore the role of the practitioners. One of the strongest themes in Canadian medical historiography, both old and new, has been the changing nature and status of those who practised medicine: the successful push on the part of one group of practitioners to control medicine and to become regarded as professionals. It is easy to chart this progress through the legislative process. In 1788, the first step to regulate the practice of medicine in Canada occurred in an Act to "prevent persons practising physic and surgery within the Province of Quebec or midwifery in the towns of Quebec and Montreal without a license."[12] In 1795, the Legislature of Upper Canada insisted that all physicians in the colony have a licence to practise granted by a board of surgeons licensed by the newly-created Medical Board.[13] These early laws were an attempt to protect the public from quackery, but they also reflected the desire of physicians, already present in the colony, to regulate and limit the practice of medicine to those who had achieved a specific training.

The efforts of the profession to take charge did not go unchallenged; not everyone saw monolithic control by only one type of health practitioner as desirable or even practical. In the early part of the nineteenth century, the majority of people were treated at home by members of their family using time-honoured folk medicines. Some of those rendering treatment were faith healers. Others were simply individuals who had a skill they were willing to share. Still others were trained physicians who had been refused licences or who could not be bothered to apply for one. In the middle of the nineteenth century, they were joined by the homeopaths who believed that the less medicine given, the more potent it became, and by the Thomsonians who were users of natural or botanical remedies. But, by the end of the century, most groups had to conform to the standards set by the regulars. This resulted partly from a very strong and persistent campaign on the part of the regulars but also from a general change in the perception of medical practice. From the mid- to late-nineteenth century, there was a growing acceptance of the ideal of science as an objective evaluator of what was wrong with society – in the case of medical science, of what was physically wrong with the body. Canadians increasingly were turning to experts for aid.

If science was an objective evaluator, then the need for an objective determination of a person's scientific expertise was desirable. Throughout the nineteenth century, medical education became more stringent and focused upon educational institutions rather than on apprenticeship. By the end of the century, medical training in a university was the only way in which a doctor could be trained. Thus, within a century, those practising medicine had gone from a rather eclectic group of individuals competing amongst themselves to a cohesive group with a monopoly. Members of that monopoly have tended to perceive this development as a natural evolutionary step.

It is this perception which some historians have begun to criticize.[14] By the 1960s, there was an unwillingness to accept the idea of unalloyed progress in the medical field.[15] Health-care institutions such as asylums came under attack. Members of the women's movement were particularly forthright in their criticism. They were joined by persons espousing a more holistic approach to individual health, persons who felt that the bureaucracies controlling medical care had shifted the focus away from the patient, and persons who saw amelioration of environmental abuse rather than curative treatment as the greatest hope for mass physical well-being. These interest groups sprang from a society which has become more health conscious in general, as witnessed by the fitness boom and the anti-smoking campaign. The same types of criticism were made by historians as they turned their eyes to the medical history field. This new historiographical approach began to examine the vested interests of the medical profession, especially in regard to the control of patients.

Medical historians first questioned the increasing medicalization of society which attended the growing prestige and status of regular practitioners and their monopoly over health care. They did not view the pervasiveness of medicine as simply a consequence of progress or of realization on the part of Canadians that medicine was of some value. A prime example of the type of medical subject to come under new scrutiny is the expansion of hospitals. For most of the nineteenth century, only the most destitute went to these institutions. Anyone who could afford to be was treated at home. Obviously, a physician could not have total control over a patient in the home environment. Hospitals, however, were arenas where the doctor held sway. The belief that hospitals were the proper places to care for patients was aided directly by the advance of technology and increased dependence on expensive machinery. The movement toward centralization of health care was also aided by the successive waves of epidemic disease which followed on the growth of trade and emigration during the nineteenth century. The community hoped to protect itself more effectively by providing permanent institutions with which to deal with these onslaughts. It hoped that by providing facilities where the sick could be quarantined and cared for, society would not be destabilized at each wave. The desire of physicians for increased status and their belief that better patient care extended as a natural consequence from tighter control over patients fitted neatly with the community urge to concentrate the sick away from "healthy" society. As a consequence of this combination of concerns, the clientele of hospitals expanded greatly. In the mid nineteenth century, a hospital was seen primarily as an institution for poor relief, and if by the end of the century it was often for the care of the sick poor, by the 1920s the hospital was being put forth as the only place for treatment of all people who were seriously ill. As a result, hospitals began to dominate health care and the repercussions of this for society were great.

> They are the most costly component of medical services and the one whose expenditure is most difficult to control; they are the centres of research and training and have the influence derived from these activities; and since the arrangement of buildings and plant has a powerful influence on research and practice, they largely determine the direction of medical effort.[16]

The bureaucratization of medicine on a vast scale had begun to be established.

Another aspect which seemed to upset those most critical of medicine was its interventionist nature. This was particularly true when historians focused on patients. To historians not trained in medicine, the treatment meted out to patients often appeared cruel and unnecessary. Until the mid nineteenth century, regular physicians, despite the fact that they could do little for their patients, nevertheless felt the need to do something. As a result, they purged, bled, and often gave extreme doses of medicine, all of which activities have been subsumed under the term "heroic" medicine. With the acceptance of the germ theory of disease propagation came the realization that diseases had specific causes and could be quelled only by specific methods. Only then did blatant intervention of this type become less common. The rise of surgery at the end of the century provided historians with a similar target. Ironically, this kind of interpretation belittles the very people historians seek to defend. It depicts the patient as a victim, with no say in how he/she is treated. Ignored is the fact that patients often demand the intervention being criticized.[17]

Also underlying much of early revisionist literature was a dislike of medicine in contemporary society. This was read back into the past, sometimes causing distortion. Current beliefs that the medical profession lays too little emphasis on environmental and social causes of disease and instead stresses factors of benefit to its own health and welfare have been allowed to colour perceptions of past medical experience. A more disciplined historical aproach indicates that this is not necessarily the case. Suzann Buckley's paper "The Search for the Decline of Maternal Mortality: The Place of Hospital Records," reveals that by the 1920s and 1930s, physicians concerned about the high mortality rate among childbearing women had initiated studies into the problem. These studies suggested that environmental and socio-economic factors were significant causal factors. What Buckley's study reveals is the ebb and flow of medical knowledge and information, its loss and its rediscovery.

Past criticisms of medicine have led to creative research which has illuminated the harshness of much of medical treatment from the patient's perspective and underlined the class and gender bias of medical practitioners. It has focused historians' attention on asylums, hospitals, and other health-care facilities and the reasons for their existence. However, this emphasis on control by an elite profession has never been as strong in Canada as in the United States. Perhaps this is because social control as a model was already undergoing criticism when historians finally turned their attention to the study of the Canadian field.

Ken Pryke's article, "Poor Relief and Health Care in Halifax,

1827-1849," is a good example of how social control has been integrated into the field rather than allowed to dominate it. This paper traces the attempt to establish a hospital in Halifax and acknowledges the desire of some physicians to increase their influence as a relevant factor. But Pryke also makes it clear that the medical profession was not united on this. This meshes with other recent medical historiography which has established that the medical profession was never the monolith that the social control model suggested nor did it have the power that was claimed for it. In fact, as Pryke's paper makes evident, doctors were motivated by a multitude of factors.

If the essays in this volume reflect the concerns of earlier medical historians – medical institutions, medical practitioners, the scientific nature of medicine, and great discoveries – they do so from the perspective of social history. The overwhelming emphasis is not on medicine alone but on its interaction with society. The model of social control is evident, although not in a determinist way.

To aid the reader, the essays have been grouped both chronologically and thematically. The first four essays concentrate on the nineteenth century and the last three on the twentieth century. The first introduces the reader to the general health problems of Canadians through an analysis of mortality in nineteenth-century Montreal. Whereas the next two are specific case studies of attempts to respond to those problems – in Halifax through the building of a hospital and in Toronto through the development of a public health structure – the fourth essay examines the response to a more defined issue, namely insanity. The fifth introduces the reader to the complexities of and personal conflicts engendered by medical research through a study of the insulin team. And the final two papers focus on how medical research is actually implemented or applied in the specific cases of pregnant women and patients suffering from venereal disease.

While medical history in Canada has come of age, there is still much more work to be done. Studies of health-care workers, such as nurses and paramedics, are needed, as are studies of alternative medicine. We need to know more about the general health patterns of Canadians and specific groups within the population. To date, much of the research has focused on the period 1850 to 1940. What was the situation before this time, particularly in the period of New France? Other areas, too, pose research possibilities: the legal side of medicine, the relative worth of health provisions *vis-à-vis* welfare provisions, the development and introduction of medical technology, how change occurs in medical beliefs on the part of professionals and lay people alike, and the increasing medicalization of ordinary events such as unhappiness and death. It is hoped that the essays in this volume will stimulate the reader to continue his/her own reading and research in these and other areas.

Wendy Mitchinson,
Bright, Ontario
Janice Dickin McGinnis,
Calgary, Alberta

1

The City of Wealth and Death: Urban Mortality in Montreal, 1821–1871

Jean-Claude Robert

This paper will use a case study to analyse nineteenth-century urban mortality within the framework of social history. Mortality is of dual interest to historians. As a demographic phenomenon, it throws light on one of the basic realities of a life in which social cleavages were very much apparent. It also shows how contemporaries reacted to the phenomenon: alongside those who accepted a high mortality rate as natural, there were groups of individuals who had started to reflect upon the problem. Gradually, a situation once considered natural and ineluctable became instead a focus for investigation and corrective action. In Canada, physicians were among the first ones to study mortality and out of their reflection emerged both development of medical knowledge and commitment to the political life of the society.[1]

Recent Canadian historiography on the subject of urban mortality has focused mainly on the period after 1875, showing the linkage between industrialization and declining living conditions among the working class.[2] However true this linkage is, it is important not to overestimate the quality of life in preindustrial cities. The nineteenth-century city did carry over some of the traits of the eighteenth-century experience and, as Jean-Claude Perrot wrote about public health, "industry did not innovate, it simply aggravated an age old physiological misery."[3] In that sense, industrialization, by accelerating urban overcrowding, only exacerbated all sorts of existing tensions. Cities had always been "man-eaters" and only gradually would urban mortality be brought under control. This paper will show that some salient features of mortality were already in existence before the advent of industrialization. In this respect, the Canadian city was not very different from those in other countries.[4]

This study will try to establish and analyse the components of mortality in the city of Montreal between 1821 and 1871. There are three main reasons for choosing this city. First, Montreal became during this period the most important city in British North America, its population growing from 19,000 in 1821 to 107,225 fifty years later. Second, the city experienced during those same years the process of industrialization. Third, since Montreal had a Roman Catholic majority, population records were kept with some degree of accuracy and continuity. These records are all the more important because in the field of public health this was still a pre-statistical era; it was not until the 1870s and 1880s that reliable statistical series began to be collected.

Data is the first problem to face when analysing urban mortality. In order to calculate gross rates, one has to ascertain with some precision the total population and the total number of deaths on a yearly basis. This is not always a simple operation. Sources vary fundamentally: some enumerate the inhabitants of a given place, others count the faithful of only one religion, and others analyse population characteristics based on boundaries different from the area under study. Moreover, during the period considered, registration of births, marriages, and deaths was usually not compulsory or if it was, was not generally seriously enforced.

Montreal is a good illustration of these points. Dependable statistical series for the city start only in 1875. In 1826, the provincial legislature passed an act derived from the Bills of Mortality of the United Kingdom, obliging ministers of the various religious denominations to report annually the total number of baptisms, marriages, and deaths.[5] Figures were collected in each district of the province and published yearly between 1826 and 1857.[6] Unfortunately, many ministers did not comply with the act. There are few reliable statistics with which to supplement these data. At the municipal level a regulation dating from 1845 asked that a weekly report stating cause of death, place of birth, and residence of the deceased be submitted to the chief of police by the cemetery wardens.[7] However, the regulation concerned only burials in city cemeteries. This means that people dying in the city but buried outside its limits were not taken into account. The data are also skewed by the fact that some dead from outside the city were brought into town for burial, most notably Protestants living in other parts of the island of Montreal who were customarily interred in the city's Protestant cemetery. Furthermore, according to critics in the medical journals of the time, these reports were badly filled out and the information was not always accurate. Still, it is unfortunate that these reports could not be found in the municipal archives.

We are, therefore, left with the religious reports and their use is plagued with problems. The first arises from the sheer number of religious denominations. In 1861, twenty different "religions" – ranging from the traditional Roman Catholic and Anglican churches to Methodist groups and the less conventional Church of the Order of the Countess of Huntingdon – claimed to have registers. Another problem stems from the fact that, while registers are complete for the Roman Catholics and the Anglicans, this is not so for the other denominations, thus rendering any analysis of the city's Protestants more difficult. Even the Roman Catholics, who left the best-kept records, pose problems. First there was a discrepancy between the territory of the Parish of Montreal and that of the city, the parish being larger. In 1825, Roman Catholic Montrealers accounted for only 84.4 per cent of the Roman Catholics of the Parish of Montreal and only 81.8 per cent in 1871. Second, the Roman Catholic population was not homogeneous. If, generally speaking, the statement that Roman Catholic equalled French Canadian can be made for Lower Canada as a whole, it is certainly false in the cases of Quebec City and Montreal. The impact of Irish immigration is particularly obvious in the latter. While in 1825 French Canadians accounted for 80 per cent of the Roman Catholics, the proportion fell to 62.8 per cent in 1852 and rose again to 72.5 per cent in 1871. To balance these faulty records other sources such as censuses, various summaries and abstracts, parish registers, and nineteenth-century studies have been examined. It is possible, through employment of several types of data, to use the strengths of one to offset the deficiencies of another.

During the period under consideration, there were seven official censuses: 1825, 1831, 1842, 1844, 1851–52, 1861, and 1871. In this paper, the censuses were used for the calculation of the average population of the city and for controlling some population estimates. This is not the place to evaluate each of them,[8] but it should be noted that before 1871, Canadian censuses do not have a very high reputation among scholars as far as the quality and reliability of data are concerned. Some regard the census of 1851–52 as the first "modern Canadian census."[9] For the first time all individuals were reported separately, the formulation of the questions was better and the coverage more comprehensive. Apparently the operation proceeded with greater care and benefited from transformations in transportation and communication. Further improvement came with the census of 1871 which provided greater accuracy of enumeration brought about by the organization of Joseph-Charles Taché. He implemented reforms which enhanced the reliability and coherence of the operation, in particular providing census-takers with some available information beforehand. For example, thirteen census officers were called to Ottawa to take part in the preparation of the census and to receive instructions they were later to give to other census officials and enumerators.[10] Still, some scholars regard the 1891 census as the first dependable one.[11] Certainly it demonstrates a better quality of data: its comprehensive questionnaire is a far cry from the twelve questions of 1825.[12] As for the earlier censuses (1825, 1831, 1842, and 1844), they are considered by many to be somewhat prehistoric, their value diminishing as one goes back in time. These general qualifications notwithstanding, the quality of all the censuses, particularly the earlier ones, varied from place to place. In Montreal in 1825 one zealous census-taker produced a first-rate document that stands out from the otherwise poorly taken census.[13]

Among the various summaries and abstracts used were cemetery reports. Published in abstract form from 1846 in the various medical papers they were cited by public health reformers in their articles and pamphlets.[14] Also used were accurate summaries prepared by the Abbé Cyprien Tanguay, published in Volume v of the Census of Canada for 1871. These served to establish the natural movement of the Roman Catholic population. The parish registers for Notre-Dame de Montréal proved valuable for the period 1821–46, as were the various papers of interested physicians and reformers. The earlier papers date from the 1830s with the analysis of the cholera epidemic of 1832 and with Dr. William Kelly's study on medical statistics. Later medical papers published in Montreal contain a wealth of information about public health and for the late 1850s and the 1860s, there is the well-documented analysis of Philip P. Carpenter.

Before turning to mortality in Montreal, it is necessary to put the city in context by looking at the overall natural change of population in Lower Canada. Since Cyprien Tanguay's work a century ago, scholars have variously estimated the growth of the Roman Catholic population in Lower Canada.[15] The oldest figures computed from Tanguay's data are the highest:[16] the birth rate dropped from 60.1 per thousand in 1830–40 to 47.3 in 1870–75, while the death rate fell from 30.5 per thousand to 25.1 during the same time. Fernand Ouellet in his 1966 book, *Economic and Social History of Quebec, 1760–1850*, calculated that the birth rate increased from 50.9 per thousand in 1817–21 to 52.6 in 1847–51 and that the mortality rate went from 25.5 per thousand to 23.1 during the same period.[17] In 1972, demographers Jacques Henripin and Yves Peron estimated that the birth rate was 52.5 per thousand in 1821–25, falling to 45.4 in 1871–75 whereas the death rate fell from 25.6 per thousand for the first period to 24.6 for the latter.[18] Obviously, the general trend was downward for both the natality and mortality rates. The only exception is Ouellet's natality rate but it must be remembered that it is for mid-century, not the 1870s.

Before the rates for the city of Montreal can be calculated, the difficulty created by the discrepancy between the territory of the city and that of the Parish of Montreal must be offset. Table 1 shows the growth of the population of the Parish of Montreal.

Table 1
Population of the Parish of Montreal

	Total Population	Mean Annual Growth Rate	Roman Catholic Population	% Total Population	Mean Annual Growth Rate
1822	22,095		15,909	72.0%	
1825	26,154	5.78	18,133	69.3%	4.46
1831	31,783	3.3	21,401	67.3%	2.8
1844	49,909	3.53	33,361	66.8%	3.47
1851–52	62,653	2.88	45,561	72.7%	3.97
1861	100,723	5.42	74,776	74.2%	5.66
1871	127,616	2.39	95,283	74.6%	2.45

SOURCES: Censuses; for 1822: Archives du Séminaire Saint-Sulpice de Mont-réal, dossier statistique; *Rapport de l'archiviste de la province de Québec*, correspondance de J.-J. Lartigue.

Table 2 gives an overview of the growth of some components of the population of the city of Montreal. By comparing the two, it is possible to see the rhythms of development for those components of the population.

Using figures for the Roman Catholic population of the parish

Table 2
Population Growth in Montreal

	Total Population	Mean Annual Growth Rate	Roman Catholic Population	% Total Population	Mean Annual Growth Rate	French Canadian Population	% of Roman Catholic Population	Mean Annual Growth Rate
1825	22,540	–	15,300	67.9	–	12,273	80.2	–
1831	22,297	3.24	17,953	65.8	2.7	–	–	1.97
1842	40,290	3.6	25,699	63.8	3.31	17,108	66.6	5.50
1844	44,591	5.2	29,821	66.9	7.72	19,041	63.9	3.98
1851–52	57,715	3.28	41,464	71.8	4.21	26,020	62.8	5.88
1861	90,323	5.1	65,896	73.0	5.28	43,509	66.0	2.66
1871	107,225	1.73	77,980	72.7	1.7	56,577	72.5	3.38
1825–71	–	3.45	–	–	3.6	–	–	3.38

SOURCE: Censuses.

of Montreal and the annual number of baptisms, marriages, and deaths,[19] we can calculate gross rates on a five-year basis. The results, shown in Table 3, are quite high, even given the high rates normal in nineteenth-century cities.[20]

Table 3
Roman Catholic Parish of Montreal:
Gross Rates (Natality, Nuptiality, Death)

	Natality per 1000	Nuptiality per 1000	Mortality per 1000
1822–26	59.1	10.5	43.3
1827–31	57.8	10.5	45.3
1832–36	59.7	12.1	64.6
1837–41	50.2	9.4	43.0
1842–46	68.3	13.4	52.6
1847–51	55.0	10.5	49.6
1852–56	52.2	11.4	42.4
1857–61	59.2	10.8	34.3
1862–66	60.0	9.6	39.7
1867–71	47.3	8.6	41.0

Two factors could bias these rates. The first and most important is migration. Besides immigrants settling in Montreal and influencing the rates by their peculiar age structure (mostly people in their twenties and thirties), there are those who stayed only a short while before moving on to another destination and whose experience in Montreal would be recorded only in terms of births or deaths. It is almost impossible to estimate the size of the floating population in Montreal, let alone its average stay in the city. However, we cannot doubt its existence. We have seen that from 1825 to 1871 the composition of the Roman Catholic population varied greatly. It is precisely between these dates that two migratory movements intersected in Montreal: Irish Catholics coming from overseas and French-Canadian Catholics coming from the countryside. In addition, Montreal was a point of departure for the United States. The second factor is illegitimacy. Due to its size and facilities, Montreal attracted women who were about to give birth out of wedlock. The Grey Nuns received most of the babies at their *Hôpital Général*. All were baptized into the Roman Catholic faith, thus increasing the number of Catholic births. On the other hand, the very high mortality of these babies swelled the city death rates. But even if we adjust for these factors, Montreal's rates still remain higher than those of Lower Canada.

The importance and persistence of the high mortality rate in the Parish of Montreal is striking when we look at Table 3. Over a period of half a century there is a slight downward trend but it remains slight. Graph 1, on the natural change in population, gives another view of the phenomenon. Here the mortality curve reveals peaks corresponding to epidemics: cholera in 1832 and 1834, typhus in 1847, and the return of cholera in 1854. Nonetheless, it is the high level of the ordinary mortality that is surprising. The graph clearly shows that the mortality curve follows that of natality. This situation does not seem to have attracted the attention of the authorities; they intervened only during epidemics. Physicians and reformers were the first ones to analyse the situation and the first to point out the urgent need for municipal or provincial action.[21]

In April 1834, the members of the Literary and Historical Society of Quebec listened to a paper by William Kelly, entitled "On the Medical Statistics of Lower Canada,"[22] in which the author calculated mortality rates for Montreal in the 1820s and 1830s. For the period 1826–30, he found a rate of 36.2 per thousand. For his analysis he used the censuses of 1825 and 1831 and the annual statement of returns of burials published in the journals of the assembly. As we have seen, these abstracts were incomplete because a number of Protestant registers were unreported and also because there was a significant under-registration of deaths in the Protestant community. After 1830, Kelly's figure went up: 47.6 per thousand in 1831 and 114.5 in 1832, the cholera year. Despite their approximate character, Kelly's calculations are good indicators of the level of mortality.

In July 1845, the *British American Journal of Medical and Physical Science* published a mortality table for Montreal for the period up to 1845.[23]

Rates per Thousand Population

1832	120.5	1839	45.2
1833	46.4	1840	39.1
1834	67.2	1841	47.9
1835	30.0	1842	51.4
1836	34.8	1843	47.1
1837	46.9	1844	40.4
1838	32.7		

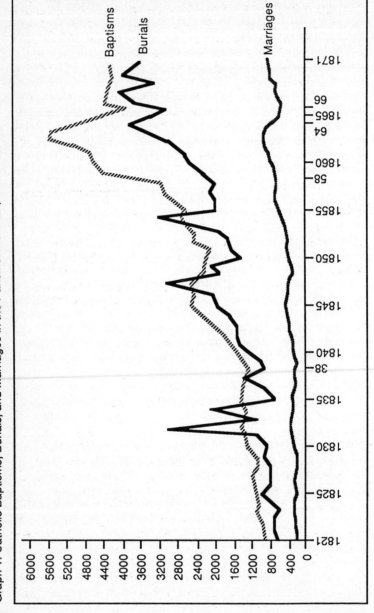

Graph 1. Catholic Baptisms, Burials, and Marriages in the Parish of Montreal, 1821 - 1871

The author stressed the relative reduction of mortality and alluded to the sanitary progress of Montreal since 1842. Here again the sources were the censuses and the annual statement of returns of burials. His calculations were more crude than Kelly's since he did not try to estimate the floating population.[24] Also, unlike Kelly's use of annual averages, he used real annual figures.

After 1845, such data could be supplanted by the reports cemetery wardens made weekly to the chief of police comprising name of the deceased, sex, age, and cause of death. However, as pointed out by the editors of the *British American Journal of Medical and Physical Science*, accuracy was reduced by the fact that the cause of death was given by relatives and friends. This was corrected by 1847.[25] Death statistics improved in quality and from that date on physicians' attention turned to the analysis of mortality. Still, no complete series of data was found and scant information exists for the late forties and early fifties. In 1846, according to Doctor A. Hall,[26] the mortality rate was 42.4 per thousand and the year after it reached 57.3 when a typhus epidemic decimated Irish immigrants.

In 1867, Philip P. Carpenter calculated with the aid of cemetery reports all rates of mortality per thousand for the period 1855–66:[27]

1855	35.2	1861	35.2
1856	32.9	1862	36.6
1857	33.3	1863	36.4
1858	32.0	1864	45.3
1859	33.7	1865	37.8
1860	36.8	1866	32.2

Two years later, in another article, Carpenter gave the rates for 1867 as 38.3 per thousand and for 1868, 39.6.[28] In 1871, the mortality rate was 37.3 per thousand. All those calculations were made on an annual basis and can be misleading. Annual variations are sometimes too great and may mask trends. This is the reason why the use of mean annual rates is preferable. In Table 4, three series of gross rates, calculated on a five-year mean, summarize the findings on mortality. The first one shows the rates for the Roman Catholic parish, the second is calculated on the basis of the data coming from the medical journals and from Carpenter, and the last is calculated from annual estimates of the population of Montreal.[29] The latter calculations were necessary because of Carpenter's high population estimates after 1861. For example, to work out his rate for 1868, he used a population estimate of 122,028 while the census of 1871 reported only 107,225. An examination of the three sets of rates shows that while there is a tendency toward the reduction of mortality, it seems to have slowed down particularly in 1862–66. This evolution can also be inferred from Graph 1. There, mortality and natality curves follow each other closely before 1850 but start to diverge thereafter.

Table 4
Gross Mortality Rates
per Thousand
Parish and City of Montreal

	Parish	City (nineteenth-century sources)	City (estimates)
1822–26	45.3	–	–
1827–31	45.3	–	–
1832–36	64.6	58.1	59.0
1837–41	43.0	42.4	43.2
1842–46	52.6	–	46.3
1847–51	49.6	–	45.7
1852–56	42.4	41.7	41.6
1857–61	34.3	34.3	34.5
1862–66	39.7	37.7	40.8
1867–71	41.0	–	–

SOURCES: Annual population estimates from the censuses; summary of deaths in *Census of Canada 1870–71*, Vol. v; W. Kelly, loc. cit.; *The British American Journal*, 15 July 1845, 110; P. P. Carpenter, various articles.

All observers who looked into the matter of population in Montreal – from Dr. Kelly, who in 1834 found the Montreal and Quebec situation abnormal,[30] to P. P. Carpenter – are unanimous in noting the very high mortality rate. Carpenter made some striking comparisons: mortality in 1851 Montreal was three times the Canadian level, higher than Boston's and comparable to that of Liverpool, which was considered the least healthy of all British cities.[31]

Analysis of this mortality shows its salient feature – the primary importance of infant mortality. This, however, was not fully recognized until public interest began to turn to this matter in the 1860s.

The relatively late date for this interest stems probably from the lack of precise statistics on mortality and from the fact that, apart from the medical community, no one seemed concerned. Even the Church, when recording the deaths or (in the case of the nuns) when taking care of the babies, never questioned the extent of this phenomenon, its possible causes, or its possible cure. It was as though for Church and public alike the high level of infant mortality was considered a natural fact, tied to the high natality.[32]

Before registration of age at death was started, only speculations could be made about the causes and features of mortality. This is what Dr. Kelly did in 1834, although he had already pointed to high infant mortality in the summer as a component of general mortality.[33] After 1845, cemetery returns show clearly the impact of infant mortality; before that date we have to use the Roman Catholic registers. To analyse the age structure of the deceased between 1821 and 1846, I have depended on an anonymous summary of all deaths in the Parish of Notre-Dame de Montréal.

Graph 2 shows clearly that high infant mortality was not a new phenomenon in Montreal. As early as 1821, 60 per cent of all Catholic deaths were children under four years of age. In 1846, the proportion was 64 per cent for the same age group. There is a remarkable stability in those twenty-five years; the two dents in the curve do not correspond to an absolute decline in infant mortality but to the cholera epidemics of 1832 and 1834. It should be pointed out that the epidemic killed mainly youths and adults, therefore changing the age structure of death for those years.[34] As for children under one year of age, the graph indicates that they represented 40 per cent of all deaths between 1821 and 1846. The inaccuracy of the data will not permit calculation of the infant mortality rate, but a rough comparison, over twenty-five years, of the average number of children under one year with the average number of births indicates that out of every four newborns in Montreal, one would die in its first year.[35]

These data are for the Roman Catholic population of the parish. After 1846, we have cemetery returns for the whole city. This same year Dr. A. Hall demonstrated that 61 per cent of all Montreal deaths were children under five and more than half of these were children under one year.[36] Fifteen years later, the situation had not changed. In a long article published in 1861 and 1862,[37] Dr. G. E. Fenwick, who tried to downplay the high mortality of Montreal, found nonetheless that 68.7 per cent of all burials in 1860 were

Graph 2. Infant Deaths in the Parish of Montreal (R.C.), 1821 - 1846

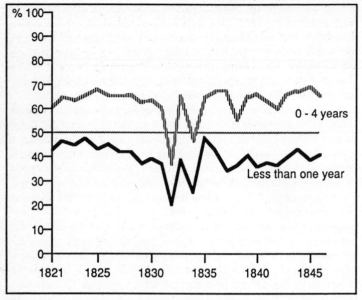

those of children under eight years of age. Unfortunately, the age breakdown used by Fenwick renders comparison difficult, especially for children under one year. However he did show that 20 per cent of all deaths were infants of less than one month old.

For 1867, the situation looks even worse. Carpenter figured out that 46.2 per cent of all deaths were children under one year and that 64.6 per cent of all deaths were children under twelve.[38] In 1868, the curé of the parish, in an annual abstract of vital statistics noted "the extraordinary mortality of the children."[39] It seems that the high level continued in 1869 and 1870 and even after. But in the seventies, the problem at least became better known. Montreal's non-medical papers allude to it,[40] as do statistical yearbooks.[41] Pamphlets were issued to give advice on child care to mothers.[42] To conclude, for fifty years infant mortality was the main reason behind the high death rates in Montreal.

Before going further, it is important to have a look at the impact of illegitimacy. The dreadful mortality among illegitimate children and the fact that illegitimate births were concentrated in Montreal, influenced the overall mortality pattern of the city. Illegitimacy was a by-product of Montreal's growth during the nineteenth century. The development of the harbour and of the transportation network combined with immigration and the presence of the garrison until the 1870s, brought to the city a large floating population. Added to that was the relative anonymity of urban life which provided an easy way to leave behind unwanted babies.

In a majority of cases, unwanted newborns were left with the Grey Nuns' *Hôpital Général*. The nuns accepted the babies without discrimination and would not ask too many questions of those who brought them in. Their only demand was that all babies must be baptized rapidly by a priest. Newborns that seemed to be in good health were sent out to country families. In case of death, the corpse was to be brought back to Montreal for burial.[43] This religious order received some provincial grants and through its annual report some information is available about the nuns' work. Unfortunately, the series is not complete.[44] In 1867, the rumour spread that more than two thousand children were dying every year in the *Hôpital*. When Montreal papers took up the matter, the Mother Superior invited the secretary of the Montreal Sanitary Association, Philip P. Carpenter,[45] to go through the *Hôpital's* registers. He brought back some interesting figures for the period 1865–69.

Table 5 shows the place of birth of the children. More than a third came from out of town. Particularly noteworthy is the importance of Quebec City. According to Carpenter, babies sometimes came by train lying wrapped up in baskets; more than a third came in carpet-bags, but most often they were brought by a carter.[46] They were generally in a pitiful state. Nearly one-half of the babies were naked and a third were sick or injured. In 1869, of a total of 668 babies received, only 16 are said to have shown signs of having received normal care. Thus it is not surprising to learn that mortality was dreadful; in early 1868, only 33 of the 652 babies received in 1867 were still alive. In 1868, 623 of the 678 babies did not live through their first month.[47] It is hard to estimate the proportion of the infant mortality that was due to illegitimacy. A certain proportion of these children belonged to the city anyway and consequently the high rate of infant mortality in Montreal cannot be explained exclusively by this phenomenon.[48] It was only one of the reasons that Montreal, as late as the mid twentieth century, had the highest infant mortality rate in North America.[49]

Table 5
Place of Birth of Newborns Left in the Care of the Grey Nuns

	1865	1866	1867	1868	1869
Montreal	443	448	413	356	385
Vicinity of Montreal	44	40	42	30	36
Saint-Hyacinthe	26	9	21	30	28
Trois-Rivières	8	6	12	19	5
Quebec	147	85	98	110	128
Ottawa	20	18	20	62	33
Upper Canada	15	11	15	26	19
United States	25	7	29	44	32
Others	1	0	2	1	2
TOTAL	729	624	652	678	668
Total from out of town	286	176	239	322	283
% of outsiders	39.2	28.2	36.6	47.5	42.3

SOURCE: P. P. Carpenter, loc. cit.

The causes of such a high level of infant mortality are not well known, apart from the fact that it is mostly the French-Canadian population that was concerned.[50] In a 1961 study on twentieth-century Montreal, demographer Jacques Henripin underlined that there remains a proportion of endogenous mortality for babies of French-Canadian origin even after social factors which can aggravate exogenous mortality have been taken into account.[51] The situation could have been the same in the nineteenth century. While it is true that French Canadians in Montreal were not all in a good socio-economic condition, they were by no means alone; Irish-Catholic Montrealers, for instance, were in a similar condition and did not show such a high rate of infant mortality. What then could have been the cause of that difference in mortality apparent as early as the first outbreak of cholera? Was it caused by different eating habits and by a particular way of life, as one group of physicians from Philadelphia thought in 1832?[52] Was it caused by a weaker physical condition?[53] There are as yet no satisfactory answers.[54]

Two other conclusions do emerge from the statistics. The first is that spatial distribution of death seems to reflect socio-economic conditions: mortality rates for the two years for which we have data (1846 and 1860) are higher for the wards outside the old city. In the

Graph 3. Seasonal Variations in Deaths, 1829 - 1831; 1855 - 1866

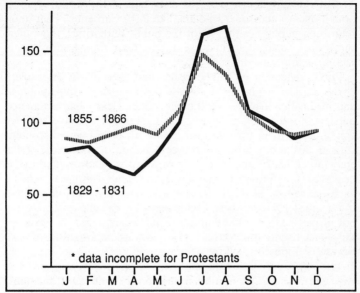

old city, where the bourgeoisie were concentrated, sanitary conditions and buildings were better. The second is the strong correlation
between time of year and death. In the nineteenth century, the
general opinion was that there were fewer deaths in winter, even
among children. Carpenter, whose descriptions became lyrical as
he evoked the perils of the springtime thaw in the backyards of the
city, underlined the fact.[55] The available sources confirm this. A
look at Graph 3 shows that mortality peaks happened in July and
August. To summarize, the salient features of the mortality of
Montreal between 1821 and 1871 were a very high level of mortality, a very high infant mortality, high mortality in the case of
illegitimacy, more death in the wards outside the old city, and peak
mortality during the summer.

During the half century between 1821 and 1871, there was a
significant change in public attitude towards mortality. It was the
beginning of a social and medical reflection that eventually led to
the idea that health is a public concern, and as such, should be
regulated. However, this awareness did not reach the authorities –

be they political or religious – until the last third of the century. Those who initiated it were, as elsewhere in the world, medical practitioners[56] and some scholars, like P. P. Carpenter, bent upon reforming public health. As for the public authorities, they intervened only during epidemics, setting up temporary health boards and providing some money.[57]

Public reflection on public health had its roots in the cholera epidemic. The origin of this disease was an issue of some political and medical controversy. Although cholera clearly had originated outside Montreal, its virulence was aggravated by local sanitary conditions.[58] It, in turn, fanned the flames of political discontent current in the city. Just a few weeks before the outbreak of the epidemic in 1832, an election riot in Montreal had resulted in the deaths of three French Canadians. Because the killing was done by garrison troops called in to restore order, the *parti patriote* claimed it was murder. Under these circumstances, when cholera came, it is not surprising to see that Papineau's party denounced the governor for his negligence and for his servility toward Montreal merchants who were opposed to all forms of quarantine.[59]

Two explanations for the outbreak of cholera were given. The *parti patriote* and, no doubt, the majority of French Canadians, felt that cholera came not just from outside the province, but specifically from Great Britain, which "vomited" thousands of immigrants.[60] This classic social conspiracy thesis that appeared almost everywhere in the world at the time,[61] had strong ethnic overtones in Lower Canada: it was not the bourgeoisie who were trying to poison the labouring classes but Great Britain trying to poison French Canadians. Even Bishop Jean-Jacques Lartigue seemed to believe it. He wrote to his cousin, on October 22, 1832:

> The other things which seem to me at the moment most worthy of your attention are: the murder of our Canadiens on 21 May, since then officially approved by the Governor; and the invasion of our uncultivated lands by British emigration which threatens to expel us from our country and decimate Canadiens regularly each year with sickness.[62]

But, for the *Montreal Gazette* and a good number of anglophone Montrealers, the cholera was of native origin and immigration was not to be blamed. In a long correspondence published in many North American medical papers,[63] Montreal physician A. F. Holmes claimed that the greater sensitivity of French Canadians to the disease was the very proof of its indigenous character.[64] A team of physicians sent by the city of Philadelphia to inquire into the Montreal epidemic in June 1832 seems to have accepted that theory at least partially.[65] Not surprisingly, proponents of the indigenous theory had difficulty explaining why, if cholera were local and contagion limited to a specific group, it spread so quickly along North American commercial routes. Thirty years later, the theory was laid to rest by a series of papers and studies confirming the exogenous origins of the disease.[66]

The impact of the 1832 epidemic on the population of Montreal was along ethnic lines. At first, the "*classes bourgeoises*," to use the expression of the paper *La Minerve*, thought that they would be spared because, as the paper wrote, the disease struck mainly the "poor and dirty classes given to intemperance, the working classes exposed to great heat and excessive work."[67] However, according to Roman Catholic parish registers, there does not seem to have been a correlation between higher mortality rates and social class. In time, all classes were struck.[68] But a comparison of francophone Catholic deaths with non-francophone Catholic deaths[69] reveals a higher mortality among French Canadians. This has been noted by all observers.

William Kelly's 1834 paper, "On the Medical Statistics of Lower Canada," marked the first time that a comprehensive survey was done, using as much statistical evidence as was available. Kelly showed the high mortality level of Lower Canadian cities, which in his view was caused by poor street conditions, poor drainage, and the poor quality of water.[70] A little more than a decade later (1845), a medical journal, the *British American Journal of Medical and Physical Science*, appeared in Montreal and evidenced concern for public health. Contributors asked for mandatory registration of vital statistics, insisted on a better control of burial registration, and, in a general manner, gave some information on the health conditions in the city. Although most of the articles dealt with pathological or surgical questions, this was the beginning of a continuous series of medical papers denoting the development of the profession and of scientific knowledge.[71]

In the 1850s, health problems began to interest people outside medical circles. This was the case with T. C. Keefer, civil engineer, and especially with Philip P. Carpenter, Presbyterian minister and specialist in natural history.[72] The arrival of Carpenter in the 1860s initiated sanitary reform in Montreal. Shortly after taking up residence in Montreal in 1865, he began to press the city council for health improvements. The following year, he wrote to his brother:

> ... and the Council have issued cleansing orders, and appointed an Officer of Health, but I know that these Bodies always want outside pressure to poke them: and I am going to give two lectures, and expect to form a Sanitary Association, in which I presume I shall have to be the chief worker.[73]

That very year, he and the Reverend Samuel Massey founded the Montreal Sanitary Association.[74]

The objectives of this association were "generally to collect and diffuse information, and take action on all matters relating to the Public Health; and especially, to assist in improving the abodes of the poorer classes."[75] Sometimes the association met with resistance from city leaders.

> Alderman Rodden wished the Association to understand that he had long been doing in the Council what they had been contending for. He suggested that they should not present memorials to the Council, but confine their labours to personal hygiene, and similar subjects on which all were agreed. He deprecated publishing statements about the great mortality of the city, lest it should depreciate property, and lessen the number of visitors.[76]

Only after years and countless "memorials to the council" did City Hall establish a real health department staffed with full-time employees. Before 1876, the department had only two physicians who bore the title of "health officers" but neither attended committee meetings nor even had an office.[77]

Carpenter was, until his death in 1877, a "chief worker" for sanitary reform. His writings reflect his concern for public health and pointed to the relationship between poverty and mortality. The motives of engineer Thomas C. Keefer might have been more related to his professional interests,[78] but nevertheless his advice had a certain impact. After the great fire of 1852 he wrote that Montrealers really did not have much choice: either conflagration or epidemic.

> You have perhaps escaped the cholera at the expense of one-third of the city in ashes. Fire is the only thorough scavenger for a city badly drained; and it is perhaps fortunate that the same poverty which causes our early towns to neglect their drainage also builds of combustible materials, thus providing the future fuel for the purifying process.[79]

Gradually, then, the reflection on mortality, which in the case of Montreal started with the cholera, passed from simply a medical point of view to a more holistic approach which held the environment accountable. At the same time, as health grew to be viewed less as an individual problem and more as a social one, doctors were able to have more say in public affairs. In the 1870s, public health became an important issue among French-Canadian physicians in Montreal and the public authorities were moved to intervene. There are then three stages in the development of the social reflection on mortality. During the first one, it was mainly physicians who tried to understand the phenomenon. In the second one the circle widened to those outside the medical profession. The last one saw the institutionalization of public health.

Between 1821 and 1871, Montreal experienced significant changes: the city became an important industrial centre, its population grew five-fold and the urban society became more complex. However, one is as struck by the high level of ordinary mortality in 1871 as in 1821. Even if there is a tendency towards reduction near the end of the period, it remains very slight. There is a striking contrast between socio-economic changes and the evolution of mortality. This is shown particularly in the infant mortality rates which, as we have seen, remained remarkably stable over these years. Indeed the annual rates for the 1821–46 period were similar to those at the beginning of the twentieth century. When we try to explain this phenomenon we do not find ready answers. The stability of the mortality pattern excludes industrialization as a key factor. Immigration has nothing to do with it, since the high level of mortality is mostly confined to French Canadians.

The slow reaction of public authorities to the high mortality rate is remarkable. During most of the period studied, there were interventions only during epidemics, and the high level of ordinary mortality was never questioned. Reflection on the phenomenon, although it started during the 1830s, only gained strength and importance in the 1860s and 1870s. It is interesting to note that it started among anglophone doctors and that francophone doctors became more involved in the seventies. It is also striking to note the attitude of the Roman Catholic Church on mortality: aside from the work of the religious communities among the sick and the abandoned, there does not seem to be any reflection about the possible causes of such a high level of infant mortality. The most probable answer is that the Church conceived those deaths as an "act of God," as something inevitably accompanying the high natality. In that context the Church's only role was to provide services and assistance.

A study of this kind of necessity raises more questions than it can answer. We should know more about the reaction to mortality of the different groups in Montreal. Likewise, the impact of medicine on the population is not known. And finally there remains the question of social inequality in the face of death; the poorer part of the population remained the hardest hit. We conclude fittingly with a quotation from one of Philip Carpenter's papers: "The people of Montreal have to this day retained their unenviable distinction as the dwellers in the city of wealth and death."[80]

2

Poor Relief and Health Care in Halifax, 1827–1849

Kenneth G. Pryke

Contagious and infectious diseases were a constant threat to the health of Nova Scotians during the nineteenth century. Epidemics, while not the leading cause of death, occurred sporadically; exposure to infection from sources outside the province, particularly from immigrants, was always possible. Nova Scotia avoided most of the devastation brought to New Brunswick and Quebec by their greater number of recent arrivals, but in no decade were contagious diseases not present in the province, and with the rise in immigration from Europe after the Napoleonic Wars their incidence increased significantly.

Health care for those suffering from contagious diseases was very limited. People unable to afford a doctor were forced either to rely on an inadequate hospital in the poor asylum or to seek a doctor's charity. Following an extremely serious outbreak of smallpox and typhus in 1827, public officials established a temporary hospital in order to protect the community's well-being. While such a facility was intended for the poor, the poor were reluctant to use it. Nevertheless, local doctors supported the idea of greater hospital facilities, in part as a means of professional development and recognition of the medical profession. In the 1830s, they renewed their request for a permanent hospital arguing that it would provide a controlled environment better suited to the treatment of disease than what was then available to the poor. It also would provide medical care to a broader spectrum of society and remove from the doctors the onus of providing charity.

A major obstacle was the cost of construction. Large sums of money would have to be raised from a public for whom health care was a low priority. In addition, many people did not distinguish between medical care and poor relief, although some doctors did. Others felt that poor relief, including medical care, should be restricted to the destitute and provided primarily through the poor asylum. Indeed, a number of people saw no reason to provide any relief to those not admittable to the asylum. The poor, even if suffering from contagious diseases, were not within society's purview. Consequently, when the doctors attempted to expand public medical facilities and medical services to the poor, their efforts conflicted with the prevailing ideas of social welfare at the time.

The ease with which contagious diseases entered Nova Scotia was well illustrated by the epidemic of 1827. Several vessels crowded with emigrants from Ireland discharged their passengers in Halifax. Before the magistrates learned that many of them were suffering from typhus, these people were lodged in various boarding houses in the town.[1] Because it had the only available health facilities, approximately sixty of them were moved into the already overcrowded poor asylum. Despite this measure, typhus was soon rampant and the situation became even more critical with the outbreak of smallpox.

As the diseases continued to spread, the magistrates urged the provincial government to establish a lazaretto, but the government was not convinced that the need warranted the cost. Instead, it provided only a little extra assistance for the relief of the sick poor and their families.[2] The poor asylum, meanwhile, was quite overwhelmed by the numbers of ill, and in July the Commissioners of the Poor persuaded the government to allow a local doctor who had no formal tie with the asylum to establish and operate a lazaretto on a farm outside the city limits. By November, when the lazaretto was closed, 361 people had been admitted, of whom 61 had died. A further 261 had died in the poor asylum and at least another 138 in the town. No accurate count of the dead was ever established, but a committee of the House of Assembly estimated that their number totaled 800.[3]

The epidemic of 1827, one of the worst to occur in Halifax in the nineteenth century, did not produce any immediate plan to improve medical care in the town. However, the magistrates were shaken by the extent of the crisis, and when smallpox reappeared in December they began to investigate means of preventing the spread of contagious disease.[4] As a result, when it became apparent in 1831 that some recently arrived immigrants had smallpox, the magistrates instructed the constables to return them to their vessels and ordered the vaccination of all children of the poor. These actions strongly indicate that the Halifax doctors believed that the community would be best protected by vaccinating children and that they were fully aware of similar existing practices and beliefs in England.[5] Despite these measures, smallpox continued to spread. When the Commissioners of the Poor refused to admit any paupers with smallpox to the asylum, the magistrates, with the consent of the government, established a lazaretto on Melville Island. During the three months that the hospital was open, the three doctors involved treated sixteen cases of smallpox. As there was no systematic method of detecting those infected or of compelling them to go to the hospital, the number of cases does not accurately reflect the extent of the disease, but it does suggest that the developing tendency of the government to intervene was not based on any pressure from those supposedly being served. Hospitals and lazarettos had a deservedly low reputation among the poor. The magistrates were responding less to any recognized need for medical care by the poor than to their own belief that the economic and social fabric of the community would be disrupted without such care.

The poor did have the most to gain from effective curtailment of contagious diseases since the morbidity and mortality rate was very high among the poor, especially the young. In England, at least one-third and up to one-half of all deaths from infectious and contagious diseases occurred among children under five years of age, then the death rate dropped sharply until approximately the age of forty-five when it rose once again. The fact that infants and children were at risk was perhaps more socially acceptable because such deaths did not cause the same immediate disruption to the urban labour force or create the same social disruption as when adults were affected. Fatalities among poor adults were frequently regarded as the result of immoral, dissolute habits and thus not a medical problem. Cholera upset this pattern of mortality because it was no respecter of age. In addition, smallpox, once vaccination of children became more common, began to bear more heavily on those aged fifteen to twenty-five. Such developments were particularly disturbing to those who suspected that it was the working class, and not paupers, who were the most affected by such contagious diseases.[6]

While the magistrates' establishment of the Melville Island lazaretto in 1831 was unlikely to have an impact on the situation in

Halifax, their willingness to intervene more quickly and more decisively than they had in 1827 indicated a shift in attitude. But the magistrates were limited in their powers and the government and the legislature were slow to support them. The immediate reaction of the government and the legislature to the epidemic of 1827 was to place the blame for the outbreak on lax British emigration regulations.[7] Rather than undertake any expansion of medical care for immigrants, the legislature tried to ensure that it would not become liable for their medical costs. A bond of £10 was imposed on any immigrant landed in the province, to be forfeited if that individual became a charge on a township in Nova Scotia within one year, as would most likely occur in the event of illness. The bond, however, proved to be too high to be enforceable and in any event it did not deal with the problem of disease and its effects on the residents of the province.

Despite its objections to expending provincial funds on the treatment of contagious diseases, the legislature did reimburse Halifax for the expenses incurred in operating the lazaretto in 1831. It was not as generous with the claims for expenses submitted by the doctors who worked in the facility. The claims were based on an unofficial scale of fees charged by the various doctors in the province.[8] The legislature did not recognize this scale and had a well-established practice of severely reducing or refusing outright claims submitted by doctors for various types of services.[9]

The dispute between the legislature and the doctors over fees was not easily resolved and was to remain an irritant for some decades. It was part of a general problem doctors faced in Nova Scotia, as well as elsewhere, in establishing an income commensurate with a professional occupation. Without it, it would be impossible to improve or to maintain a level of competency among doctors. This attempt to establish a minimum level of income conflicted with the priorities of a rising market economy, but it formed the counterpart of an effort to restrict the medical practice of those whose training did not conform to certain accepted patterns. In the late 1820s, the legislature enacted a measure which banned unregistered doctors from enforcing a contract for services rendered. Although granted with reluctance, the action was in contrast to that of some American state legislatures which, beginning in the 1830s, began revoking similar measures because of opposition to a medical monopoly and to specialization in knowledge or skills.[10] The legislature was unwilling, however, to take any action which would permit the doctors to establish, by custom, the conditions of their own services. And, despite their treatment at the hands of the members of the assembly, there were always doctors willing to work for the government – which by itself was a comment on their peripheral economic position.

The issue of fee bills revealed that for many people in the province medical aid would be beyond their means. By 1830 when the problems associated with ill health in Halifax were becoming pressing, these people had no place to turn but to the poor asylum. Yet the asylum was quite incapable of coping with the increasing numbers of ill. As well as serving as a hospital for the indigent, it functioned as a refuge for paupers, an orphanage, a lying-in hospital and a lunatic asylum. Since 1801, it had been under the control of a self-perpetuating board of commissioners who were not responsible in any way to the magistrates of Halifax. Each of the commissioners, in turn, took responsibility for the day-by-day administration of the asylum, including admission, which was based on persons being incapable of sustaining themselves. Those most likely to be admitted were the elderly (many of whom required some form of chronic care), the young, and those who were in ill health. Admittance into the asylum was not a right, however, and was determined by board policy and the decision of the commissioner in charge at any given time. Sometimes, as in the case of sick immigrants, a commissioner's policy might change from incident to incident. After 1827, when outdoor relief (or assistance given to those living in their own homes) in Halifax was abolished, the question of how the asylum's mandate to care for the destitute was carried out by the commissioners assumed greater importance.[11]

The asylum itself was a one-storey stone building, 150 feet long and 50 feet wide, erected in 1785. In 1811, an extension was added which served primarily as a hospital for the mentally ill. Renovations to the main building, including excavation of a basement, the addition of an upper storey, and repairs to the roof, began in 1831.[12] In 1802, the asylum had cared for forty-five inmates in the summer and more than seventy in the winter. By 1827, about three hundred people were in the asylum at any given time. The increase was caused by immigrants; by the 1830s, they constituted 60 per cent of the inmates.[13] Many inmates had to sleep on the floor or "two to a bed with one in the middle." Contemporary commentators did not object to the number of people using the beds but argued that one-third of the beds should be removed to prevent overcrowding.[14] There were three wards for males who were ill (including those with venereal disease), but none existed for women until 1835. Nor were children segregated from adults, a point used at the time to explain why so few children in the asylum reached the age of ten or twelve.

By the early 1830s, the asylum admitted some eight hundred people each year; of these, approximately one hundred died and one-quarter required medical aid at some time. Medical attention consisted of a daily visit by Dr. Bruce Almon, the surgeon for the asylum, plus an hour's surgery conducted daily by each of his two students. Dr. Almon altered this slightly in 1832 when he appointed an assistant in the asylum. Elderly female inmates did the nursing required. This level of medical care was considered adequate for the type of chronic care usually required by the inmates and explains the reluctance of the commissioners to admit persons suffering from contagious diseases. Nonetheless, by the early 1830s, the marked incidence of contagious disease associated with the increase in immigration, and growing public concern about the level of medical attention led a number of people in Halifax to feel that the primary function of the poor asylum's hospital was not to provide relief to the indigent but to serve the sick poor. The commissioners, however, regarded medical care as an incidental duty incurred by them in meeting the moral duty of providing for paupers. Policies adopted for the sick poor should conform, in their view, to the overall policies adopted for dealing with the poor in general. The commissioners distinguished between medical relief and poor relief; others assumed that they should provide both, especially in the event of contagious diseases. This assumption delayed the establishment of alternative facilities.

While attention centred on the dangers to Halifax from contagious diseases, the lack of health care available to the poor (which included much of the working class) was also of concern. To improve this situation, John Sterling, a forty-five-year-old former naval surgeon, and William Grigor, an 1819 graduate of the Royal College of Surgeons, Edinburgh, opened a visiting dispensary in November 1829. Such dispensaries existed in cities in Great Britain and the United States, their primary objective being to provide charity to the deserving poor. Tickets of admission, which were necessary for any treatment at the dispensary, were denied to any not considered respectable, particularly alcoholics and those with venereal diseases. Even after being admitted, a person could be dismissed if his or her conduct was judged unseemly. These dispensaries, as charitable institutions, were thus not to be confused with those end-of-the-century dispensaries which provided medical care to the poor. The stress on charity established priorities which could run counter to proper health care.

Admittance to the dispensaries was also influenced by their use as a teaching tool. They thus became a source of experience for students and of income for those who directed them. This use, which increased in importance during the century, emphasized medically interesting cases rather than medical care. Such care at the period when the Halifax dispensary was established was very limited, usually consisting on the average of two or three prescriptions for each patient. Provision of such drugs was seen by many as proof that proper treatment was being provided. Since the cost of the wide range of drugs required for the treatment customary then would have been beyond the means of most, the dispensary succeeded in serving a sizeable element of the population.

The Halifax dispensary first opened in a fifteen-foot-square room but was soon moved to the offices of Doctors Sterling and Grigor. Costs rose with increasing use and despite the patronage of the governor, a number of clergymen, and gentlemen of the town, donations failed to keep up with expenditures. Consequently, the two surgeons turned to the legislature, as did so many other promoters of charities, but found the support of the legislature tentative at best. Some members opposed any grant because of the two principals involved, while others objected to funds being granted to a charity centred in Halifax. When the legislature did provide a grant in 1831, it was for the sum of £50, which scarcely covered the cost of rent and the medicines used in the dispensary.[15]

Supporters of the dispensary in Halifax continually argued that the clinic would enable the ill to remain with their families, rather than seek admittance to the poor house. This would at once protect the sanctity of the family and reduce the charge on the county taxation rates. Moreover, the requirement that any patient had to have a certificate from a subscriber, a magistrate, or a local doctor would guarantee that only the "deserving" poor received the service. There was little doubt that a substantial number of the poor used the services of the dispensary. In 1831 about eight hundred residents of Halifax (which at that time had a population of some ten thousand) were patients. Yet these eight hundred people constituted only 40 per cent of the users in 1831. The balance were immigrants.[16] That this pattern of usage differed from the original objectives of the dispensary did not seem to create any controversy. In 1832, however, members of the assembly began to raise a charge of extravagance against the dispensary because the direct cost per patient was approximately the same as that for an inmate in the asylum. Since most of the expenses of the dispensary involved drugs, these charges were a direct attack on the level of medical care provided by Sterling and Grigor. Using the demand for economy, the critics overrode the two doctors' plea that they were only providing minimum medical care and blocked any legislative grant in 1832.[17] The difficulties in obtaining funds for the dispensary, either from private or public sources, made it clear that medical care was to be treated as a commodity. Efforts to provide protection for individuals as well as for the community would only be marginally successful at best.

Rather than make further attempts to reach those who were unable to make use of medical services, a group of doctors, including Sterling and Grigor, began a campaign to improve the professional competency of physicians in Halifax. The scheme was to use the asylum hospital as the basis of a medical college in the city.[18] The first step in achieving this objective would be to abolish Almon's exclusive control over medical care in the hospital and to open the hospital to any doctor in Halifax. Doctors could then use the inmates to gain experience and to recruit medical students who would provide an additional, and much-needed, source of income. No one questioned the propriety of using the destitute as teaching material.

The second step was to build a new hospital separate from the asylum and under the administration of doctors. This would give the doctors control over admissions policy. Supporting this ambitious scheme were several doctors who, as graduates of the Royal College of Surgeons, Edinburgh, one of the more advanced medical schools of the period, were concerned about the level of medical care available in the province and the lack of opportunities for professional advancement. Above all, they believed that medicine was a science and that its study would raise the intellectual level of the entire community.[19] But first, the poor asylum must stop administering sick relief. This would permit the commissioners of the poor to devote their energies to the care of the indigent poor.[20]

Chances of success for the proposal were slight, if only because of the expenses involved in establishing a new hospital. The scheme, however, soon achieved a modicum of political popularity because it provided a convenient platform for critics of the local government. The element of exclusive privilege enjoyed by Almon and the charges of improper administration against the asylum were readily added to the growing list of grievances against the local oligarchy.

By the close of 1831, the proposal to alter the administration of the asylum hospital received a measure of endorsement from the Grand Jury and the Halifax magistrates.[21] The most immediate defect in the campaign, however, was not with the politicians but rather with the doctors themselves. Perhaps because of their vulnerable economic and political situation, the doctors in Halifax, as elsewhere at the time, were unable to work together or to present a united front. Some felt that public criticism of Almon was unseemly, and, in view of his political influence, politically unwise. Others suspected that Grigor was acting out of pique at being replaced as health officer by Almon in August 1831.[22] Doubt was also raised as to the propriety of Grigor and Sterling criticizing Almon for enjoying a monopoly over the hospital while they benefited from a similar arrangement with respect to the dispensary. Not surprisingly, early in 1832 a group of doctors reached an accommodation with the asylum: local doctors and their students would tour the hospital with Dr. Almon at stated intervals and be able to observe such operations as took place.[23] This settlement conceded the major points of the campaign, since it neither altered the administration of the hospital nor substantially affected Almon's monopoly.

While the provision for visiting privileges effectively ended the campaign for a teaching hospital among the doctors, support continued to come from the Grand Jury[24] and some members of the assembly. Other assembly members, however, were unwilling either to assume any financial responsibility for a new hospital or to interfere with the Commissioners of the Poor and disposed of the issue by indicating that a new hospital was needed but that the matter should be studied further by the government.[25] Nothing more was heard on the subject for several years.

Although the proposal for a teaching hospital was unsuccessful, the ongoing debate had established the need for improved medical care in Halifax. This awareness was heightened by reports in the summer of 1831 that cholera might be brought into the province from the Baltic. In the winter of 1832, the government became convinced that the province would face a cholera epidemic entering the province either from the United States or by way of the Bay of Fundy from New Brunswick. It therefore prepared one bill to reorganize the quarantine regulations of the province and a second to establish and enforce sanitary guidelines.[26] Although these measures owed much to the initiative of the governor and to the fear of cholera, the concern over health issues which had been developing since 1827 eased their passage through the assembly.

Nova Scotia's adoption of the quarantine policy came at a time when the same policy was coming under increasing attack in the United States and in Great Britain.[27] Critics argued that it imposed a considerable cost on trade and their point was given added weight when quarantine failed in its stated purpose of excluding disease from entering a country. The policy of quarantine was based on a theory of contagion which postulated that disease spread by direct or indirect contact between persons. This theory was being challenged to an increasing extent by those who referred to infectious, rather than contagious disease, and who emphasized the influence of the environment on the body. While there was no agreement on the nature of those environmental factors or on how they affected the body, they did agree that diseases classified as fevers, which included cholera and smallpox, were associated with unsanitary conditions.

The basic notion was familiar and constituted an important element in English medicine. At a pragmatic level, without regard for theory, such an approach could lead to an emphasis on sanitary measures.[28] The introduction of sanitary guidelines in Nova Scotia was thus in line with measures taken elsewhere. The new legislation, however, was unlikely to effect much more than superficial changes in the immediate future. Before substantial shifts could occur, a number of changes would have to take place. One thing that was going to have to change was the belief, very strong in Halifax at the time, that fevers were a mark of personal degeneracy.

By early summer 1832 the government had established Local Boards of Health. The most important, serving as the central board for the province, was in Halifax. Because of its supervisory role, a majority of its members were doctors. In making appointments to this board, the government made considerable effort to meet the wishes of the local practitioners,[29] and those selected included several who had been involved in fighting the epidemic of 1827 and the outbreak of 1831. In comparison to those previous occasions, the doctors were now in a position to make policy and spend public funds. Expecting a major outbreak in the town, the central board arranged for the establishment of three up-to-date hospitals staffed by an ample number of doctors and attendants who would have access to such contemporary devices as a hot-air bath.[30] These hospitals would provide for the poor while those who could afford private medical care would remain in their own homes. In order to gain as much information as possible about cholera and the most recent developments in its treatment, the central board also sent a doctor to New York.[31] The stark contrast between the elaborate plans these doctors were making for the future and the conditions in which they would have to function added fuel to a new debate emerging over a treatment hospital.

The planning carried out by the central board in 1832 was an aberration made possible by the support of a governor who ignored the well-known views of the legislature toward medical care and doctors. With his departure and a lessening fear of a cholera outbreak, a reaction developed in the assembly in 1833 against the health measures.[32] This ensured that when cholera did occur, in August 1834, the new governor would be exceedingly cautious not to undertake any measure which would arouse the legislature.

The authorities were not expecting this latest outbreak, let alone prepared to cope with it. Word of cholera in Quebec City was received and, even while handbills warning Halifax residents to take precautions were being printed, Almon discovered that some of the inmates of the asylum had the disease.[33] The source of infection was unclear. Those who saw immigrants as the principal agents of disease immediately placed responsibility on survivors from a ship bound to Quebec from Ireland. This ship had foundered off Cape Breton and the magistrates in Sydney had decided, not for the first time, that the most expeditious manner of dealing with the survivors was to send them to the poor asylum in Halifax.[34] There was, however, another possible source of infection, since cholera had broken out among troops of the First Battalion Rifle Brigade.[35]

One of the first actions taken to cope with the outbreak was the forced evacuation of a number of poor into the streets and the boarding-up of their dwellings as unfit for habitation. As the cholera spread throughout the town, the governor concluded that whole areas should be cleared and the poor sent to live in tents in the country until the epidemic had passed. He offered £250 for this purpose and the magistrates organized a public subscription. On reflection, the local authorities found the project too brutal and the funds were diverted to establishing a soup kitchen.[36]

In addition to the somewhat haphazard efforts at controlling sanitation, a number of regulations were issued concerning the treatment of the cholera victims. Any poor who could not provide for their own care were to be taken, by force if necessary, to a hospital. The dead were to be buried within twelve hours and the police were ordered to seize the bodies if the families resisted.[37] Such policies, drawn up by the Central Board of Health, reflected the best scientific thinking of the day. However appropriate they might have been, they ignored the family's role in the event of death. Immediate burial clashed with the social custom, particularly strong among the Irish, of a long wake which allowed members of the families to gather.[38] The conflict between scientific reasoning and the social fabric of the community produced considerable stress, although no riots resulted in Halifax as they did in Great Britain and in the United States.[39]

Throughout the epidemic, the Central Board of Health played an active, dynamic role. At first it had been disrupted by considerable dissension between the lay members and the doctors, but the latter soon emerged as the dominant element.[40] One of the major tasks facing the board was arranging suitable hospital facilities, since the 1832 arrangements had collapsed. The only existing facility was the poor asylum hospital. The Commissioners of the Poor initially proposed that they remove all the healthy inmates to other premises and devote the asylum entirely to hospital purposes.[41] Lacking the necessary funds, they decided to use part of the asylum for a cholera hospital. Coping with the epidemic, however, was far beyond their competency, and when they were unable to find any medical attendants, they disowned any further responsibility for dealing with the disease.[42] This left the central board in control and its members quickly enlisted the support of the governor in finding a more suitable facility than the ramshackle, dirty asylum. The actual selection was left to the magistrates who decided on Dalhousie College because of its central location. Despite objections from the townspeople at having a cholera hospital in the centre of town, the college was occupied and the hospital in the asylum closed.

By the time the epidemic disappeared in early October, approximately four hundred people had died of cholera in Halifax.[43] According to the governor, the majority came from the lower classes and were principally immigrants, military pensioners, disbanded soldiers and their families – people who were of the most destitute and dissipated habits. There also had been some deaths among the blacks in Preston, but they suffered far less, said the governor, "than might have been expected considering their poverty and indolent habits."[44] Through the protestations of the governor it was possible to suspect that it was not the dissolute who had been at risk but rather the poor. There was no doubt, however, that the governor expressed the opinion of many respectable people in Halifax. It was, therefore, all the more difficult for the governor, and others, to accept that the epidemic had paralyzed the economy of the town and that many merchants had suffered losses. Even ordinary items had been in short supply, as fishermen and farmers had refused to bring produce into the market. The constant reiteration that only the dissolute had been at risk could not mask the fear which had existed throughout the entire community. During the epidemic, many people, including tradesmen and members of the government, fled the city. This exodus had caused considerable alarm in the neighbouring areas, but fortunately had not resulted in a spread of the disease.[45]

The contention that only the dissolute suffered from cholera was one means of justifying resistance to changes in public policies designed to address any future outbreak of disease. Despite the fear cholera engendered, the epidemic of 1834 did not change popular attitudes towards medical care or sanitation measures in Halifax, any more than it did elsewhere. Instead of a demand for reform, opposition to any but superficial change quickly developed. Among the most vociferous opponents were shopkeepers, a class which in England were identified with parsimony in local affairs.[46] The effect of fear was not action but paralysis and it would be some years before any significant developments occurred. Nevertheless, the discontent in the fall of 1834 did help to crystallize reaction against the magistrates, which had been developing for a number of years. While the attack on the magistrates focused on their administration of the town, it did have the unexpected result of precipitating a reorganization of the poor asylum. This occurred when Joseph Howe, in the course of his famous trial for criminal libel against the magistrates, charged some of the Commissioners of the Poor, who were also magistrates, with petty malfeasance and gross dereliction of duty.[47]

The attack by Howe was only a glancing blow, but the impact was instantaneous. Several commissioners resigned and by midsummer the government was forced to constitute a new board.[48] The new appointees, however, differed little from the former board members in social standing and attitudes toward the poor. Since the board remained a self-perpetuating body with the authority to interpret its own powers, little change in policy was likely to come from the asylum for some time. Its essential approach was clearly indicated when, after consulting with a group of protestant ministers, it declared that the asylum would in future be operated as a house of industry in which moral regeneration of the inmates would flow from a regimen of work. There was no trace in this approach of the religious or secular influences which in England were beginning to focus on the need for a pure physical environment. The notion being developed by Edwin Chadwick that moral depravity had its roots in physical depravity would have been incomprehensible to the Halifax commissioners.[49]

The commissioners' approach meant that the medical functions of the asylum would receive low priority. As an act of charity they were prepared to provide medical care for paupers, although they maintained the "black hospital" which treated venereal diseases, with considerable repugnance.[50] They were also ambivalent about treating those with smallpox or typhus, perhaps because their policy embodied the old view that epidemics were a "scourge of God." They were particularly reluctant to admit immigrants suffering such diseases. Fortunately, in the late 1830s this was not a critical problem; although no year passed without some contagious disease in Halifax, there was no serious outbreak.[51]

According to official government policy, the question of admitting sick immigrants to the asylum should not have arisen because such persons were supposed to be confined on board their vessel by the health officer and the vessel placed in quarantine. The quarantine regulations were enforced in such a haphazard fashion, however, that persons suffering from contagious diseases were able to circulate in the towns.[52] Some felt that sick immigrants should not be confined to their vessels, in part because proper medical care could not be provided on board a ship and in part to reduce the costs of quarantine to ship owners. In 1839, the legislature permitted the landing of European steerage passengers who were ill if the master of their vessel posted a bond to cover their medical expenses. Rather than undertake the expense of establishing a lazaretto or a hospital, the legislature decided that these sick immigrants should be sent to the poor asylum.[53]

The new provincial policy was put to the test the following June when the barque *Edward*, bound for New Brunswick from Cork with 290 passengers, entered harbour. The foremast had been lost in a storm and the captain and several passengers were suffering from typhus. The vessel was removed to the quarantine ground but permission to land was granted fifty passengers who seemed to be well. The boat sent to collect them was rushed by the other passengers and many managed to reach the shore. The master of the vessel was suddenly threatened with a fine of £1,300 for the illegal discharge of immigrants into the province.[54]

Although the government did not usually respond to the presence of typhus in Halifax, it took this outbreak seriously because of the large number of people involved. The inherent danger in the situation was driven home when the health officer, Dr. Almon, died in the course of treating the immigrants. Both the Central Board of Health, which had been reorganized in June,[55] and the government were convinced that on-shore facilities had to be found for the newly arrived ill. The poor asylum was filled, and the Commissioners of the Poor refused to admit any of the immigrants despite the legal requirements of the 1839 statute. The Central Board of Health felt that the time was opportune to establish a separate facility with its own board of management. The government, however, saw no need for such a hospital and ordered the commissioners to establish a lazaretto. The commissioners complied by establishing a temporary facility, known as Waterloo Hospital, in a small barn near the corner of Robie and South streets. It remained open for two months.[56]

With the closure of Waterloo Hospital, Halifax was again without a permanent arrangement for the handling of immigrants with contagious diseases. This lack was emphasized by the new health officer, Dr. Matthias Hoffmann, who was more energetic than his predecessor had been in tracking down immigrants and seamen who were suffering from contagious diseases.[57] Responding to Hoffmann's request that some arrangement be made to assist transients suffering from contagious diseases, the government urged the Commissioners of the Poor to reopen Waterloo Hospital. Before this could occur, the ship *Europe* bound for New York put into Halifax with sickness on board. Faced with an emergency, the government met the commissioners' objections to having any of their staff treat persons who were not paupers by placing Hoffmann in charge of transients, including immigrants, and admitting them to the reopened lazaretto.[58] The compromise worked satisfactorily in 1841 and Hoffmann treated nineteen of the thirty patients admitted to the reopened Waterloo Hospital.[59] In 1842, however, the commissioners became increasingly restive about the arrangement. Since the lazaretto was under the administration of the poor asylum, any immigrants in Waterloo Hospital were legally inmates of the asylum. The commissioners therefore decided that the arrangement with Hoffmann violated their rule that only a commissioner could admit a person to the asylum and their policy that only surgeons on their staff could treat inmates. After months of debate, the commissioners finally decided to enforce their exclusive control over the asylum. They terminated the arrangement whereby Hoffmann treated sick immigrants in the lazaretto.[60] Thus the commissioners protected their own jurisdiction and the monopoly of their surgeon, Dr. William I. Almon, son of the late surgeon and health officer. The seemingly endless dispute over the operation of Waterloo Hospital illustrated the difficulties of altering existing practices of medical care of the poor.

Even had there been no dispute over the management of the lazaretto, a derelict barn could not be a suitable facility. Yet for some years, this served as a hospital for both residents and transients who were suffering from contagious diseases. Apart from whatever medical care was provided as an act of charity, the only other medical care for many of the poor was provided by the dispensary. This continued to suffer from a chronic lack of funds and the legislature remained uncertain whether to support it.[61] In 1838, Joseph Howe revived the earlier proposal to turn the asylum into a teaching hospital, but, as before, he was met by the continued intransigence of the Commissioners of the Poor.[62] The only concession which they were willing to make was to iterate their proposal, first made in 1832, to allow local doctors and their students to tour the hospital.[63]

Despite the obvious difficulties of obtaining support (and especially needed funds), a number of people, including Dr. Robert Hume, a respected doctor and a long-time member of the Central Board of Health, recognized that the only way of improving hospital facilities was to build a new one. He and some other doctors petitioned the legislature in 1839 for a hospital that would be separate from the poor asylum, but they received little support.[64] In 1841, however, Hume returned to the subject, this time with the assistance of the health officer, Dr. Hoffmann, and Dr. Grigor of the dispensary. By 1843, the proposal had attracted the support of prominent people in Halifax.

As the project for a hospital took form, it emerged as a plan to build a 100-bed unit on a three-acre site at a cost of £2,500. Costs of operating this hospital would be covered by fees from medical students, annual subscriptions from private benefactors, fees from paying patients, and a tax on shipping. Although concern over contagious diseases acted as a stimulus for the project, and treatment of such diseases constituted an essential part of it, the objectives of the proposed hospital included general medical care of the poor. Ambitious though it was, the project would remain merely a suggestion unless some philanthropic support was forthcoming. In the fall of 1844 a series of public meetings were arranged at which public figures – such as the Mayor of Halifax and the Speaker of the Assembly – made pledges of support.[65] The promotion failed and the efforts to obtain a hospital diminished for a time, although they by no means died away completely.

The campaign of the early 1840s increased cohesion among the doctors. In arguing for a hospital, they managed to avoid the personal recriminations and internal division which had marked the proposals for a hospital in the previous decade. Organizing petitions to the legislature and arranging public meetings brought home the need for an organization which would include all the doctors in the city. The Central Board of Health provided Hume with a useful and logical base, but it only included a handful of the city doctors. Moreover, the formation of a Local Board of Health at the time of the incorporation of Halifax as a city in 1841 limited the role of this board in dealing with the health issues of the city.[66] Consequently, the doctors established the Medical Society of Halifax, with Hume as president, simultaneously with the organization of public meetings in 1844.[67]

The growing cohesion among the doctors and their insistence that a hospital should serve the general health needs of the poor indicated that a hospital was assuming more significance. In 1832 much stress had been laid on the need for a teaching hospital as a device for elevating the status of the profession. A decade later this point was subordinated and the principal emphasis was on improving the medical care given to the poor, as opposed to the destitute. This shift in emphasis enhanced the political appeal of the project and was designed to obtain the needed public support. It also prevented any confrontation with the poor asylum; the Commissioners of the Poor, recognizing that it would release them from providing medical aid to those who were not destitute, lent their support to the campaign.[68] The Medical Society argued forcibly that members of "the middle station of society" who were not admittable to the poor asylum were unable to provide "the care and comforts which are absolutely indispensable for those in ill health." The health of the city would improve, argued some doctors, if they had a hospital where they could provide a regular regimen and a measure of cleanliness and fresh air for the poor. The issue was a critical one because a large though unspecified number of the working classes were unable to afford medical assistance or to provide care for the ill in their own residences. At the same time, in order to secure their professional position, which included their economic status, doctors needed to expand their potential clientele beyond that narrow spectrum of society which was able to afford their services. While some were concerned with the problem of dealing with medicine as a commodity, others saw the institution of a hospital as a benefit in the relationship between a doctor and his patients. If local mechanics and shopkeepers, mused one doctor, could see the advantages of treating contagious diseases in a hospital, they would put aside their prejudices against doctors and willingly seek medical aid.[69]

The suggestion that a hospital was needed so that doctors could control the behaviour of the ill could arouse suspicion that the doctors looked on a hospital as a means of control. Elements of social control, however, are an integral part of any society. Moreover, Nova Scotia at mid-nineteenth century bore many aspects of a deferential society and control was advocated by some as an essential element of social order. In considering the doctors' intentions, a distinction must be made between their objectives and the methods used to achieve those objectives. In seeking to control diet, hygiene, and ventilation, the doctors' objective was to remove the particular symptoms affecting the patient. With the decline in heroic treatments the management of the patient had become the essence of the doctor-patient relationship.[70] In the case of the poor, this type of control could, on occasion, be best carried out in a hospital.

Interest in broadening the clientele of doctors was apparent throughout the agitation for a hospital. This was particularly true with respect to the inclusion in the project of provision for sick mariners. Under existing legislation, ships' captains were required to provide medical aid during the life of a contract, but they had no liability once it had expired. Nor was there any stipulation that such medical aid that was supplied must be provided by a doctor. Thus, a crewman who had signed on a voyage which would terminate in Halifax, and who had been injured or become ill during the voyage, could not expect to receive any medical aid once the vessel had arrived in port. In view of the importance of shipping to the province, the lack of any regular facility was perhaps surprising. Other ports in British North America had them and they had long been features of ports in the United States and Great Britain.[71] Creation of a marine hospital would be to the professional advantage of the doctors. It could also, with the appropriate arrangements, result in considerable savings to the employers. While the support of the shipowners strengthened the proposal politically, there were always those in the assembly who insisted on maintaining the full discipline of the market economy.

Had the doctors been primarily interested in providing medical care to the poor, they might well have concentrated on developing the dispensary. Such an expansion would probably not have cost as much as a new facility and would have required fewer expenses to operate. Moreover, it had a far better image than did the hospital, which like similar institutions elsewhere at that time, was regarded with considerable hostility. Although the doctors admitted that people would take advantage of any opportunity to avoid going to a hospital, they persevered with the proposal. In part, this emphasis on a hospital recognized that some people in the city lacked suitable physical facilities to deal with illness. For these individuals, the dispensary was not sufficient. The stress on institutional care thus reflected, in part, a response to the reality of developing urbanization.[72]

Two other factors may have played a role in focusing doctors' attention on hospital care but they are difficult to document. By mid-century, hospitals were seen as part of the medical education system. To what extent the Halifax doctors anticipated using a hospital for teaching opportunities and thereby increasing their income was uncertain. While the subject was raised, it was presented as a means of raising revenue for the hospital rather than as a source of income for the doctors. If the latter had been of vital concern, there would surely have been some agitation, as there had been in 1832, to loosen the monopoly of the Almon family over the hospital in the poorhouse. Use of the hospital for teaching purposes would also affect the asylum hospital and the dispensary, yet both the Commissioners of the Poor and Dr. William Grigor of the dispensary were supportive of it.

In addition, a new hospital would have been important in the development of clinical medicine. Unfortunately, the extent of any such focus in Halifax in the 1840s is difficult to determine. So too is an interest in pathology. To what degree, if any, Dr. Almon carried out autopsies in the poor asylum is unknown, and, at best, other doctors would have had a limited opportunity to do so. This situation changed slightly in 1848 when Dr. William Grigor was appointed as a coroner, probably the first doctor to fill that position in the province. Other doctors were soon appointed and by the mid-1850s they were using their positions to teach pathology to their apprentices.[73] Whether this developing interest played a role in the early campaign for a hospital, however, remains uncertain.

Whatever the reasons the doctors had for supporting a hospital, to be successful they needed widespread support. While there was a considerable degree of public approval for the idea of a new hospital, not everyone endorsed the specifics of the doctors' proposal. The Halifax City Council requested that the governor support a grant to help defray the estimated cost of £2,500 for a hospital but the facility it envisioned was not a general hospital but one for sick immigrants and sick seamen. This was perhaps because the council was primarily responsible for dealing with immigrants rather than with the sick poor. Moreover, an outbreak of typhus and dysentery brought in by immigrant ships that summer made council painfully aware of the dangers to the community. Some 203 immigrants were treated in a lazaretto established by the city[74] and 920 people were admitted as paupers to the poorhouse, as compared with 502 in 1846.[75]

Support by the City Council for a hospital to treat contagious and infectious diseases among immigrants was a response to an immediate crisis. The various diseases then classified as fevers, whether they be smallpox, cholera, or typhoid, were an obvious threat to the community. Moreover, dealing with this threat was straightforward, for it did not require a close examination of the relationship between filth, disease, and poverty. The proposal to help the sick immigrants, unlike that for a general hospital, did not raise the issues of who the poor were and whether illness was a cause of poverty. Nor did it provoke discussions concerning the doctrine of self-help. The doctors' proposal did, for they contended that charity should not be confined solely to the destitute. For example, some suggested that it was unreasonable to expect certain groups, such as apprentices, to be completely responsible for their own well-being. Charity, then, should be extended to include the sick poor.

City Council's request for an immigrants' hospital was rather surprisingly endorsed by the governor, Sir John Harvey, who had previously opposed any permanent facility. His change of opinion undoubtedly reflected the influence of the Reform government which had taken office in February 1848. Introduction into the legislature of a proposal to advance a loan to the city provoked a predictable series of attacks on the motives, conduct, and professional practices of doctors.[76] Some county members were jealous of any funds given to Halifax and others denied that public monies should be spent on any such purposes. Despite such animosity, the members could not ignore the actual threat created by sick immigrants. Even while the issue was under debate in the assembly, seventy-three survivors, many of them suffering from typhus, from the ship *Omega*, which had foundered in a storm off the coast, arrived in Halifax.[77] This was the beginning of an epidemic which affected both Halifax and Dartmouth until late fall and defeated the sometimes frenzied efforts of the Local Board of Health and the Commissioners of the Poor to deal with it.[78] The response of the assembly was to vote £750 to Halifax for an immigrant and seaman's hospital, provided that a matching grant be made by the city.[79]

Given the mood of the legislature, no hospitals would be built in Halifax without considerable public support. It was not forthcoming. Little, if any, progress was made in qualifying for the 1848 legislative grant for an immigrant and seamen's hospital, although interest in the subject did continue, especially in 1849 when a serious and long-drawn-out epidemic of smallpox occurred. In a classic example of a charitable endeavour, one of the city aldermen, on his own initiative, arranged funds through a public subscription and with assistance from the government established a lazaretto on the city commons. This facility was open to both residents and immigrants. Those judged able to pay would be charged a fee and those who could not would be supported by funds raised by public subscription. This policy had been advocated for several years by the doctors.

Although all reports indicated that smallpox was prevalent throughout the city, by the time the lazaretto closed only 50 patients had been admitted, of whom about one-half were Halifax residents. This was far less than the number of cases known to the local doctors, and several doctors cited instances of people refusing to go to the hospital.[80] Later in the fall, with smallpox once more on the increase, doctors surveyed indicated that there were 70 cases under medical treatment. One doctor connected with the dispensary and who had been in charge of the lazaretto during the summer, speculated that only one case out of five was under a doctor's care. According to this estimate, 280 undetected cases existed in the city. Several doctors believed that these undetected cases were frequently among the poor and often among groups, such as the blacks, who suffered from a far more serious form of the disease than those being treated. Although some sought aid from druggists, they often would go to considerable lengths to prevent their neighbours from knowing that they, or their families, had smallpox. Shopkeepers and tradesmen feared that publicity of their illness would lead to a loss of trade. Others preferred anonymity in order to prevent any interference by the authorities.[81] A general hospital would not have changed this situation.

City Council's idea of a hospital for infectious and contagious diseases was not the only competition the doctors' proposal for a general hospital faced. At the same time that doctors were making their plea, critics of the all-purpose asylum were advocating several different specialized institutions. Of these projects, it was clear that one for a new insane asylum enjoyed a higher priority than did that for the hospital. The reason for such a preference may well have been due to the horror with which loss of reason was regarded. Moreover, a growing confidence that the mentally ill could be cured by proper institutional care lent strong support to the demand that assistance should be provided to those unable to aid themselves.[82] This attitude did not necessarily apply to the proposal for a general hospital. In England, for example, considerable attention was focused on creating a pure physical environment in order to prevent disease. This approach, in the form of the public health movement, was intellectually influenced by the Benthamite philosophy.[83] The work of English promoters of the public health movement such as Edwin Chadwick were followed closely in Nova Scotia and had a definite appeal to Reformers such as Joseph Howe.[84] While the impact of such an approach lent support to the notion of state action to enhance public health, it did not necessarily provide a high priority to proposals to help cure the sick poor as advocated by the doctors.

The ultimate reason for the defeat of the doctors' proposal for a general hospital was that it reflected the priorities of the medical profession rather than of the general community. It would enable the doctors to provide a type of personal care which the ill would be unable to provide for themselves. It would also provide an opportunity to those interested in clinical medicine and pathology to develop their skills. A hospital would also advance doctors' professional interests. In the first instance, it would provide them with an institution they could control. Secondly, it was seen as a means for broadening their clientele by reaching persons who at that time were unable or unwilling to make use of their services. Furthermore, it was one means of reconciling the care of the poor with the problem of increased specialization of function. Rather than have much of the direct and indirect cost of the care of the poor absorbed by the doctors as an act of charity, the cost would be transferred to a public institution.

There undoubtedly was public concern over health issues in Nova Scotia, particularly after the formation of the Reform ministry. The doctors, however, did not enjoy sufficient credibility to have their arguments publicly accepted and their proposals implemented. This was due, in part, to a lack of unanimity within the profession itself. Another aspect was that political attitudes placed more emphasis on preventative than curative methods in dealing with illness among the poor. The overriding presumption that medical care should be treated as a commodity seemed to be questioned only with respect to the care of contagious and infectious diseases. When faced with an extended outbreak of diseases, the various bodies involved became more supportive of a hospital, in theory, if not always in fact.

The extended struggle for a hospital might not have taken place if it had been viewed as critical for medical care. It was not. Despite the danger to the poor and to the community from contagious diseases, Halifax proved reluctant to abandon traditional attitudes towards the poor and the medical profession. Actual construction of a hospital in Halifax would not take place for another decade and then only because City Council took the initiative and constructed the facility as a civic project. This hospital, which remained under the control of city council, was administered in the tradition of a charitable institution, such as an alms house. Denied control of the hospital, most doctors boycotted it and the hospital remained virtually empty for some years.

3

Public Health and the "Sanitary Idea" in Toronto, 1866–1890

Heather MacDougall

During the quarter-century after Confederation, public health reformers in Toronto attempted to persuade all levels of government, particularly municipal authorities, to adopt the British "sanitary idea." Sanitarians believed that the state should be responsible for the prevention of outbreaks of infectious diseases through regulation of the urban environment and provision of essential amenities such as pure water and efficient waste removal. In their efforts to improve living and working conditions for all Torontonians, however, the public health advocates overlooked two significant factors: the differing public perceptions of the nature and extent of health problems and the dissimilarity of the British and Canadian institutional settings. Studying the evolution of preventive medical services in this major Canadian centre from their origin on the eve of the cholera epidemic of 1866 to their widespread public acceptance by the end of the 1880s reveals the challenges and pitfalls involved in applying to one milieu an idea that was designed especially for another. Indeed, the public health developments in Toronto in this period demonstrate the distinctly local nature of social problems and efforts to cope with them.

Prior to the 1860s most towns and cities in Upper Canada devoted little attention to public health matters except when threatened by epidemics of cholera or typhus. Toronto was one of the few exceptions. From its incorporation in 1834 the city had possessed a council committee known as the Local Board of Health. The board had been created in response to administrative difficulties which had hampered the fight against cholera in 1832. Moreover, By-law 8, "An Act to establish a Board of Health" which was passed on June 9, 1834, in preparation for another cholera onslaught, contained fifteen clauses regarding disease control and environmental sanitation. To ensure that disease control was efficiently undertaken, the Board of Health was given the power to provide hospital accommodation and medical supplies. Its responsibilities for environmental sanitation included encouraging citizens to clean up their premises, to abate any nuisances such as overflowing privies and cesspools, and to dispose of the by-products of noxious trades such as slaughtering. However, the board was only activated whenever Toronto was faced with a potential disease threat, and even then its disease-control efforts were often superseded by regulations emanating from the provincial administration. This development made disease prevention a very minor aspect of municipal life, with the result that from 1834 to 1866 public health activities were fundamentally responses to external forces – namely, epidemics and accompanying provincial compulsion to deal with them.[1]

As Toronto's population grew from approximately ten thousand inhabitants in 1834 to roughly forty-four thousand in 1861,[2] some citizens, notably British-trained doctors, became concerned about issues such as slums, polluted water supplies, and the lack of effective waste-removal systems. Such environmental problems led these professionals to question the limited role of the Local Board of Health and to agitate for more permanent forms of preventive services, including the appointment of a full-time medical health officer.[3] To support their demands, Toronto's sanitary reformers turned to the British model from which they derived both a sense of the urgent need for health reform and a methodology – the "sanitary idea."

The sanitary idea had emerged in Great Britain during the 1830s and 1840s in response to the increasing ill-health and poverty that had accompanied rapid urban-industrial growth and that had been so starkly revealed by the high death toll in the first great nineteenth-century cholera epidemic in 1831–32. The concept embodied an extremely complex process consisting of investigation, legislation, and administration. Initially, the impetus for public health reform was a result of the revelations of massive urban insanitation documented by the Secretary of the Poor Law Commission, Edwin Chadwick, in his *Report on the Sanitary Conditions of the Labouring Population of Great Britain* (1842). Chadwick argued that environmental pollution led to disease which in turn produced degradation.[4] He based his conclusions on the miasmatic theory of disease causation. Proponents of the miasmatic theory argued "that conditions of insanitation were able to produce locally an atmospheric state which itself was the causative agent of disease."[5] Chadwick and his supporters claimed that the removal of animal and human wastes from British cities would lower mortality and morbidity rates from "filth" diseases such as cholera, typhus, typhoid fever, scarlet fever, and diphtheria.

Chadwick's theory of disease causation was only one variant in the spectrum of nineteenth-century viewpoints on this issue. Between 1850 and 1875 the most popular theory was *contingent-contagionism*. It claimed that the state of the atmosphere alone was insufficient to bring about disease, but that it was an important factor working in concert with specific or non-specific contagion in spawning the various infectious diseases. This position extended the miasmatic approach to incorporate aspects of the new germ theory. Supporters of the latter believed that only one specific micro-organism produced each epidemic disease. However, until the research of Robert Koch and Louis Pasteur in the 1870s and 1880s confirmed this supposition, most doctors and the public preferred to accept a more all-embracing theory like contingent-contagionism.[6] Supporters of either the miasmatic or contingent-contagionist positions dominated the evolution of public health services in the English-speaking world and concentrated on direct sanitary action rather than scientific research.[7] In this intellectual climate, the major contributions of the Anglo-Saxon world to the development of preventive medicine were to be a nation-wide system of vital statistics which was used by the British after 1837 to measure national "healthfulness,"[8] and methodical investigations of urban and rural living and working conditions which served as foundations for further policy development at the municipal and central levels.[9] In Great Britain, the United States, and Canada, preventive medicine was an empirical discipline which reflected local and national needs and interests far more than medical theory. Consequently, in the 1840s and 1850s Chadwick and his fellow sanitary enthusiasts maintained their faith in the ultimately fallacious miasmatic theory because it legitimized their demands for government intervention and their emphasis on disease prevention.

In response to sustained agitation and additional publicity regarding unhealthy urban living conditions, Parliament passed Britain's first formal public health legislation in 1848. This introduced the second component of the sanitary idea – legislation. Tentative as the 1848 statute was, it set the pattern for the development of public health programs for the remainder of the century through the establishment of a central administrative body whose primary function was the supervision of local sanitation and disease prevention.[10] To ensure that central initiatives were carried out, the Public Health Act encouraged the appointment of a qualified local medical officer of health. As an administrative instrument at the municipal level, he represented the third component of the sanitary idea because he was expected to investigate health problems, to present solutions, and to prevent the spread of infectious diseases.[11] The challenge for Toronto supporters of this system lay in modifying it to suit the city's circumstances.

In the autumn of 1865 Toronto's leading newspapers, the Liberal *Globe* and the Conservative *Leader*, reported the presence of cholera in the Mediterranean. Both papers also printed circulars, sent by British health officials in an effort to arouse interest in sanitation measures,[12] and pressed the civic government to begin cleansing Toronto's notoriously dirty streets and back lanes. In November the cholera question assumed new importance as the disease arrived in New York City on board the steamer, *Atalanta*. The *Leader* urged municipal action, arguing: "There must be cleanliness [because cholera] finds in the atmosphere and in the filthy houses and habits of its victims, the material on which it feeds."[13] Citing both British and French examples, the paper stressed its belief that cholera was preventable if sanitation policies were implemented.

The *Leader* doubted that city authorities took the impending epidemic seriously. Like the *Globe*, it was irritated by City Council's slowness in appropriating $1,500 for scavenging in Toronto before the winter set in and applauded Councillor Spence for stating that "it would be better to spend the money now in cleaning the streets than buying coffins for the poor next year."[14] It also made reference to widespread voter belief that city hall's failure to act was partly due to the fact that this type of expenditure provided little opportunity for patronage.[15] Such vehement criticism from a party paper was unusual and indicated the depth of public concern.

Both of Toronto's major dailies continued to inform their readers of the extent of disease and suffering in England and New York City. Early in 1866 the papers carried articles which outlined the heroic medications deemed necessary to cure cholera[16] and in February the *Globe* printed an investigative exposé on the city's slums. In prose that imitated Chadwick at his most vehement, readers were asked to commence a little east of Victoria street on the south side of Stanley, and look at the rear premises of the miserable hovels which in themselves, are better fitted for pig-styes, and cow pens than residences for human beings. The corners of yards are filled with refuse of cooking – the yards are a mass of slops and decomposing filth. . . . On Stanley street from Victoria to Nelson, there are no fewer than twenty-eight closets in such a state that it is hard to comprehend how any man, however low and degraded in social position, could eat, drink or sleep within gunshot of them.[17]

MIASMATIC.

The writer was concerned that his audience understand that "miserable drainage, bad air, bad water, filth, dirt and refuse of the worst kind . . . are . . . the main causes of epidemic disease."

To focus the discussion on a practical level, the *Globe* offered a variety of sanitation suggestions drawn from the British experience. These included flushing the main sewers to prevent the accumulation and putrefaction of supposedly disease-producing waste water, the frequent inspection of homes and businesses to ensure adequate sanitary standards, and the extensive use of quicklime to disinfect heavily polluted areas. Furthermore it was urged that houses of the poor be inspected and whitewashed if necessary and that both landlords and tenants be forced to keep them in better condition.[18] Concentration on regulating the living conditions of the poor extended beyond the factors of class prejudice and humanitarianism; it was of real practical value. As the *Leader* would later point out, "there are many respectable families . . . who in the case of an epidemic would suffer equally with those less cleanly in their habits, unless the authorities take some measures for purifying the locality."[19]

Another area of great concern to both newsmen and the public was the quality of Toronto's water supply. The *Globe* noted the poor quality of the city's well water and requested that municipal authorities take steps to provide the indigent with pure water for "cleaning and cooking." Above all, the paper stressed City Council's obligation "not to fritter away time" but to strengthen the powers of the Board of Health to enable it to undertake "a thorough and radical cleansing" of the city.[20] By demanding that the authorities take preventive action, the *Globe* highlighted one of Toronto's major sanitary deficiencies – an inadequate legal foundation from which to protect its citizens' health.

In response to interest aroused by the *Globe*, Alderman Nathaniel Dickey, the chairman of the Local Board of Health, called a public meeting for the evening of February 14, 1866, which was attended by representatives of the regular and homeopathic branches of Toronto's medical profession, the City Council, and the business community. Dickey opened the gathering with the admission that the city was not prepared to deal with an epidemic, a circumstance which he blamed on lack of public support for the Board of Health's activities. He then asked for public approval of a set of sanitation proposals. In general, the participants supported Dickey's proposals. Dr. Edward Hodder, a leading teacher and surgeon, stressed the potential danger of using a contaminated water supply such as Toronto's during an epidemic and urged the improvement of the city's drainage system. He was followed by G. W. Allen, a prominent businessman and philanthropist, who seconded Dickey's observation that the health inspector was unable to carry out his duties effectively, gloomily concluding that "the health by-laws . . . were a dead letter." Alderman Samuel Harman "thought it would be well if Corporations had full power to compel persons to keep clean yards etc.," while Alderman William Edwards called for the appointment of a medical health officer to provide expert advice to civic authorities.[21] Although these individuals did not demand the implementation of the sanitary idea *per se*, they were recommending two of its essential ingredients in an effort to protect all Torontonians from a dreaded scourge.

To ensure that these recommendations became part of the municipal disease-fighting strategy, a resolution was passed at the meeting requesting the formation of a medical committee to assess the city's health problems and to devise solutions. This was not unexpected. Toronto's doctors were at the centre of both medical education and politics in the province and had traditionally been consulted about the implementation of curative measures. This new committee was to be composed of instructors from Toronto's competing medical schools, staff members from the Toronto General Hospital, and the leaders of the homeopathic and regular practitioners.[22] Such a broad-ranging coalition was designed to attract the widest possible support from doctors and the public and to carry out the first phase of the sanitary idea – investigation of local circumstances and needs.

The medical committee completed its task and presented its recommendations to another public gathering on March 2, 1866. The members opened their report by emphasizing their belief that cholera could be prevented. The methods they suggested were the use of pure water and the construction of a "proper system" of drainage. To corroborate their demand for an immediate extension of the water supply and the closure of polluted wells, they referred to the famous Broad Street pump incident during the 1854 cholera epidemic in London, the investigations of John Simon, the Chief Medical Officer of the Medical Department of the Privy Council, and the research of Dr. William Budd of Bristol.[23] They expressed concern about dumping untreated sewage into Toronto Bay and suggested that a filtration system comparable to those advocated by Edwin Chadwick for cities in England be considered for the Canadian centre. Approving the efforts of Londoners "to benefit by the suggestions and improvements of science," the members of the committee exhorted their fellow citizens to recognize that "ere it be too late it is our manifest duty to secure for ourselves some of those advantages, and to profit by the failings as well as the wise acts of others."[24]

By emphasizing the British sanitarians' practical approach to urban water supplies and waste-removal systems, the medical committee was not only reiterating the suggestions made in the *Globe* but striving to convince Torontonians to emulate their counterparts in the mother country. Since the committee members recognized the difficulty and expense which both waterworks and drainage systems entailed, they also advocated adopting New York City's garbage-collection system as a temporary solution.[25] By basing their suggestions for short- and long-term sanitation policies on systems that were successful elsewhere, the sanitarians demonstrated the international nature of public health problems and policies. They were also being very pragmatic. They were well aware of the limitations of municipal spending powers and were therefore realistic about the speed at which their proposals could be adapted to meet local needs.

The final suggestion which the medical committee made was the appointment of a qualified medical officer.[26] This recommendation reflected the members' understanding of the third component of the sanitary idea – administration. In their opinion, successfully combating the threat of infectious disease and eradicating long-standing sanitary problems required the expertise of a committed sanitarian who would model his behaviour on British precedents.[27] But were there underlying motives as well? Professional prestige might be enhanced by the creation of a senior administrative post but City Council's shabby treatment of its previous health officers[28] did not augur well for an increase in status. Similarly, the doctors' personal concern for their individual interests during an epidemic no doubt made them support the proposal. Neither of these factors, however, was dominant. Instead, the arguments which the committee used to justify its recommendation demonstrated humanitarian concern allied with a desire to apply their medical knowledge to a pressing social problem.

The medical committee offered several arguments in order to obtain the public support necessary to implement its proposals. First, it argued that disease did not observe class barriers, noting that the wealthy were just as likely to have improperly constructed drains and cesspools as the poor and hence to suffer from filth diseases. Second, it asserted that all residents ought to "be thoroughly impressed with the knowledge that epidemics may burst out in a community when the terrene and atmospheric conditions combine to render the season . . . unhealthy." Third, the committee stated that it had not recommended expensive remedial measures because it did not think that spending alone would solve Toronto's health problems. And finally, it appealed to the citizens' self-interest.

> The principle is admitted that our neighbour has no right to keep a match box and combustibles against our premises. Why should he be permitted to keep on his premises a putrified poison to be always on hand, so that the first shower may bring down into our wells of water, or the first stirring breeze bring into our houses pestilent draughts?[29]

By the beginning of April 1866, Alderman Dickey and the other members of the Board of Health had come to agree with the doctors' arguments in favour of a more planned approach to protecting the city's health. Many of the Board's efforts to clean up Toronto had been thwarted by lack of funds and opposition from the Board of Works which was also responsible for garbage collection and street cleaning.[30] To overcome these difficulties, By-law 431 was introduced. Its purpose was to amend all preceding health legislation focusing on disease control, nuisance abatement, removal of night soil, and impounding of stray animals. The new ordinance contained fifty-four clauses delineating the basic functions of the Local Board of Health, outlining offences against health, setting construction standards for vaults and drains, establishing regulations for noxious trades and the disposal of offal and ashes, and imposing heavy fines for disobedience. The most significant aspects of the ordinance from the sanitarians' viewpoint, however, were the two lengthy sections describing the duties and activities of the medical health officers and the sanitary inspectors.[31] By including these provisions the aldermen who supported the by-law indicated their faith in medical expertise and their willingness to implement the second component of the sanitary idea – legislation – as a means of protecting the health of the city.

But it was these very aspects of professionalism and efficiency which were at the root of much of the opposition. Control of patronage and limited public expenditures on municipal services were at the heart of mid-Victorian civic politics in Toronto because of the desire to maintain Tory control and of the uncertain economic climate created by the crash of 1857.[32] By-law 431 clearly threatened traditional ward politics and upset the delicate task of balancing Toronto's budget because it transferred garbage-collection duties (and the attendant patronage) from the Board of Works to the Board of Health as well as expanding the municipal bureaucracy through the appointment of four new officials.

As the discussions dragged on, Toronto's papers, notably the *Globe*, became increasingly strident in their condemnation of the Tory aldermen. Ascribing the opposition to "petty jealousy," the Liberal organ supported the appointment of a medical officer versed in sanitary science, arguing that "far more depends upon the sanitary precaution than upon all that medical skill can do after the epidemic has made its appearance."[33] As well, the *Globe* objected to Mayor Medcalf's efforts to stall the by-law by arguing that the province would soon be implementing a revised version of the 1849 Public Health Act. The *Globe* decried this tendency to depend on central initiatives and called for a municipal health by-law which would "include many provisions of a permanent character, intended not merely for a time of threatened epidemic, but for the preservation of public health at all times."[34] In effect, the paper was asking City Council to reassess its role in the provision of health services – to replace the limited response which had characterized previous epidemics with an administrative structure based on the application of the sanitary idea.

The *Leader* added its contribution to the debate by pointedly reminding the Local Board of Health of its duties.

Many of the minor streets and back lanes and vacant lots are in a most filthy condition. The carcasses of putrid dogs and cats are lying freely about, exposed to the rays of the sun and emitting a

> very unpleasant effluvium during all hours of the day. . . . Complaints are numerous and well-founded. The Board of Health must see that these causes of offensiveness and danger to the public health are speedily removed.[35]

Although not as harsh as the *Globe* in its condemnation of the Council's delaying tactics, the *Leader* consistently reminded its readers of the politicians' shortcomings and demanded sanitary reform. Still, it recognized the political difficulties inherent in implementing public health legislation.

> In some respects the fulfillment of this duty will not be very pleasant, inasmuch as it will interfere with the ordinary course of certain trades and callings; but, however disagreeable this may be, the public health, in times like the present, is a consideration of paramount importance to all others. . . . [36]

Such objections had at present, moreover, to be overcome: cholera had appeared in Halifax in mid-April.[37]

After vitriolic discussions and grudging passage of the by-law on April 27, 1866, Toronto City Council's attempt to implement some aspects of the sanitary idea as a means of combating cholera was quickly rendered superfluous. On May 4, 1866, the Governor General issued a proclamation which created a Central Board of Health and suspended municipal health ordinances for the duration of the impending cholera epidemic. Although the provincial body's regulations were somewhat more stringent than Toronto's ordinance, they paralleled the latter's emphasis on prevention.[38] In response to these central initiatives, the City Council appointed two medical health officers, Doctors William Tempest and James Rowell, for the eastern and western portions of the city. Both men had the requisite interest, training, and political connections. Tempest had already acquired prominence as a leading member of the medical section of the Canadian Institute and was one of the moving spirits behind the medical committee's report. Rowell was a British-trained lecturer in surgical anatomy and one of the three honorary medical advisors to Toronto's St. George's Society.[39] He had also been one of the practitioners singled out to give a public address on cholera at the March meeting.

In order to organize the city's defences, Tempest and Rowell arranged for publication of a pamphlet containing the most up-to-date information on cholera causation and treatment. Entitled *To the Citizens of Toronto*, the pamphlet opened with the comment that its purpose was to inform the citizens about the cause, cure, and prevention of cholera. Tempest and Rowell stated that

> The almost universal testimony of medical men, in the civilized world, is, that from uncleanness of person, dwelling or premises, or locality, combined with improper food and intemperate or irregular habits, arises the chief danger from Cholera or other epidemics; hence the importance of paying strict attention to sanitary precautions.

They supported their contentions by citing British and American cities such as Worcester, London, Liverpool, Salisbury, and Philadelphia as examples of places which had lowered their death rates by improving sanitation. Edwin Chadwick was quoted on the benefits of sanitation and the British Privy Council on effective disinfectants. But, like their British counterparts, Tempest and Rowell discovered that even the fear of cholera did little to alter deeply engrained habits.[40] Tempest was particularly concerned about waste-disposal practices, remarking in his final report

> In former years the garbage thrown on the streets appears to have been allowed to decompose until all was mud together. Notwithstanding the large quantities taken up this year, and the cautions issued by the Board of Health, the habit of making use of street and land as a deposit for house refuse of every kind is so established in this City, that inhabitants of even respectable houses, or at any rate their servants, regularly violate the Bylaws in this respect, often selecting the vicinity of their neighbors [sic] back gate as a specially eligible spot.[41]

To mitigate this health hazard, Tempest suggested that all city scavenging be carried out by the Board of Health and that the refuse collected be sold as fertilizer. He also called for improvement of the quality of Toronto's water supply and construction of an efficient drainage system. Tempest's forceful advocacy of these remedies demonstrated his belief that City Council had a dynamic role to play in improving living conditions in Toronto. He observed that, although cholera had appeared in Toronto five times during the summer, the death rate from filth diseases had actually declined in 1866 because of the preventive measures which he and Rowell had introduced.[42] By using his annual report to publicize the success which the Local Board had achieved and to agitate for further activity, Tempest was imitating proven British tactics and providing his successors with a model.

With the cessation of the epidemic and the conclusion of the central board's region, Toronto's council moved speedily to dispense with the services of its health officers.[43] The impetus to do this came from the cost-conscious aldermen who had objected to By-law 431, but the lack of comment from either the lay or medical press or the council members who had supported the ordinance indicates that support for the concept of continuous supervision of the health habits of Toronto's citizens was not yet accepted. During the spring of 1867 concern about a possible reappearance of cholera led the Local Board of Health to request council's approval for the reappointment of its medical health officers. Again, a sustained campaign was necessary before Tempest and Rowell were reinstated. They immediately began to undertake preventive measures such as cleaning the city, surveying the back lanes prior to ordering the abatement of long-standing nuisances, and collecting death statistics in an attempt to discover the extent of preventable disease.[44] This work was quickly overshadowed by the outbreak of smallpox and medical relief problems associated with the closing of Toronto General Hospital.[45] The medical officers were responsible for vaccinating large numbers of Torontonians and for caring for those afflicted with smallpox and other diseases. Once again, the needs of the moment took precedence over any long-term system of prevention.

Over the next three years, further attacks were levelled at even those few preventive measures already in place. During 1867 and 1868, the discontented councillors who had objected to the expansion of the Board of Health's activities in 1866 began a series of attacks on the probity of board members and the effectiveness of their activities. Francis Medcalf, now an alderman, charged that D'Arcy Boulton, the board's chairman in 1867, was indulging in the "vicious and corrupt" practice of letting contracts without public tenders. This partisan slur on the board's business principles was paralleled by Alderman Harman's attack on its sanitation policies.[46] In 1868, other council members voiced their constituents' criticisms of the Board of Health's laxity in failing to keep cows and pigs off the streets and to remove nuisances promptly.[47] Two of the aldermen appointed to the Board of Health in 1869 had been its staunchest opponents in the 1866 debates on By-law 431. Having failed to prevent its inception, Aldermen John Baxter and William Strachan determined to exert council control over the board from the inside. With the disappearance of cholera and typhus, some aldermen and their voters agreed that there was little need for expensive permanent preventive services. Consequently, one of the first motions which the 1869 Local Board of Health introduced was a demand for its own abolition.[48] Next, it recommended dismissing the health officers and transferring all sanitary activities to the Board of Works.[49]

These proposals prompted an outcry from the *Leader* and its independent Conservative rival, the *Daily Telegraph*. The former argued: "The medical health officers have done so much to preserve the health of the city and in so many ways, that we cannot suppose that the Council will be rash enough to dismiss them for the sake of making a show of saving the small salaries they are paid."[50] The *Telegraph* echoed its counterpart, commending Rowell and Tempest on their diligence and saying that, while

> The lanes – the great sanitary curse of the city – are certainly not so cleanly as they might be, but they would assuredly be in a much worse condition than they are, if we dispensed with the services of the health officers.[51]

Like the *Leader*, the *Telegraph* was concerned that "a buncombe cry of economy – mingled with a little personal ill-feeling" was the principal reason for dismissal.[52] The *Telegraph* stated that, furthermore, it had failed to find substantiation of charges of negligence and incompetence levelled against Tempest and Rowell.[53] Instead, it offered as proof of their efficiency the increased death rate and the filthy state of the lanes and alleys which had supposedly followed the elimination of the positions. Finally, it commented:

> The neglect of proper scavenging and the cramping of the health officers has a great deal to do with this state of things. We know that last summer was a very hot one and some few deaths might be ascribed to it. But the heat was not confined to Toronto nor Canada. In England the heat of summer was intense. Yet in Liverpool the densest peopled of English towns, the death rate was materially lessened through the exertions of its Medical Officer and the help of the civic authorities.[54]

Although the *Telegraph* evidently wanted Toronto to copy the British example, its pleading was in vain, and by June 1869 the medical health officers had been fired.[55] The Local Board of Health straggled on until November when it too was disbanded.[56]

From one perspective, the successful campaign to abolish the Board of Health and its officers can be viewed as political revenge for the removal of the Board of Works' traditional hegemony over civic patronage. From another perspective, it demonstrated how great an anomaly the 1866 by-law had been with its emphasis on disease prevention and use of medical experts. Fear of cholera may have led to the imposition of some aspects of the British sanitary idea on Toronto prior to the epidemic but this did not necessarily indicate appreciation or understanding of that idea. Once that concern receded, efforts to dismantle the administrative apparatus commenced. It simply did not reflect the city's limited health needs as the public and its elected representatives saw them.

For the majority of Torontonians, the sanitary idea was an overly complex and expensive approach to a relatively minor aspect of urban life in the 1860s. With only the limited sanitary surveys carried out in 1866 and 1867 to guide them, most citizens had little knowledge of slum life and its potential threat to their health. This lack of knowledge was in emphatic contrast to the British experience. There, lobbying groups such as the Health of Towns and Social Science associations vied with government agencies in producing studies and reports which graphically detailed the environmental problems facing British centres. Exposure of these appalling conditions usually resulted either in private bills brought forward by the parliamentary representatives of great cities like London or Liverpool, or in the expansion of the central authorities' supervisory powers. In both instances, municipal corporations made long-term commitments to alleviating the environmental pollution. It was recognized that such problems undermined their inhabitants' health and were not remediable without sustained planning and financial backing.[57] Since Toronto had not yet experienced the pressures of rapid demographic expansion, its council was unwilling to do more than respond to the threat of epidemic disease and the fiats of the provincial administration.

Similarly, views about the role of the medical health officer were markedly different on either side of the Atlantic. In Britain, from 1848 onward there was a clear division between urban-based preventive and curative services; Poor Law physicians supplied the latter while medical officers of health provided the former.[58] In Canada, no provisions had been made for a formal system of poor relief, with the result that Toronto's health officers were expected to combine both functions. As mentioned earlier, Doctors Tempest's and Rowell's acceptance of this duty in 1867 undercut their efforts to promote the sanitary idea among their fellow Torontonians. Nevertheless, the health officers had attempted to focus public attention on disease prevention rather than curative activities when they noted in their annual report that during 1866

> a considerable sum was expended in precautionary measures, an expenditure which some may deem unnecessary, in view of the fact that we were spared any severe visitation of Cholera, but in consideration of the diminished mortality and relative sickness, an amount that should be grudged by no one. The requirements of Public Hygiene will yet engage more seriously the attention of civilized people, and have a more important place in their municipal arrangements.[59]

Dr. Tempest, however, may inadvertently have contributed to his own downfall when he assessed the medical relief problem in February 1869 and suggested that City Council use municipal taxes to fund city patients in the Toronto General Hospital.[60] This recommendation may well have been seen as an unwarranted extension of the health officers' activities and along with the tradition of routinely dispensing with the services of medical advisors after an epidemic was over, undoubtedly provided the justification for eliminating the positions.

The 1870s, however, proved to be a turning point as the various strands of the sanitary idea began to be woven together. At the local level, the health problems facing Torontonians multiplied as the city's population expanded from around fifty-six thousand in 1871 to about eighty-six thousand in 1886.[61] This extensive growth occurred in spite of a depression from 1873 to 1878 which was sufficiently severe to bring civic politicians and the public to discuss methods of rationalizing Toronto's social services, specifically funding of poor relief and medical relief. Meanwhile, the provincial government also passed Ontario's first post-Confederation public health act in 1873. This legislation reinforced the crisis-response mentality by providing for the appointment of a Central Board of Health only during epidemics. The act reiterated the view that public health was a municipal responsibility but did not require civic authorities to appoint medical health officers or to undertake preventive activities.[62] To the vanguard of the Ontario medical profession, the 1873 Public Health Act seemed regressive, and they pressed the government to investigate the sanitary state of the province and to establish a permanent provincial health board modelled on the British example.[63]

At the federal level, the Canadian Medical Association sought to encourage federal support for preventive medicine by lobbying for the creation of a Central Bureau of Health and the collection, analysis, and publication of nation-wide mortality statistics.[64] The Medical Association's Committee on Vital Statistics and Public Hygiene believed that public support for government intervention would be forthcoming if the true extent of preventable disease deaths were known. Committee members hoped, through investigation and legislation, to create a climate of opinion conducive to the development by the municipal, provincial, and federal governments of effective preventive services. As central Canada became more and more industrialized during this decade, the health costs which the medical practitioners had warned were associated with this phenomenon became more obvious and led to a growing public appreciation of the sanitary idea.

As one of the major beneficiaries of the industrial expansion which occurred after 1867, Toronto required a more sophisticated administrative structure. In 1871 City Council created a new officer known as the Commissioner of Works and Health (usually referred to as the city commissioner) to oversee public works projects and to carry out the city's sanitation policies.[65] In August 1871, John Carr, the city commissioner, submitted a lengthy report to council in which he outlined the sanitary problems which plagued Toronto. Given the environmentalist emphasis of medical theory as laymen understood it, Carr was particularly concerned about the lack of systematic scavenging, the presence of nuisances caused by poor drainage, and the danger of offal from slaughterhouses polluting the adjacent neighbourhood. The city commissioner reiterated his anxieties with increasing stridency throughout the fall of 1871 because cholera was once again on the move. By January, unable to obtain any funding or rouse the Board of Works to action, Carr began to agitate for the recreation of the Board of Health.[66] A further impetus was provided when smallpox erupted in January 1872, and the civic government was unable to contain it without medical assistance. Sustained pressure from both the *Globe* and the *Telegraph*, along with Carr's recommendation that his political superiors on the Board of Works rescind their jurisdiction over health matters, led to the re-establishment of the Local Board of Health in February 1872.[67]

Like its predecessors, the newly created Board of Health had a limited role and limited prestige within the municipal hierarchy. It was to be served by a health inspector who was expected to administer health-related works projects, investigate sanitary problems, analyse well water, prevent public sewers from becoming nuisances, and ensure that slaughterhouse proprietors maintained appropriate standards of cleanliness. In addition, the enabling by-law provided for the appointment of medical health officers "to hold office during the pleasure of the Council, and whose duties and remuneration shall be specially defined from time to time by resolution of the Council or the said Committee [the Local Board of Health]."[68] Clearly, the British emphasis on medical expertise and guidance in the formulation of municipal health policy had not yet been adopted by Toronto's aldermen. Carr set up a temporary smallpox hospital and arranged for the appointment of a medical superintendant, Dr. A. A. Riddell, while at the same time maintaining a semi-supervisory role in the institution's administration until he was stricken with the disease.[69]

After its resurrection, the Local Board assumed control of the hospital and also organized public vaccination for the city.[70] The latter preventive measure was applauded by the *Globe* and the *Telegraph*, both of which exhorted their readers to take advantage of the free service.[71] Gradually, the epidemic was brought under control and, although smallpox appeared sporadically throughout the remainder of the decade,[72] it did not assist to any great extent in advancing the sanitary idea. The reasons for this are two-fold: first, in spite of the *Globe's* contention that bad sanitation contributed to the outbreak, most Torontonians seem to have accepted the *Telegraph's* view that smallpox was not a filth disease,[73] and second, it would appear that Dr. Riddell made no attempt to make the sanitary concept a viable aspect of civic policy.[74] During the 1870s, the medical superintendant provided curative services in the smallpox hospital and arranged for public vaccination, but he did not actively pursue other preventive activities.

As the decade progressed, however, several aldermen began to question the effectiveness of using the medical health officer only for disease-control purposes. In 1876, Alderman Thomas Gearing asked permission to introduce a motion for the appointment "of an officer ... whom the sick poor can approach in times of distress." Although this suggestion was not acted upon, it may well have helped prompt Alderman Morgan Baldwin to make a similar resolution in 1877. Baldwin wanted to see a more equitable system of poor relief and more predictable levels of municipal spending on health problems.[75] Like its 1877 counterpart, Baldwin's second motion in 1878 perished in committee, but all three of these efforts did bring the question of the duties of the medical health officer back into the political arena at a critical moment.

Baldwin's and Gearing's motions indicated the ambivalence or confusion which members of the City Council apparently felt when addressing this issue. Did they want a public servant whose major duties were preventive or curative? Did they want to continue to combine both types of activity? Although the Toronto *Mail*, a Conservative organ, had argued as early as 1872 that "to wait until disease actually appears is false economy," and that it would be "better to employ competent medical skill to prevent than to cure," Toronto's elected representatives were still endeavouring to unite both functions in 1880.[76] Shortly after his inauguration that year, the new mayor, businessman W. B. McMurrich, indicated that he supported the appointment of a medical relief officer primarily to prevent chronic cases from being treated in Toronto General Hospital at the city's expense.[77] McMurrich's attempt to rationalize Toronto's health services in this manner demonstrated the way in which local needs influenced the development of health services.

Beyond the council, however, there was a growing understanding of the price of urban growth. Toronto's papers, especially the *Mail*, warned their readers about the deteriorating quality of meat and milk supplies, questioned the potability of Toronto's water supply, and criticized the municipal corporation for its inability to cope with the vast amounts of household and industrial wastes that were polluting the city.[78] Within the civic bureaucracy Robert Awde, the General Inspector of Licenses, and Emerson Coatsworth, the city commissioner, both began to agitate for an extension of their powers to protect the city's food supplies and its sanitation activities. In their monthly and annual reports to the Markets and Health Committee and the Board of Works these overburdened civil servants tried to foster a sense of the magnitude of the sanitary problems facing the aldermen and their constituents. Again and again, they stressed the council's responsibility to protect the health of the public through the provision of pure water, effective waste removal, and close supervision of the production and sale of Toronto's food supplies.[79] Awde even cited European chemists and British health officers to buttress his demands for stricter by-laws. With typically Victorian fervour, the General Inspector of Licenses urged municipal politicians to action.

> To you, gentlemen of the Board of Health this [public health reform] is a subject of vital importance, and intimately associated

with the high interests that you are as a body appointed to conserve, and one which would justify an increased expenditure, promoting the highest results – the health and happiness of the masses.[80]

As a result of such prodding, the City Council moved slowly to increase its involvement in the lives of its citizens.

During the 1870s interested citizens, notably Toronto's medical elite, participated in the effort to obtain federal and provincial support for public health services. After their disillusioning experience at the municipal level, it was hardly surprising that they, like many of their British counterparts, turned to the senior levels of government to attain their goals. By 1878, Toronto-based practitioners and teachers such as Edward Playter, the editor of the *Sanitary Journal* (1874) and Parkdale's first Medical Health Officer (1876), William Oldright, a professor of sanitary science at the Toronto School of Medicine, and Charles W. Covernton, Oldright's opposite number at Trinity Medical School, had persuaded Premier Oliver Mowat to appoint a select committee of the Ontario legislature to investigate existing health services in the province. In its final report, the committee tabulated the sanitary deficiencies of towns and cities throughout the province and called for the creation of a Central Board of Health to supervise local efforts and to formulate policy for both municipal and provincial authorities.[81] This recommendation paralleled the development of preventive medicine in Great Britain and demonstrated the international nature of health problems and their solutions. Further agitation by Ontario's doctors and the formation of the Ontario Medical Association was necessary before the Mowat government passed the Public Health Act of 1882. This statute set up a permanent Provincial Board of Health whose mandate encompassed the supervision of specific preventive efforts at the municipal level as well as disease prevention and control in the central sphere.[82] Fear of unwanted provincial interference was therefore another feature of the debate on the appointment of Toronto's first permanent medical health officer in 1883.

But the medical profession was at the same time gaining concessions from the federal government which were of distinct value to Toronto and its aldermen. In 1879 the Macdonald administration passed a Census and Vital Statistics Act which supplied federal funds not only for the 1881 census but also for the collection of mortality statistics in cities with populations over ten thousand.

The grant, however, was conditional upon the existence of an active Local Board of Health with a permanent, salaried medical health officer.[83] Since this section of the 1879 statute was to come into effect in 1883, Toronto's council found itself once again compelled to think seriously about the role of the medical health officer within the structure of municipal affairs.

In January 1883 Toronto's Local Board of Health began the delicate task of defining the responsibilities of the medical health officer it was legally obligated to have in order to qualify for federal funding. On the one hand, leaders of the sanitary movement, like Doctors Playter and Oldright, urged the aldermen to take this opportunity to bring Toronto to the forefront of North American cities by adopting the preventive approach dominating major British centres.[84] On the other, old-guard politicians saw the new appointment as a way to overcome medical relief problems for both the sick poor and injured municipal workers. Not unexpectedly, By-law 1317 mirrored the views of the aldermen with the result that the officer was expected to examine the sick poor, provide curative services to injured city employees, offer public vaccination on a monthly basis, and collect the federal government's statistics. He was permitted to undertake preventive efforts such as investigating nuisances and providing advice on sanitation, disease control measures, and food supplies only at the request of the mayor, the Markets and Health Committee, and the General Inspector of Licenses. Although sanitary enthusiasts were disappointed by By-law 1317 because of its limited preventive provisions, they were immeasurably heartened by the appointment of Dr. William Canniff to the post.[85]

Underlying discussion on the by-law was the question of patronage. Toronto had a long history of rewarding faithful Tories with civic posts, and for some council members the new position was merely an addition to the civic spoils. Others, however, were more concerned with the degree of professional training and expertise required than with the party affiliation of the candidates whose names they were presenting. For both camps, Canniff was the ideal choice. Conservative in temperament and political allegiance, the new Medical Health Officer was also a well-known figure in Toronto society, a noted historian, and a prominent Canadian nationalist. His medical credentials were equally impeccable – including as they did initial training at Victoria College Medical School, post-graduate work in New York City and London, a teaching career in Toronto, and the presidency of the Canadian Medical

Association in 1880–81. He had also been the chairman of the Association's Committee on Vital Statistics and Public Hygiene which had convinced the Macdonald government to provide the funding for the collection of municipal mortality statistics.[86]

In hiring Canniff, however, the City Council was getting even more than it anticipated. The new medical officer was a committed contingent-contagionist. He intended to try to educate Torontonians in all aspects of the sanitary idea. From 1883 until his resignation in 1890, Canniff investigated and publicized Toronto's health problems, devised and implemented legislative and administrative solutions to them, and expanded the services which his department provided. Under his expert tutelage and guidance, Torontonians of all social classes and political persuasions were gradually convinced that preventive medicine was an integral aspect of municipal life.

In the summer of 1883 Canniff began his efforts to implement the sanitary idea. He borrowed five policemen for a house-to-house survey of the city. As he indicated to Mayor Boswell, the purpose of the investigation was "to ascertain the sanitary state of each place visited" and "to impart information to the citizens as to the sanitary requirements of houses and premises." Like his British counterparts, Canniff believed that good drainage, the use of city water, the closure of foul wells, cisterns, and privies, and the development of efficient garbage-disposal practices were essential to public health. Since he recognized that many citizens were not aware of the by-laws relating to household sanitation, he instructed his inspectors "to exert themselves to accomplish sanitary reform by persuasion rather than coercion or threat." When investigators uncovered "serious unhealthy nuisances," an interview with the person responsible was undertaken "to inform the party of the nuisance, to secure, if possible, his willing promise to abate the evil, and to supply this office with the knowledge of what might be reasonably expected to be done."[87] By emphasizing co-operation instead of compulsion, Toronto's medical officer was not only imitating John Simon's approach to municipal health work but also educating his fellow citizens in their sanitary responsibilities. Such behaviour was both politically expedient and a reflection of Canniff's faith in the rationality of Torontonians.

Proof of the medical officer's success in this area was the increase in the number of citizen complaints concerning nuisances such as rotting garbage and improperly flushed and ventilated sewers, and major environmental pollution problems such as distillery refuse and manure in Ashbridge's Bay, sewage in Toronto Harbour, and unauthorized waste dumping in the Garrison and Rosedale creeks. In 1883 Canniff's staff responded to approximately five hundred citizen complaints. By 1889 the yearly total had risen to roughly six thousand.[88] This vast increase in public awareness can be attributed to the sustained agitation by Toronto newspapers through the 1870s and 1880s, the publication of annual reports by the medical health department, and the ever-increasing pollution problems associated with urban growth.

Citizen complaints, however, were not the major component of the health department's investigatory efforts. With the amendment of the Provincial Public Health Act in 1884, Toronto's health officer found himself empowered to examine the sanitary condition of the city's schools, factories, and homes and, in particular, to focus his efforts on its noxious trades and food suppliers.[89] Recognizing that these duties overlapped with the work of existing departments, Canniff sought allies within the civic bureaucracy. As a result, the health department undertook school inspection with the blessing of the Board of Education in 1886, shared milk inspection with the General Inspector of Licenses, provided a sanitary patrol for Toronto Island with the approval of the Property Committee, and assessed the quality of Toronto's ice supply in conjunction with the city commissioner.[90] By sharing his inspectorial functions with other municipal departments, Toronto's health officer was inculcating the sanitary idea among his fellow bureaucrats and thus expanding the concept's influence.

To ensure that the work of the health department reached the widest possible audience, Canniff made ceaseless efforts to publicize his staff's activities. His task was made easier by the Public Health Act of 1884 which required the Medical Health Officer to present an annual report to his local board. Canniff used this opportunity to outline in graphic detail the continuing sanitary problems which he saw as causing much unnecessary illness and death. In addition, he provided a statistical tabulation of the inspections which his men had carried out and appended copies of his correspondence with citizens, members of council, and the Local and Provincial Boards of Health.

Not content with official channels alone, Canniff also used the lay and medical press and various interest groups to obtain public support. The Toronto *News*, the working-man's paper, was especially assiduous in interviewing him about sanitary matters and disease-causation theories.[91] Both the Conservative *Mail* and its party rival the *Empire* printed comparative national mortality statistics[92] while the Liberal *Globe* occasionally commented on the quality of Toronto's water supply and contentious local issues such as the high cost of constructing a trunk sewer.[93] Toronto's leading medical journals, the *Canada Lancet* and the *Canadian Practitioner*, also kept their readership informed about the health department's endeavours. The latter even went so far as to remind the city's doctors of their duty to report cases of infectious disease without delay in 1887.[94] Public lectures on sanitary issues at the Canadian Institute,[95] the formation of the Toronto Sanitary Association in 1884,[96] and the visit of the American Public Health Association to Toronto in 1886 for its annual meeting[97] all contributed to the expansion of citizen awareness of both the sanitary idea and the activities of the city's health department.

With the election of a reform-oriented municipal government under William Howland in 1886, Canniff was able to move more forcefully into health administration. Indeed, the choice of Philip Drayton, a Toronto lawyer and son-in-law of the chairman of the Provincial Board of Health, as chairman of the Local Board of Health meant that the health department now had an articulate champion within the council chamber.[98] Together, Howland, Drayton, Canniff, and their supporters began to develop a series of by-laws to regulate the quality of Toronto's meat, milk, and ice supplies and to combat enduring environmental problems such as sewage contamination and garbage disposal. In each instance, every opportunity for collaboration between the health department and the trade or group being regulated was exploited in order to devise legislation appropriate to the Canadian context. An example of this can be found in Canniff's regulation of slaughterhouse sanitation.

In April 1886 Canniff's men discovered that only 5 of 25 slaughterhouses and 103 of 143 butcher shops within the city limits were kept sufficiently clean according to the standards established in 1884. The health department sent written notification and a copy of the by-law to the offending operators. This action was followed by further visits from the inspectors to remind the owners of their legal duty. When "even this failed to arouse those addressed," the medical officer informed the Local Board of Health that as the law had been ignored, "one or more public slaughterhouses should be established, and the private ones closed up." Having taken this extreme position, the proponents of reform then prepared to negotiate a settlement with the Butchers' Association. On November 1, 1886, By-law 1769 to regulate slaughterhouses was passed. Under this ordinance, clauses 8 and 9 of the 1884 model health by-law were repealed and were replaced by a permit system supervised by the health department. The medical officer and his inspectors were empowered to visit any city slaughterhouse at any time and to revoke its licence if the sanitary conditions were not acceptable. To ensure that this did not occur, the Butchers' Association appointed its own inspector and encouraged members to keep their workplaces clean.[99] This episode illustrated the gradualist approach which the health department adopted towards its administrative duties. Rather than taking a doctrinaire stance based on the latest scientific advances, Toronto's health officials preferred to work to achieve consensus.

This gradualist approach, however, had limitations which became apparent when public health enthusiasts attempted to resolve major environmental problems. As early as 1884 Canniff issued warnings about the quality of Toronto's well water and recommended that citizens purchase their supply from the city waterworks instead. Growing doubts about the purity of the municipal product undercut his advocacy and led to demands that the waterworks department itself upgrade the quality.[100] Canniff felt that one of the most effective ways to improve the quality of Toronto's water was to construct a trunk sewer to prevent household wastes from being deposited in the city harbour. During 1886 and 1887, Howland, Canniff, and the members of the Toronto Sanitary Association all agitated in favour of building an intercepting sewer at a cost of $1.4 million. Their efforts were in vain as the city's ratepayers rejected the proposal twice.[101] In an attempt to salvage something from the situation, Canniff got the Local Board of Health to support his suggestion that foul wells, cisterns, and privies in downtown Toronto be closed by April 1, 1888.[102] More ambitious reforms in this area would have to wait.

In 1889, Canniff paused to assess his department's history. He felt that, although there had been some headway made in overcoming public and political indifference to sanitary reform, much remained to be done.[103] Clearly the department had expanded in terms of both personnel and budget since 1883. In 1885, the health department consisted of the medical officer, a single secretary, six borrowed policemen, and six summer employees.[104] By 1890 the staff included one senior inspector supervising seven inspectors whose duties involved responding to public complaints, controlling contagious diseases, investigating the cleanliness of slaughterhouses, cow byres, and ice houses, serving legal notices, and prosecuting court cases. There were also junior and senior office clerks, and occasionally a veterinary surgeon was hired to assist in milk inspection.[105] As the table below indicates, public health spending on preventive measures increased markedly throughout the 1880s, suggesting that even municipal politicians had come to find some value in the sanitary idea.

Local Board of Health Expenditure as a Proportion of Toronto's Public Health Spending in the 1880s*

Year	LBH	Health Dept.†	Total	Percentage
1883		$31,463.25	$31,463.25	100%
1884	$ 1,006.06	$29,951.40	$30,957.45	3%
1885	$ 6,672.84	$35,783.96	$42,456.80	16%
1886	$ 4,960.32	$40,727.18	$45,687.50	11%
1887	$ 4,165.89	$47,858.61	$52,024.50	8%
1888	$19,926.90	$60,288.16	$80,215.06	25%
1889	$12,645.17	$69,153.84	$81,799.01	15%
1890	$21,957.17	$59,476.19	$81,433.36	27%

* Does not include the amount spent on health department staff salaries.

† In addition to the preventive work carried out by the Local Board, the health department was also responsible for street watering, street cleaning, and scavenging.

By the end of the decade all three components of the sanitary idea – investigation, legislation, and administration – were in place. Torontonians had become accustomed to investigations carried out by the health officer and his staff leading to revisions in civic by-laws and improvements in municipal disease-prevention administration. Visible proof of the complete acceptance of the concept occurred in the wake of Canniff's resignation in September 1890. In contrast to its behaviour in 1869, the Toronto City Council immediately moved to appoint an interim successor and then held an open competitive examination to choose an appropriate candidate.[106]

Such behaviour indicated how completely the "sanitary idea" had been adopted over the preceding quarter century. As the threat of cholera receded, basic sanitation problems assumed great importance because with the rapid population growth of the 1870s, they intensified. Clearly the episodic, piecemeal approach to public health which had characterized the 1860s was no longer viable. As the public slowly recognized the permanent and intractable nature of environmental pollution, the warnings and recommendations of the medical community acquired greater validity. In such a climate William Canniff became both a catalyst and a rallying point for sanitary reform during the 1880s. Using the contingent-contagionist disease causation theory to support his activities, he modified each aspect of the sanitary idea to suit the political, economic, and ideological interests of his fellow Torontonians. By 1890 this British concept had been successfully Canadianized and had become an integral part of Toronto life.

— says nothing concerning actual reduce of risk.

— undercuts argument early in essay

4

Reasons for Committal to a Mid-Nineteenth-Century Ontario Insane Asylum: The Case of Toronto

Wendy Mitchinson

Mid-nineteenth-century Ontario saw the emergence of a variety of institutions for the care and treatment of targeted groups in society. Schools emerged to teach proper values to young people, reformatories to discipline those who rebelled, orphanages to care for those without parents, prisons to punish those who committed crimes, and hospitals to care for the sick poor. Asylums for the insane were a significant part of this movement. In pre-Confederation Canada, the public purse gave more to asylums than to any other form of social service.[1] In 1874, provincial monies to asylums exceeded allocations to institutions for the blind, the deaf and dumb, the provincial reformatory, general hospitals, and common gaols.[2] The 1871 census estimated that in the province 1 person out of every 397 was of unsound mind and that 1 per 1,120 of the population was either in a prison or an asylum.[3]

The historiography of the asylum has focused primarily on its purpose. Was the asylum designed to cure the insane – that is, did it stem from a reform impulse? Or was the asylum designed to provide custodial services as a form of social control? The former interpretation dominated nineteenth- and most twentieth-century writing and emphasized the change which occurred with the acceptance of moral treatment in the early nineteenth century. Moral treatment was predicated on the belief that insanity was curable and that the insane were human. It resulted in the removal of mechanical restraints from those incarcerated, the provision of adequate food, a modicum of freedom and activity, surrounding the insane with a pleasing and restful environment, and, above all, treating them as people who were sick but not hopelessly so. When compared to the horrendous conditions which had preceded this, it is not surprising that those involved with asylums believed that they had witnessed a revolutionary change for the better.[4] Little challenge to this interpretation occurred until the 1960s with the publication of Michel Foucault's seminal work, *Madness and Civilization: A History of Insanity in the Age of Reason*. Foucault saw the beginnings of the new asylum system as a result of rising capitalism and the needs of the middle class and argued that asylum reformers such as Pinel and Tuke, while freeing the insane from physical restraint, did so in return for the insane accepting responsibility for their actions. "Fear no longer reigned on the other side of the prison gates, it now raged under the seals of conscience."[5] The insane were free of bondage as long as they did not disturb the middle-class morality of society.

Foucault's concept of control proved very popular with American historians, although they added their own refinements. While believing that the asylum was established as a form of social control, David Rothman argued it was not because of economic forces but rather to "promote the stability of the society at a moment when traditional ideas and practices appeared outmoded, constricted, and ineffective."[6] Christopher Lasch also stressed ideology. He maintained that the rise of egalitarianism led to a heightened awareness of deviancy, social differences, and intolerance "which expressed itself in a determination to compel or persuade all members of society to conform to a single standard of citizenship" which stressed self-reliance and self-support.[7] The recent work of Andrew Scull on asylums in Britain continued the attack.

> But far from asylums having been altruistic institutions . . . detached from the social structures that perpetuate poverty, one must realize that they were important elements in sustaining those structures; important because of their symbolic value, and as a reminder of the awful consequences of non-conformity.[8]

Not all historians have accepted the social control perspective.[9] For his part, Gerald Grob believes that historians critical of the asylum have confused outcome with motivation. The failure of the asylum masked its original purpose, which Grob argues was humanitarian and reform in nature. The asylum was a product of the desire to cure, not control, and this desire came out of a context of changing ideas about the insane and the belief that they could be cured.[10]

Recently Michael Katz has attempted to shift the debate by asking why the asylum as an institution emerged and not whether it was good or bad. Expanding on the economic model utilized by many of the social controllers, he argues that the asylum, among other institutions, was a product of the commercial/capitalist stage of development.[11] Capitalism is based on wage labour and those without work are consequently seen as non-productive and therefore dependent. The problem for the commercial/capitalist stage of development was what to do with the non-productive in society; the solution, make them productive, that is, cure them of their non-productivity. At one time, such people had been grouped together in poorhouses or gaols, but with the division of labour that accompanied capitalism came similar divisions in social life and the rise of institutions catering to the needs of specific groups.[12] In arguing this way, Katz seems to share the historiographical determinism of the social controllers. But if the economic structure determined the form the asylum took, Katz is careful to point out that people's ideas were still of influence. Thus, it can be argued that humanitarian impulses could motivate the actual running of the institution and determine people's involvement with it.[13]

Other historians have gone beyond Katz's concerns and have shifted the focus away from the origins of the asylum, the motivation of its promoters, and why it took the form it did.[14] Instead, they have begun to concentrate on what was occurring within the asylum and by doing so have added to our understanding about the complex functions the asylum performed and the often conflicting demands which were placed upon it. They have tended to steer a middle course between the unquestioning optimism of the Whig historians and the cynical approach of the social control historians. In addition, they have begun to redress the balance of the historiography by focusing on the people who used the asylum: the patients, their families, and the authorities. It is the purpose of this paper to continue that effort.

Who were the insane? What were the definitions of insanity which could bring about a committal? Was it non-productivity in society, as Katz suggests, or was it something else? In an attempt to analyse why people were committed to an institution for the insane, this paper examines the Provincial Lunatic Asylum (PLA) in Toronto from 1841 to the end of 1874. The focus is on why people viewed others as insane and not on whether those committed were actually insane or not. After all, as the 1873 *Canada Lancet* pointed out, sanity and insanity are relative terms.[15] In the years under review, 4,280 patients entered the asylum. The records of every tenth patient have been examined, giving a total of 428 cases.[16] Of particular interest were the descriptions of the insanity exhibited by each patient *before* admission to the asylum. The various records on each patient were studied and the symptoms of insanity categorized, listed, and tabulated in an effort to assess the symptoms of insanity in mid-century and the reasons for committal to the asylum. What the analysis reveals is the inadequacy of the cure/custody debate.

The Toronto institution originated in an 1839 decision by the legislature of Upper Canada to build an asylum for the insane. However, no immediate action took place and the insane continued to be cared for by their families and friends or placed in local gaols. In 1841, the old York gaol became a temporary asylum, and, in 1850, the long-promised new facility finally opened.[17] More often than not, treatment of patients in these early years was deficient. When J. H. Tuke, the noted British asylum reformer, visited the temporary asylum in 1845, he was appalled at what he saw.

> The doctor pursues the exploded system of constantly cupping, bleeding, blistering and purging his patients, giving them also the smallest quantity of food and that of the poorest quality.[18]

Fortunately, by the mid-1850s "moral treatment" was beginning to hold sway and by the mid-1870s it totally dominated care of the insane. However, moral treatment leading to cure was restricted by the asylum's overcrowded conditions. Experts believed the optimum size of an asylum was 250 patients, yet in 1853 there were already 373 in the partially completed building.[19] Thus from the beginning of its existence, the PLA's ability to provide optimum curative care was restricted. In an attempt to limit the number of patients, Joseph Workman, superintendent of the asylum from 1854 to 1875, considered admitting only the curably insane. The incurable would be left to their own devices, which meant care by their families or placement in gaols or whatever institution for the indigent existed.[20] But not all who were insane had families who would or could care for them, and Workman viewed alternative institutions as providing poorer custodial care than that of the PLA. Thus, for what he argued were humanitarian reasons, he continued to accept both the curably and incurably insane into the asylum.[21]

The only apparent solution to the overcrowding was to provide additional accommodations, and from the late 1850s on, branches of the Provincial Lunatic Asylum were opened and new asylums built. In 1856 a wing of King's College in Toronto became a branch asylum as did the military barracks of Ford Malden in 1859 and the Orillia Asylum in 1861. Each of these branch asylums became a holding institution for the chronically insane in an attempt to maintain the central asylum as a curative facility, but even they could not offset the increasing number of incurables under care. More institutions were consequently opened and built. In 1856, the Rockwood Asylum in Kingston became an institution for the criminally insane. In 1870 the London Asylum opened, in 1876 Hamilton, in 1890 Mimico, in 1894 Brockville, in 1902 Cobourg, and in 1904 Penetanguishene. By the end of the century the asylum system in Ontario was in place. At that point Ontario had 69 per cent of its estimated 7,552 mentally ill in asylums.[22] While the growth of the asylum system was impressive after 1870, its direction had already been determined by that date. The system would be based on moral treatment, but its curative effect offset by continuing overcrowded conditions.

What were the characteristics of the people admitted to the asylums? By January of 1850 the Provincial Lunatic Asylum had admitted a total of 889 patients: 536 men and 353 women. The difference in the admission rate between the sexes in part reflected the reluctance in the early years to commit females to an untried institution, particularly one that was a converted gaol. Women were also less likely to be dangerous than men and consequently better suited to home care.[23] Nevertheless, by 1870 the discrepancy between the sexes was declining. Between 1851 and 1870 the total admitted was 3,830: 1,991 men and 1,839 women.[24] In October 1874 the asylum held 640 patients, equally divided between male and female.[25] By the end of the period under study, no distinction between the sexes in the number admitted existed; a difference remained, however, in their marital status (see Table 1).

Table 1[26]
Patients Admitted 1841 – September 1875
Marital Status

	Male	Female	Total
Married or Widowed	1,055	1,339	2,394
Single	1,277	730	2,007
	2,332	2,069	4,401

As Table 1 indicates, over the years there were more married women admitted to the asylum than single women and more single men than married men. Joseph Workman was struck by this and in 1864 argued that, while married women outnumbered single women in the asylum, when compared to their percentage in the population, married women were under-represented. He reached this conclusion by comparing figures for women in the general population in the thirty- to forty-year-old age bracket (the group in which the percentage of married women would be highest) with the entire female asylum population of all ages.[27] Perhaps he realized the fallacy of his analysis, for in his 1873 Report he simply noted "That as far as liability to insanity is concerned, marriage is very dangerous to women and single life very dangerous to men, whilst married men and single women enjoy comparative immunity."[28] While he attempted no analysis, it is possible to argue that single women, more than single men, were more likely to have recourse to their parental families when in need and that the pressures of marriage fell more heavily on women (given the stress of childbirth and the ideology of domesticity) than on men.[29] It also may have been more difficult for a man to care for his wife at home than it was for her to care for him.

While the marital status of the patients is intriguing, the place of residence of the patients was predictable. The asylum catered to those who could conveniently use it. People living in Toronto or the surrounding counties dominated, even in the years when the PLA was the only asylum in the province.[30] Those admitted were usually non-paying patients; indeed, the asylum was really designed for them in the early years. Thus it is understandable that the male patients were mainly farmers and labourers and the female patients were mostly domestics.[31]

Also predictable was the ethnic origin of the patients. In 1842, most of the 126 admissions had been born outside the country. Little else could be expected since Canada West at that time was an immigrant province. The Irish headed the list with 68, followed by the English with 36, the Canadian-born with 11, the Scots with 8, and Americans with 3.[32] Over time, the number of Canadian-born patients increased as did the native-born population in the province (see Table 2). Unfortunately, there is no indication of how long those born outside Canada had been in the country – that is, whether they were recent immigrants or not. According to Workman, one reason for the high representation of the Irish was their tendency to inter-marry which left them with an hereditary taint resulting in an incurable form of insanity. He also believed that the

Irish were often in trouble with local authorities who used the asylum as a cheap lock-up for them. However, more significant was their poverty. Irish-Canadian families simply could not afford to take care of their insane and thus sent them to the asylum.[33] Certainly poverty was a factor which Workman believed encouraged people in general to commit others to the asylum.[34] But as will be seen, poverty was only one of the factors which pushed families and friends to have loved ones committed and Workman's focus on it may have reflected the scarcity of paying patients in the early years and the consequent lack of funding for the asylum.

Table 2[35]
Patients Admitted 1841 – 30 September 1875
Ethnicity

Irish	1,499
Canadian	1,105
English	721
Scots	632
American	156
Others	138
	4,251

What the poverty of the patients did suggest, however, was that the public viewed the asylum, in part, as a custodial institution. This is supported by Workman's perception that the institution attracted the chronically insane, the people for whom little could be done except to provide custodial care. "Very few persons, who are at all able to detain insane friends at home, consent to send them to any Asylum, until this step has become a matter of dire necessity; and too often when this conjuncture has been reached, the disease has passed on to a hopeless stage."[36] The reason for his frustration is evident. Alienists could do nothing significant for the chronically ill; they could not cure them; they could only act as guardians. This custodial view of the asylum persisted, despite the efforts of Workman and others to persuade the public to see the asylum in a more positive light and to encourage them to commit the insane early in their disease, the time when alienists believed the best chance for a cure existed.

If the insane were not committed early enough to please Workman, they nevertheless were being committed – the overcrowded conditions attest to that. Families became less willing to keep their insane relatives when an alternative such as the asylum appeared. But what actually prodded them to make that move? What were the actions of the insane with which the families no longer could cope or were willing to cope? What symptoms did an individual have to exhibit to be considered insane, and how severe did the insanity have to be before commitment was considered necessary either by the family or by the authorities? And did the symptoms suggest what use was being made of the asylum?

Certifying physicians made little distinction between the symptoms and the causes of insanity. For example, intemperance, jealousy, anxiety, idiocy, epilepsy, and religious delusions were seen as both. In addition, mania, melancholia, and dementia, the major classifications of insanity, were also considered symptoms.[37] For the purposes of this study, the tendency to group symptom with cause and classification proved helpful in cases where patient records were limited, for it allowed some insight into why the patient was perceived to be insane.

Symptoms of insanity were varied. Violence, excitement, depression, delusions, and what modern analysts would classify as paranoia seemed quite common. Some patients swore more than usual, refused to work, drank to excess, were jealous without reason, were epileptic, suffered from hypochondria, or engaged in masturbation. Others wandered, were dirty, or exhibited erotic tendencies. Idiocy was also mentioned.[38] Most, if not all, symptoms could be placed under at least one of the three major classifications. For example, violence, delusions, paranoia, jealousy, quarreling, drinking, and swearing were all symptoms of a manic personality. Paranoia, depression, and refusing to eat or sleep or work could be symptomatic of melancholia. Incoherency, wandering, being dirty, and refusing to engage in any activity could be indicative of someone suffering from dementia. Each symptom could go under more than one classification and often it was the specific combination of symptoms which determined the classification. All symptoms, however, reflected some form of excessive behaviour when compared to the middle-class norms of society.

Another way of viewing the symptoms of insanity is to decide whether they made the individual dangerous to society or to self. Violence, excitement, delusions, and paranoia could cause a person to be dangerous to society. Depression, drinking, idiocy, and unwillingness to work would made an individual dysfunctional in society and unable to maintain himself/herself. Obviously there could be great overlapping between the two. What this seems to suggest is that any form of lack of control pre-disposed society to view a person as insane. This conclusion gains credence when an analysis is made of how often the records mentioned the various symptoms.

Between 1841 and the end of 1844, 40 per cent of those patients admitted whose records were checked were described as violent in one way or another. Forty-four per cent of the patients exhibited some form of excitement and 28 per cent suffered from some despondency, depression, or melancholia. Since a patient could have more than one symptom, I made an attempt to determine which of the symptoms brought about the committal. Of the twenty-five patients for whom descriptions were available between 1841 and 1844, ten were violent and six exhibited signs of abnormal excitement including drinking to excess and having epileptic seizures. Three were idiots, four suffered from some form of depression, and two had "drink" as the only description. This confirms the order which emerged from simply going through the patients and seeing how often each symptom was mentioned as done above. An analysis of the entire period 1841 to 1875 reinforces this (see Table 3).

Violence was the symptom mentioned most often in patient records. The frequency of violence indicates one of the main purposes of the asylum – the protection of society. However, the asylum also protected the insane from retaliation by society and, if they were suicidal, from themselves. This focus on violence increased over time, reflecting the increasing custodial use being made of the asylum. But even granting that, the friends and relatives of patients, in their letters to the asylum, indicated that they kept hoping for more than humane custody, they hoped for a cure and return of their loved ones.

Violence in the insane took three forms. The first was violence towards some other person, as in the case of Elias S. (#410), a thirty-one-year-old farmer who had been ill for three months before entering the asylum in September 1846. He refused food and suffered from depression caused by a misunderstanding with his father who had prevented him from joining a religious society. His insanity was increasing and had reached the point where he attempted to kill both his father and his brother. The second form of violence was violence towards self, particularly attempted or threatened suicide. John A. (#3,890), twenty-three years of age, suffering from epilepsy and ill for four years before entering the asylum in March 1872, had at one time tried to jump out of a window and at another to drown himself. The last form of violence mentioned was destruc-

Table 3[39]
Major Symptoms of Insanity
1841–1875

Symptom[†]	1840s		1850s		1860s		1870s	
Number of Patients With Symptoms Mentioned*	81		124		132		72	
	N	%	N	%	N	%	N	%
Dangerous	12	14.8	50	40.3	52	39.3	33	45.8
Suicidal	9	11.1	16	12.9	41	31.0	18	25.0
Destructive	17	20.9	12	9.7	28	21.2	22	30.5
Violent (all 3)	27	33.3	61	49.2	88	66.6	49	68.0
Excitement	27	33.3	24	19.4	48	36.3	40	55.5
Depression	17	20.9	12	9.7	13	9.8	8	11.1
Paranoia	7	8.6	13	10.5	28	21.2	18	25.0
Delusions	6	7.4	22	17.5	34	25.7	32	44.4

* The total number of patients whose records were checked was 428. However, nineteen of the records did not contain enough information to determine symptoms.

† A patient could exhibit more than one symptom. The number and percentage simply indicate the number and percentage who exhibit a specific symptom among others.

tion of property, often the patient's own. Euphonia B. (#3,830), aged thirty-eight, was described as talking, singing, and being generally wakeful except for one day a week when she was dull, sleepy, and quiet. She also had a proclivity for tearing her own clothes.

In the 1840s, the percentage of patients deemed dangerous was not large. Between 1841 and 1845, only 16 per cent of the patients were described in a manner which suggested they were dangerous. Between 1845 and 1850, it was 14.3 per cent. However, after that period, the percentage considered dangerous increased, with some ups and downs until it reached a high of 45.8 per cent between 1870 and 1875. The low percentage in the 1840s could be a consequence of the large number of chronic cases which were admitted to the asylum in the early years. These were individuals kept in gaol or at home for years simply because there was nowhere else to send them. After being insane for a long time, it is quite likely that these patients had gone beyond being dangerous or violent and had become harmlessly demented. After the 1840s, the increase might reflect patients coming to the asylum in the early stage of their illness. However, Workman felt that this was seldom the case and the increase was more likely a function of needing to satisfy certain criteria in order to gain admission. Very soon after the asylum opened it became overcrowded. If the asylum had to turn back patients, it had to decide on what grounds to do so. Applicants who were dangerous were given high priority, if only to remove them from society to an environment where they posed less of a threat and where they could be helped. Yet, patients described as dangerous in the certificate of insanity did not always show indications of it once they entered the asylum, suggesting that the symptom was put down only in order to get the individual admitted.[40] Admission procedures support that supposition.

Admission to the asylum was relatively straightforward. It was a public asylum which meant that it was inspected on a regular basis by government representatives. As well, medical certificates of insanity were needed before commitment could occur. The 1839 Act insisted that three physicians practising in Ontario certify any proposed patient and the Board of Commissioners of the asylum or any one member of the board, if the board was not sitting, had to be satisfied about the insanity.[41] The 1853 legislation basically left certification the same as in the 1839 Act. Three physicians had to certify the insanity and the reeve or mayor in the patient's township or town had to sign the certificate.[42] Dangerous lunatics could be committed to gaol by a Justice's warrant, and, after evidence was given on the insanity of the prisoner, he/she could be held in gaol until moved to the asylum by authority of the Lieutenant Governor.[43] Because it was sometimes very awkward to get three physicians to fill out a certificate of insanity, families often resorted to having the patient declared "insane and dangerous to be at large" so that he/she would be placed in gaol and then removed to the asylum. In 1860, one-third of all patients admitted to the Provincial Lunatic Asylum came from gaol.[44]

Of the 147 cases deemed dangerous in one way or another out of the 428 cases checked, 94 were males and 53 were females. The sex differential is in keeping with the social context of an era which emphasized gentleness in women and aggressiveness in men. Nevertheless, 13 of the female patients actually attacked someone, 12 of them threatened to do so, and 28 simply were termed "dangerous" with no further detail offered. Of the 94 men, 20 attacked, 20 threatened and 54 were deemed dangerous. Threatening violence was considered significant, even though threats do not necessarily mean that the individual is actually dangerous. However, those who threatened did so against some specific individual. This made the threat believable, especially when it coincided with some other expression of violence, either to property or to self. The number of dangerous cases where no detail was given reinforces the suspicion that being considered dangerous eased entry into the asylum.

Despite the apparent willingness of women to attack as well as to threaten to attack, the perception of the danger posed by women was different from that posed by men. The records describe women simply as "attacking" whereas men are described as "assaulting," "stabbing," "injuring," "striking violently," and "attempting to kill." Male violence was seen as brutal and detailed extensively. Both sexes concentrated their violence on their families, although males were able to direct some at others. Of the thirteen women who actually attacked someone, not one attacked an individual outside the family. This reflected the isolation of women within the confines of their homes. They only infrequently came into contact with anyone outside the family with whom they could establish a relationship intense enough to lead to violence. Men, on the other hand, had more contacts outside the family through their work.

Suicide, unlike attack, was a form of violence utilized almost equally by the two sexes and it increased over time.[45] Forty-three female and forty-one male patients were suicidal. Of the forty-one men, eleven attempted suicide, thirteen threatened, and the remaining seventeen simply were described as suicidal. Among the forty-three women, nine attempted and nine threatened suicide while twenty-five were described merely as suicidal. As in the case of threatening attack, threatening suicide was seen as a sign of insanity. When accompanied by other acts of violence, the threat became believable. The number of cases designated simply "suicidal" lends support to the theory that the symptom of violence to self was also attributed to patients in order to gain them entry to the asylum.

Many patients were not suicidal and neither attacked nor threatened to attack others but were still violent. They tended to be destructive towards property, both their own and others'. The incidence of this form of violence remained relatively stable over time. The differences between male and female patients were minimal and it is only in the early years that more men than women were viewed as destructive. This can be accounted for by the majority of male patients over female during that period. As with those who were labelled dangerous, those deemed on admission to be destructive do not always appear to have shown signs of it once in the asylum.

Linked closely with violence was excitement. It was a major symptom of insanity and was found in patients like Euphonia B. (#3,830 above) or Thomas C. (#3,100), a twenty-four-year-old single man, ill nine weeks before being admitted on November 11, 1864. He was described as singing, whistling, talking too much, dancing, shouting, and preaching. Such antics were considered symptomatic of a maniac. Excitement remains a significant symptom of insanity throughout the period, although it declines drastically in the 1850s. It is difficult to account for this unless it is simply a reflection of the record-keeping during that decade. Whatever the reason, by the end of the 1870s 55 per cent of the patients exhibited some signs of excitement. Since the nature of the excitement, whether it be singing, dancing, swearing, or restlessness, was often episodic or sporadic in nature, it was seldom the sole reason for a person's committal. Unless constant, it was a symptom which could be coped with by the family and which did not endanger society or the individual in any way.

In many respects, depression was similar. A typical case, Mary B. (#2,010), was committed to the asylum for the third time in 1857. At that point she was a forty-seven-year-old married woman, mother of ten children and described simply as despondent over the death of one of them. Depression could make an individual unable to care for themselves and thus a prime candidate for the asylum. However, the percentage of patients suffering from depression decreased over time. This was probably linked more to the overcrowded conditions of the asylum and the difficulty in gaining entry than to an absolute decrease in the number of people suffering from severe depression. If the violent were admitted as top priority, people exhibiting other symptoms, especially those suffering from depression, would experience more difficulty in obtaining committal; unless their depression was accompanied by some sort of violence they would more than likely be harmless. Certainly very few admissions are listed as having suffered from despondency alone. Out of the 428 cases examined, of the 50 cases indicating depression 27 exhibited signs of violence, 4 were deluded, 3 suffered from mania, and 1 patient wandered from home. In the case of the 15 remaining patients, it was circumstances in addition to their own depression which may have directed them to the asylum. Some patients had families who could no longer cope. For example, Margaret M.

(#1,180), a widow aged sixty-seven with nine children, was committed in April 1852. She previously had been in the asylum suffering from bouts of depression or melancholia but had been committed only because of the illness of a son. If not for that, her family would have continued to care for her, since her attacks were sporadic and she was essentially harmless. In other cases, those suffering from depression had no family at all to care for them. Still others like William S. (#210) had come to the attention of the authorities and were sent to the asylum from gaol. William was a thirty-five-year-old Irishman, single and a pauper. He had been in gaol for some time and had led the life of a recluse since coming to Canada. A few patients entered the asylum, not simply suffering from melancholia, but in what appeared to be a dying condition. For example, James S. (#1,860) came to the asylum on February 16, 1857, suffering from partial paralysis caused by disease of the brain. He died eleven days later.

The scarcity of inmates suffering from depression could mean that family and friends simply did not view such a symptom as requiring incarceration – that is, it was a symptom which could be coped with within the family. But coping and curing are not the same. If families were not sending their relatives to the asylum for depression, it meant they did not see the asylum as a place to cure these individuals but rather as a holding institution for those who were unruly. On the other hand, if it was the asylum which refused to accept these people, it was a function of overcrowded conditions and the perception that dangerous lunatics had priority over the safe ones. In either case, it means that the asylum was perceived as an institution designed first for the protection of society and only secondarily as a place to cure the insane.[46]

Patients suffering from delusions and what appears to be paranoia increased over the 1841–75 period. Patrick K. (#480) is an excellent example of both. A young man (aged twenty-six), born in Ireland, single and a labourer, he had been ill for nine weeks before being committed in March 1847 suffering from melancholia. Apparently witty and temperate when sane, he was now suffering at times from elevation of spirits, although more often from depression. He frequently made threats and once ran at his brother with an axe. He also imagined that people were anxious to have him marry their daughters, that they kept making him good offers and that he was to marry the queen. Not all of his delusions were so happy; he feared he would be murdered by those he associated with and as a result refused to take tea, alleging it was poisoned.

Most of the inmates exhibiting symptoms of paranoia, like Patrick, focused their attention on fear of being poisoned, murdered, injured, or of losing their soul. Others were characterized merely as fearful or suspicious. The delusions were usually religious in nature or grandiose or a combination of both. John B.(#500) believed he had a special way of curing people and of banishing devils. John D. (#1,920), a twenty-five-year-old single labourer, believed he was going to make the world new and have plenty of hounds and horses. That the delusions centred on religion and on wealth suggests their importance as facets of mid-century society, itself obsessed with these matters. As with depression, well over 50 per cent of the patients exhibiting signs of paranoia and delusion exhibited signs of violence as well, with paranoids slightly more likely to be violent than the deluded.

One symptom of insanity was mentioned infrequently even though its repercussions were grave, and that was the refusal of an individual to work. This is interesting given Katz's and others' argument that nineteenth-century institutions emerged as places to contain those who were economically unproductive. Perhaps it went without saying that the insane could not or would not work. Certainly their willingness to do so was viewed as a symptom of sanity and emphasized by asylum superintendents when considering the discharge of patients. What is noteworthy, however, is that in the few instances when the records specifically refer to refusal to work, it was usually with reference to a woman neglecting her housework and her children. Sarah C. (#4,060), as one certificate of insanity put it, paid no attention whatever to domestic arrangements and left her children entirely uncared for. This focus on women as opposed to men may have been a result of the different positions the sexes found themselves in when in need of assistance and the repercussions of this for their spouses.

Because men, by and large, worked outside the home, whether as farmers, labourers, or even artisans, they would have had difficulty coping with a sick wife. The case of Elizabeth M. (#3,270), whose illness forced her husband to miss work, was a good example of the predicament in which a working man with a sick spouse could find himself. Charity would not come to his assistance because he had employment, but because he was not making very much he could not afford to pay someone to help. A wife with an ill husband, however, would more than likely be at home to care for him. This clearly placed her in some financial stress. There would be little money coming into the house but, in that case, charity would be sympathetic towards her. With her husband ill, she became part of the deserving poor. She also would have more access to help from friends and family simply because her situation appeared desperate. If the above analysis is correct, it would help explain the larger number of married women in the asylum compared to married men.

Examination of the stated symptoms of insanity makes it obvious that violence in its various manifestations was the most significant. It clearly demonstrated the need for incarceration from the point of view of the protection of society and indicated the individual's need for help since violent actions transgressed acceptable and therefore "sane" behaviour. It was the combination of the two which the asylum found difficult to resist. Other symptoms, such as depression, posed no threat to society and those suffering from it were less likely to be committed. When the depressed were admitted, factors in addition to their depression played some role. These factors must be examined to gain a more complete picture of why people were committed to asylums in the mid-part of the nineteenth century.

If individuals had no family, it was convenient to place them in an institution like the asylum when their actions prevented them from being able to care for or to control themselves. Widows were particularly vulnerable as were deserted wives and husbands. The 1842 report of the asylum pointed out that four of the females in the institution had been deserted by their husbands and nine were widows.[47] Nancy H. (#20), an Irishwoman, aged forty, became insane after her husband drowned. Pregnant at the time, in her grief she apparently turned to drink for consolation and eventually exhibited signs of mania. Being a pauper, with seemingly no one to turn to, she was committed to the asylum on April 8, 1841, and was in and out of the asylum constantly. Where else was there for her to go? George P. (#60), a thirty-year-old printer and resident of New York, became ill while visiting Toronto. His insanity, caused by drink, was obviously mild since he was only incarcerated for three months. The fact that he was separated from his family and had no one to care for him meant there was no alternative but the asylum for him. Nicholas M. (#2,100), aged thirty, married with three children, had been ill for two years before he was admitted in 1858 suffering from mental stupor and partial paralysis. His wife left him after the first year of his illness which suggests that he was alone. In all these cases, the individuals needed extra care which they could not provide themselves. For these people, the asylum did not usurp the role of the family, but rather filled a vacuum left by the absence of the family.

Even if a family was present, it could not always cope with the problems of the insane. Many families tried to help but were not successful. Fanny F. (#3,020), thirty-two and married, had been ill for eight weeks prior to committal. In an effort to help her and get her mind off her troubles, her family took her for visits from one friend to another. At one point she really seemed to be improving but then suffered a relapse and was committed. In some cases it was obvious why families could not cope. The husband of Elizabeth H. (#3,270), a thirty-six-year-old mother of six children, wrote to the superintendent on November 16, 1866 (just before she was committed) explaining why he was forced to take such a drastic step. He had had to move closer to his place of work so that he could see his wife more often when she became excited. He had also removed his sixteen-year-old daughter from her employment so that she could look after her mother, but, because the girl was so young, she had difficulty controlling her. He tried to employ a woman to look after Elizabeth but was unable to, since, as he explained, he found people had peculiar ideas about the insane. In any case, his wife would not have allowed another woman in the house and he really would not have been able to afford it. He had five children at home and only one dollar a day to support seven people. He had been absent from work quite often because his wife would not sleep unless he was there and he worked at night. If this state of affairs continued, the family as a whole would suffer. Another case, thirty-nine-year-old Michael S. (#3,480), was married and a store-keeper. He had attempted to shoot himself and his wife had had to bring in a man to watch him at night. After nine months of Michael's illness, the asylum appeared as a way out for her and protection for him. It is understandable why the families of such patients felt they could no longer cope with the situation presented by having an insane person living with them. Where the insane were dangerous to both themselves and others they should not have had to cope.

Still the asylum should not be dismissed as a last desperate resort. In many cases, it helped improve the condition of patients and in some instances cured them. In 1874, just over 40 per cent as many patients were discharged cured as were admitted and an additional 14 to 15 per cent were discharged improved.[48] In some cases, the asylum could provide even better custodial care than could the family. Ann S. (#3,950) was admitted in July 1872 shortly after having had a baby and her doctor wrote a private letter to the superintendent explaining that, while she normally was a very industrious woman, her husband was basically lazy and was frequently absent from home. Within her family she would find little care. For Margaret B. (#3,070), the asylum would be a welcome relief from her husband, who was a drunkard, and from her home, where she was confined in a straitjacket. For Bridget C. (#3,380), as well, who had been nine years insane and was brought to the asylum after having been handcuffed and confined at home, the asylum could only appear to be a safe haven. From these examples, it is obvious that family care should not be idealized.[49] It also emphasizes a more positive view of custodial care provided by the asylum than many historians have been wont to give.

Another factor which often motivated committal and which has been suggested in some of the cases mentioned is alcoholism. Although the asylum was not designed to care for inebriates, excessive use of alcohol was perceived as a cause of insanity as well as a symptom. Alcoholics were persons at risk and therefore eligible for admittance. Richard O. (#370), committed in April 1846 after being ill only two days, remained in the asylum only ten days. It is noteworthy that he entered the asylum suffering from a case of delerium tremens. Mary T. (#90), a drunkard, came to the asylum on February 25, 1841. She was discharged on April 5, readmitted May 29, discharged July 15, readmitted July 31, discharged September 20, readmitted October 22, discharged November 13, and readmitted on May 10, 1842. It is difficult to avoid the conclusion that she was sent to the asylum to dry out, was released and then readmitted each time she went on another drinking spree and became unmanageable.

If some people used the asylum as an inebriate care institution, others used it as a terminal care facility. At least thirty-three of the over four hundred cases examined died within twelve months of entering the asylum. While many reasons may account for this,[50] it is obvious that some patients entered in a dying state. Certainly Mr. M. (#2,470) did. Committed at the age of seventy after being insane for over ten years, he died within two weeks. John A. (#4,240), aged seventy-four years, was suffering from senility and was weak and totally helpless when he entered. He died within two months. These patients were insane, but often it was a case of long-standing insanity which, as they grew older, was compounded by their ill health or, as in the case of John A. (#4,240 above), by their senility. The asylum could offer these patients only refuge. In caring for the old, the inebriate, and the ill, the asylum had gone beyond its original purpose, suggesting its "clientele" had their own view of what benefits it had to offer. In some respects, the asylum had usurped the gaol as a custodial facility for the dependent in society who had nowhere else to turn.

The last factor examined in this study to ascertain why people were being committed to the asylum was the length of illness they had experienced before committal. Particularly intriguing were patients who had been ill a short period. This suggests that they were admitted in the hopes of cure. This is what Workman and other alienists had been trying to convince the public was necessary. Equally curious were those who had been ill for many years before being finally committed. This group, according to physicians, had little chance of being cured. Therefore, why were they being sent to an asylum touted as curative?

Of the fifty-one patients admitted after only two weeks of insanity, twenty-four had either experienced a previous attack of insanity or had been in an asylum before. Once a pattern of attacks emerged, it was probable that an individual would be committed to an asylum; once labelled insane an individual had difficulty avoiding the asylum. Such patients needed the regulated environment of the asylum in order to gain some control over their actions. Once this occurred, the asylum would release them as recovered since it could not afford to keep patients longer than necessary in its overcrowded wards. If they lost control or exhibited signs of insanity again, they were readmitted and the process repeated itself. These readmissions indicated that, while the asylum could not permanently cure such people, it was perceived as a place which could best care for them and help them. The second factor which prompted a quick admission to the asylum was violence, and 25 per cent of the patients had exhibited this in one form or another. This is not surprising; it was the symptom of insanity that society and the family found most unsettling. Altogether, thirty-nine out of the fifty-one records for patients with insanity of short duration referred to the existence of a previous attack, a previous committal, or an act of violence. Of those remaining, ill health often was mentioned as the cause of the insanity and was possibly the reason for the committal. Marie G. (#680) was in poor health and admitted after being insane for only nine days, her insanity being connected with the weaning of her youngest child. She died less than a month later. Ann B. (#1,480) came to the asylum suffering from delusions on December 2, 1853, after five days of illness and died twenty-seven days later from pleural adhesion on the left side.[51] For some patients, committal was used as an object lesson. Mary Jane A's. (#1,520) husband committed her after a week's illness caused by drink but withdrew her after only a week in the asylum. Perhaps other patients, like Sarah N. (#1,570), who was single and a servant, had no one to care for them. For the patients entering the asylum after a short period of insanity, then, cure seemed to be only one motivation for committal. Other factors involved the protection of society and the provision of a refuge for those with no one willing or able to care for them.

An examination of the fifty-nine people entering the asylum after more than two years of illness reinforces that conclusion.[52] In some cases it would appear that the asylum was the last hope. Richard W. (#4,150) was a harmless twenty-nine-year-old who had been cared for by his father for four or five years before his committal in January 1874. After only two months, his father removed him. Perhaps he had hoped the asylum would be able to do something for his son. Perhaps he was just tired of caring for him, but, after committing him, was overcome by guilt. Lois P. (#3,600) had been ill for nine years and had been under the care of at least three doctors during that time with no effect before finally being committed in April 1870.

Other factors leading to a late committal have already been suggested. Some, like Hanna B. (#2,330), a widow suffering from senility and partial paralysis, or Mr. M. (#2,470) who, according to his record, arrived in a dying state, entered after a long insanity in order to die. Some could no longer care for themselves like Nicholas H. (#2,100) who suffered from partial paralysis and whose wife had left him. Others were becoming worse. James G. (#670), ill for two years off and on, was never considered dangerous until three weeks previous to his committal when he tried to cut his throat and drown himself. William M. (#3,720), ill for three years and under the care of numerous doctors, had recently attacked his son. All these cases suggest that the motivation for committal was not the expectation of a cure but the last desperate attempt at one, or the last resort for a family tired of coping or no longer able to cope with insanity within its circle.

From the examination of the patients in the Provincial Lunatic Asylum from 1841 to 1875, it is clear that moderation was the key to being considered sane. Any individual exhibiting extremes in behaviour was a likely candidate for committal. However, not all extreme behaviour was equally significant. Depression was a symptom of insanity but not a reason for committal, unless the depression led to suicidal tendencies. Unlike depression, violence was both a symptom of insanity and a reason for committal. Violence removed control from the family's hands because it brought the insane to the attention of authorities and the family lost its say about whether the individual should be committed or not. Abnormal excitement was also a strong indicator of insanity. Victorians abhorred excessive emotions and actions and the emphasis on mania as a classification of insanity reflected this.

The asylum designed to cure patients was also the protector of society. With the overcrowded conditions, priority had to be given to those who were deemed dangerous either to themselves or to others. This did not negate the curative aspects; these patients needed care and treatment, but it meant that many who were only marginally or harmlessly insane could not profit from the controlled environment supplied by the asylum, either because, being harmless, they did not often come to the attention of the authorities, or because their families preferred to keep them at home. Taking into account the crowded condition of the asylum and its focus on the dangerously insane, the curative aspects of asylum care would not appear to have been strong and the reluctance of some families to commit one of their members, especially if harmless, is understandable. Only when factors other than insanity (such as poverty) intervened, did they utilize the asylum.

The fact that more patients were not sent to the asylum earlier in their illness suggests that the asylum was not viewed as a curative institution, as does the sending of patients after a lengthy illness or to die. The high incidence of previous admissions, 17 per cent, suggests that the asylum, once tried, was resorted to again and again, if not as a vehicle for complete recovery, at least as a place where the patient could be helped through the worst of the attack.[53] This is also true for those patients sent because of drinking and who stayed only until recuperated from its effects. The existence of all these patients lessens the curative emphasis of the asylum and underlines the use being made of it by many segments of the public as a welfare institution. While not the original purpose of the asylum, does this necessarily make it a failure? Surely, offering care and protection to those who needed it is not to be dismissed lightly.

Much of the historiography of asylums, in its attempt to find an either/or answer to the issue of social control or social reform has been overly simplistic. The overcrowded conditions indicate that the asylum was fulfilling a need in society. It was a place which, most agreed, could cope with the problems of the violently insane better than gaols or families could. For the harmlessly insane, the asylum offered a refuge only if their domestic circumstances dictated it. For both the superintendent and the patients, the goal was cure, and, indeed, that is how asylum officials measured their success. Cure meant release from the asylum as a self-sufficient and supporting individual. If a relapse occurred it was not indicative of failure to cure the original insanity but rather of the emergence of a new case of insanity. Just as an individual could have many colds and recover from each, some individuals re-experienced insanity. However, if asylum officials saw the goal of the asylum as cure, those sending patients to it (both families and authorities) viewed it in a different light. It was a welfare institution to care for the poor, the ill, the old, and the inebriate. It was a holding institution to care for the as-yet non-criminal, violent insane. The asylum in the mid-nineteenth century had a multiplicity of purposes. Whether its function as a welfare and holding institution made it a vehicle for social control is a question that historians can debate *ad infinitum*. While neither purpose negated the desire for a cure, although limiting its chances, both dictated whom the focus of that cure would be – those with whom society could not cope. That same concern determined the recipients of other types of institutional care in mid-century Ontario. Just as the asylum wanted to contain and help cure the violent insane, schools wanted to socialize and educate the young, reformatories wanted to punish and reform delinquents, prisons wanted to punish, control, and rehabilitate criminals, and hospitals wanted to segregate and help the sick poor. In all cases, the welfare and stability of society were uppermost in the minds of the mid-Victorians. This did not negate their reform impulse but did determine its direction.

5

J. B. Collip: A Forgotten Member of the Insulin Team

Michael Bliss

Even people with a medical background generally share the common belief that the greatest achievement of medical research in Canada, the discovery of insulin in 1921–22, was made by Frederick Banting and Charles Best. Those who are vaguely conversant with the literature on the discovery know that some considerable debate exists about the contribution of Professor J. J. R. Macleod, head of the University of Toronto laboratory in which insulin was discovered, formal director of Banting and Best's work, and co-winner of the 1923 Nobel Prize with Banting. Did Macleod deserve to have shared the Nobel Prize with Banting? Banting obviously thought the award to only the two of them – perhaps to Macleod at all – was a mistake, for he immediately announced that he would share his half of the prize with Best. Macleod, as very few people realize, then announced that he would share his half with J. B. Collip.

Who was Collip? Certainly he was the forgotten man in the discovery of insulin, for even those who remember his name have no idea of his contribution to the work. Others, who know of Collip's later achievements as a medical researcher and administrator, know little or nothing of his participation in the insulin work. This neglect of Collip's role in insulin is undeserved and unfortunate. Not only was his contribution to the work absolutely vital, thereby giving him a reasonable claim to more historical recognition than he has received, but a consideration of his role in the discovery usefully reminds us of the collaborative nature of the research that led to insulin. While this essay is ostensibly a study in the achievements of an individual researcher, it actually leads towards an understanding of the curious, fractious teamwork that gave the world insulin.[1]

James Bertram Collip, a florist's son, was born near Belleville, Ontario in November 1892. Collip developed an interest in chemistry during his high-school years that he pursued through the honours physiology and biochemistry course at the University of Toronto, graduating at the head of his class in 1912. Influenced by Professor A. B. Macallum, the first professor of biochemistry at a Canadian university, Collip remained at Toronto to complete his MA in 1913 and his Ph.D. in biochemistry in 1916. He was hired as a lecturer in the Department of Physiology at the young University of Alberta for the 1915–16 session, and remained in Edmonton during the war and afterwards, being promoted to professor and head of the new Department of Biochemistry in 1920.[2]

Collip was a prolific researcher, working on several problems involving blood chemistry. By the end of 1921 he had a respectable list of twenty-three academic publications. One of his long-standing interests was in the functions of the endocrine glands such as the thyroid, thymus, suprarenals, pituitary, and others whose primary function is to secrete hormones internally into the bloodstream. In 1916 he had published a very good summary article on scientists' knowledge of the internal secretions of the endocrine glands. Endocrinology was a field of growing interest and one of the key problems in the area, mentioned briefly in Collip's article, was whether the pancreas, whose *external* secretion was important in digestion, also produced some kind of *internal* secretion which controlled carbohydrate metabolism. If an animal's pancreas was removed, it rapidly developed severe diabetes mellitus, a functional breakdown of the system the chief characteristic of which is the body's failure to be able to utilize or burn carbohydrates. The observation of diabetes following pancreatectomy (which had first been made by Minkowski and von Mering in 1889) led immediately to the hypothesis that the pancreas somehow, probably by producing an internal secretion, enables the body to metabolize carbohydrates and other sources of energy. As Collip noted in his 1916 article, however, many attempts to supply the missing pancreatic function by organ therapy, i.e., by feeding or injecting extracts of pancreas, had failed. After almost thirty years' research, the hypothetical internal secretion had yet to be found.[3]

For a 1921–22 sabbatical year Collip was awarded a Rockefeller

Travelling Fellowship. He planned to spend part of his time working with Professor J. J. R. Macleod in the Department of Physiology at the University of Toronto, then go on to the United States and Britain. In May 1921, while in Toronto making his arrangements with Macleod, Collip sat in on a discussion between Macleod and a young surgeon, Frederick Banting, about research Banting was planning to attempt that summer. Banting, a medical graduate of the University of Toronto who was not doing well in his practice in London, Ontario, had come to Macleod with an idea for a new approach to the problem of finding the internal secretion of the pancreas. Although Banting had no experience with either diabetes or animal research, Macleod had been persuaded to give him surplus lab space, dogs, and student assistance for work during the summer, during which time Macleod would be absent on vacation. Collip seems to have been only an accidental observer at Banting and Macleod's meeting, but may have expressed interest in the research. Either for that reason or because Collip possessed considerable biochemical expertise, Banting recorded his summer address next to that of Macleod's in his research notebook. He may have considered Collip someone he could turn to for help or advice while Macleod was abroad.[4] When Collip returned to Toronto after spending the summer at Wood's Hole, Massachusetts, he found that Banting and C. H. Best, the student assistant, had produced interesting results by injecting pancreatic extracts into dogs made diabetic by depancreatization. Taking up residence in Toronto, Collip began working on a quite different problem in the pathology department, several blocks away from Banting's and Best's lab. He saw the two every few days, however, took a great interest in their experiments, and often left them with the comment, "Well, if I can be of any assistance let me know."[5]

Very excited by the results of his research, believing from the beginning that he was onto something that might be used to treat diabetes in humans, Banting several times asked Macleod if Collip could help with the work. Macleod at first resisted these suggestions, urging Banting and Best to be absolutely sure of the validity of their work before rushing into new territory, but in early December he finally agreed that the time had come to expand the work on pancreatic extracts.[6] By Monday, December 12, Collip was involved in the research, though continuing to work in a separate lab.

Collip joined the team after Banting and Best had compiled a long series of experimental results indicating that injections of aqueous extract made from animal pancreases which had been caused to degenerate through surgical ligation of the pancreatic ducts reduced the amount of sugar in the blood and urine of diabetic dogs, therefore apparently reducing the severity of the diabetes. They had given a preliminary talk about this work, written a paper, and arranged to present a summary of it at a meeting of the American Physiological Society in New Haven at the end of December. In the few weeks before Collip started work, they had made particularly exciting progress. They had found that extracts made from the pancreases of fetal calves worked just as well as their earlier extracts of dog pancreas and did not require major surgery and a long waiting period to produce. Taking up an idea Macleod had first suggested – he had known from the literature that it had been tried before – they had also begun using alcohol instead of water as their main extractive. Fetal pancreas was ground up in alcohol, filtered, and then the alcohol evaporated off, leaving the extract in a concentrated form. With alcohol seeming to work so well as an extractive, Banting and Best had decided on December 8 to try fresh adult beef pancreas. Once again, the results, as measured by blood-sugar readings on December 11, seemed good.[7] This was an important breakthrough in the work, for it meant that the research could go forward using virtually unlimited supplies of pancreas obtained from local abattoirs. An oft-told story in Canadian medical circles to the effect that Collip was asked to help with the research because Banting and Best were bogged down and going nowhere is not accurate. Collip seems to have joined the team partly because much good progress now paved the way for more experiments requiring more researchers. As a trained biochemist, experienced in work with tissue extracts, Collip was an ideal and logical addition to the group.

Collip immediately began making extract from whole beef pancreas.[8] His first experiment started in pursuit of a suggestion Macleod had made to the three of them that it would be useful to try the extract on rabbits made diabetic by routine experimental methods. Collip quickly found that the extract effectively lowered the blood sugar – not just of diabetic rabbits, but of normal ones. This observation had immense practical importance, for it gave the group a quick, easy way of testing the potency of any particular batch of extract; for several years the basic insulin unit was defined with reference to the rabbit test. Banting and Best had not tried their extract on normal animals.[9]

Collip next volunteered to tackle the complex question of the extract's effect on the workings of the liver. As Banting had suggested from time to time, it was important at some stage in the research to see whether the extract restored the liver's capacity to convert and store glucose as glycogen, one of the vital processes in carbohydrate metabolism which was largely lost in the diabetic condition. On December 13, Banting and Best depancreatized a dog which Collip took back to the lab for this experiment. He also undertook to record observations of the extract's effect on the amount of ketone bodies (partially burned fatty acids, another indication of severe metabolic breakdown) excreted in the urine of a diabetic animal. In both cases Collip was undertaking the first measurements of the extract's potency beyond Banting and Best's studies of blood and urinary sugar. As diabetes researchers knew at the time, these sugar tests were too easily subject to other interpretations – perhaps the extracts were having some kind of toxic effect which depressed the sugar readings; other substances seemed capable of doing this – to be convincing without more precise supplementary experiments.

On December 21, Collip found that the diabetic dog's urine became completely ketone-free after injections of extract. The next day, the last before the Christmas break, he chloroformed the animal, measured its liver for glycogen, and found an incredibly high reading. The experiment was a clear demonstration that the extract enabled a diabetic animal's liver to store glycogen, and was the first evidence in the Toronto experiments that the extract could restore a function known to be lacking in the diabetic state.

During the same weeks in December that Collip's experiments were working so well, Banting and Best were having a very frustrating time trying to produce pancreatic extract that would work at all. Their experiments also ended for a Christmas break on December twenty-second, after the seventh consecutive failure to make a potent extract. There had been some failures earlier, but nothing this bad. A few days later, when Banting presented his and Best's first paper to the American Physiological Society conference in New Haven, he had another discouraging experience. He gave a very weak presentation, was subjected to tough questioning from a highly critical audience of leading American experts, and had to be rescued by Macleod, the chairman of the session, who jumped in and answered the questions as best he could. Except for the enthusiasm shown by Dr. G. H. A. Clowes, the research director for Eli Lilly and Company of Indianapolis, the general reaction to this first presentation of the University of Toronto work seems to have been cool interest. The experts would await further developments.[10]

The New Haven experience, hard on the heels of his laboratory failures, was something of a trauma for Fred Banting, an inarticulate, inexperienced, and very insecure young man (much less articulate, experienced, and secure, for example, than Collip, who was the same age). Banting had had a serious argument with Macleod in September about facilities and the future of his work. At the best of times, Banting, the earthy Canadian farmer's son, had little in common with the urbane, reserved Scotsman, Macleod. Macleod was the internationally known expert in carbohydrate metabolism and the director of Banting's work. Banting felt, however, that the idea for the research had been his alone, and that all the important research, notably the early demonstrations of the extract's ability to lower blood sugar, had been done that summer while Macleod was holidaying in Scotland. At best, Banting believed, Macleod and Collip were now helping somewhat in the development of the discovery. After New Haven and Macleod's frequent use of the word "we" while answering questions about the research, Banting seems to have begun to believe that Macleod was trying to appropriate credit for all the work done by himself and Best.[11] He began to worry, too, about Collip, who was achieving so much, who had Macleod's confidence, and who, according to the division of labour Macleod had set up, was beginning work in the New Year to see if he could take the crude extract Banting and Best were making and purify it sufficiently to permit trials on human diabetics.

Collip was working with immense vigour and enthusiasm. His feelings are evident in the extremely important letter he wrote on January 8, 1922, to H. M. Tory, president of the University of Alberta:

> I will never regret having decided to spend a year near Professor Macleod. . . . Last spring the old problem of diabetes was again taken up for re-investigation in his laboratory. During the summer such encouraging results were obtained by Dr. Banting and Mr. Best that in the fall the scope of the work was much enlarged. I was given the chemical side and a good part of the Physiological to push along with.
>
> I planned a series of experiments the results of which when obtained gave me a direct lead to the solution of the basic functional derangement in diabetes. The crucial experiment was tried out just before the Christmas break and the results were so

striking that even the most skeptical I think would be convinced. I have never had such an absolutely satisfactory experience before, namely going in a logical way from point to point into an unexplored field building absolutely solid structure all the way. However to make a long story short we have obtained from the pancreas of animals a mysterious something which when injected into totally diabetic dogs completely removes all the cardinal symptoms of the disease. Just at the moment it is my problem to isolate in a form suitable for human administration the principle which has such wonderous powers, the existence of which many have suspected but no one has hitherto proved. If the substance works on the human it will be a great boon to Medicine, but even if it does not work out a milestone has at least been added to the field of carbohydrate metabolism.

Professor Graham was in my laboratory today discussing the whole matter and in the course of a few days time we hope to have had a clinical test made. If it works we will turn over in all probability the formula to the Connaught Anti-Toxin laboratories for manufacturing purposes.[12]

As the prospect of clinical testing moved closer to reality, Banting became more worried that he was being pushed aside. Was he becoming just the group's experimental surgeon? What role would there be for him in the clinical testing, which had always been one of his keen interests? Banting began to press Macleod to allow clinical tests of the extract that he and Best were making. About this time he applied for privileges at Toronto General Hospital, the university's teaching hospital where any clinical tests would take place. Banting's tendency to view events through a paranoic lens could only have been reinforced when Duncan Graham, head of medicine at the university and hospital, refused. Graham, a tough-minded autocrat when it came to protecting his patients, adopted the position that Banting, a surgeon not currently in practice, had no qualifications to experiment on human diabetics.[13]

Banting was nothing if not persistent, and he finally persuaded Macleod to intervene with Graham to make possible a clinical trial of extract prepared by Banting and Best. The test took place on January 11, 1922, when a house doctor injected 15 ccs of a murky, light-brown fluid into the buttocks of a severely diabetic fourteen-year-old boy, Leonard Thompson. Banting and Best were not present at the test, but were among the authors of the paper summarizing its results. Leonard Thompson's blood sugar dropped from

.440 per cent to .320. The twenty-four-hour excretion of glucose in his urine fell very slightly. Tests for ketones continued to be highly positive. "No clinical benefit was evidenced." A sterile abscess, caused by impurities in the extract, developed at the site of the injection.[14]

The clinical test was a failure. Banting and Best found ways of putting a favourable gloss on it in later accounts,[15] but the fact was that the extract's very modest impact on the sugar content of the blood and urine did not outweigh the reaction it caused. (There is also some evidence that it was tried on two other diabetic patients, with no effects at all.) Although Leonard Thompson was a very sick little boy, the doctors decided not to give him further injections of Banting's and Best's extract.[16] They would wait until Collip came up with something better. In the aftermath of the test a *Toronto Star* reporter learned about it, published the story, and by the wording of his article caused the first confrontation between Banting and Macleod over credit.[17]

As Collip worked to try to make a purer extract, he could not have been very happy about the odd behaviour of Banting, who seemed to have undermined the job assignments Macleod had specified for the members of the team by turning the purification problem into some kind of competition between Banting and Best on the one hand and himself on the other. That competition had led to a premature clinical test, which is always something of an embarrassment for researchers. Just about this time, Collip made another important discovery: a large dose of potent extract could lower the blood sugar so drastically that rabbits went into convulsions leading to death. While this hypoglycaemic reaction to an overdose of the extract could be controlled quickly by the administration of sugar, its discovery made a careful handling of the extract in human cases all the more necessary. Collip's discovery was made sometime just before or after January 11.[18] If it came after the first clinical test, the realization of the recklessness of that course would have been heightened. Finally, Banting's and Best's method of producing extract in January incorporated minor but not insignificant improvements in technique which had been suggested to them by Collip. Collip may have wondered whether Banting and Best, who appeared to be racing against him for priority in the testing of their extract, would give full credit for the help they had been given. Collip spent long hours in his laboratory in mid-January mixing, filtering, distilling, concentrating, diluting, centrifuging, blending, etc., as he made batch after batch of pancreatic extract, testing each one, perhaps several times at different stages, on his rabbits. The fresh pancreatic tissues consisted of fats and proteins, water, salts, and the mysterious unknown active principle or ingredient. Collip's problem was to produce an extract free of fats, salts, and as they all thought, proteins. (Only several years later was it finally shown that the active principle, insulin, is itself a protein.) Collip knew how to get fats and salts out of this kind of solution, and he also knew that the solubility of proteins in aqueous alcohol varies according to the percentage of alcohol and according to the acid-base balance. He knew, too, that at the approximately 50 per cent concentration Banting and Best had hit upon, the active principle was soluble in alcohol. Most of his work involved fiddling with the concentrations of alcohol, trying to precipitate out the contaminating proteins while keeping the active principle in solution, and then figuring out how to concentrate the solution (i.e., get rid of most of the alcohol) without losing the active principle.

Late one January night (probably that of January 16), Collip made his breakthrough. He found he could "trap" the active principle, first by producing a concentration of alcohol in which it was soluble but most of the other proteins were not, then by increasing the concentration to a point just over 90 per cent, at which the active principle itself precipitated out in more or less pure form. The night he discovered this, Collip wrote in 1949, "I experienced then and there all alone in the top story of the old Pathology Building perhaps the greatest thrill which has ever been given me to realize." Collip tested his extract's potency on rabbits, waited a few days to check for abscesses, and then sent it over to the clinic. Treatment of Leonard Thompson with pancreatic extract, Collip's extract, resumed on January 13. It was spectacularly successful, and the testing was expanded to other patients.[19]

The triumphant purification of insulin was accompanied by a tragic collapse of civility among members of the insulin team. Sometime between January 17 and 23, there was a violent confrontation between Collip and Banting, with Best present. In 1940, Banting described what happened as follows:

> Collip had become less and less communicative and finally after about a week's absence he came into our little room about five thirty one evening. He stopped inside the door and said "Well fellows I've got it."
>
> I turned and said, "Fine, congratulations. How did you do it?"

Collip replied, "I have decided not to tell you."

His face was white as a sheet. He made as if to go. I grabbed him with one hand by the overcoat where it met in front and almost lifting him I sat him down hard on the chair. I do not remember all that was said but I remember telling him that it was a good job he was so much smaller – otherwise I would "knock hell out of him." He told us that he had talked it over with Macleod and that Macleod agreed with him that he should not tell us by what means he had purified the extract.

An independent account by Best supports Banting's story in most of the essential details, with Best adding that it took all his strength to stop Banting from seriously hurting Collip.[20]

It will probably never be known exactly what was said in the confrontation that night. Collip apparently did refuse to tell Banting and Best his method, and said he had Macleod's permission not to tell. He may also have threatened to leave Toronto, as Banting elsewhere claimed, and patent his method. All of the men were tired after days of hard work and extreme pressure. The atmosphere was charged with distrust. Banting had shown his distrust of Collip and Macleod by arranging an advanced clinical test, and then had accused Macleod of trying to steal credit; now Macleod and Collip had decided not to trust him and Best. Banting thought Macleod and Collip were trying to steal his and Best's credit. Collip and Macleod probably thought Banting would deny them credit for their contributions. Paranoia begat paranoia. Whatever he said, Collip was foolish to have talked so bluntly to the unhappy, suspicious, frightened, and angry Banting. As many young veterans of the Great War would have done, Banting chose to fight back.

The result of the fight was an agreement signed by Banting, Best, Collip, and Macleod on January 25 establishing formal, written ground rules for a collaborative effort to develop the extract in cooperation with the university's Connaught Laboratories. None of the four would independently try to patent or develop the process. After the agreement, the work of production, laboratory research, and clinical testing continued. Collip, who had dropped his other sabbatical plans, was placed in charge of manufacture of the extract. Some time in March the group chose the name *insulin* for the extract; the choice was based on the correct assumption that the extract was produced in the pancreatic cells known as the Islands of Langerhans. In the ongoing research and testing effort, both

Banting and Best seemed relegated to minor roles; it could seem as though a couple of lucky amateurs had had their work taken over by the professionals.[21]

About the same time in March that insulin got its name, the good fortune Collip had been enjoying since starting the insulin work suddenly ended. He lost the ability to make insulin. First he could not make it in the enlarged quantities they were trying to obtain, then he started to have trouble making it by any method, even in his own lab. Toronto suffered an insulin famine in the spring of 1922, which led to the suspension of clinical testing, the death of a diabetic patient who needed insulin to survive, and a frantic struggle by every one on the team to find some way to regain the knack of making insulin.[22]

Collip's failure only increased Banting's anger at what seemed to him to be gross bungling. He thought Collip probably had neglected to write down his methods because he was being so secretive.[23] Actually, failures like these were not uncommon in primitive extractions working with unknown substances – Banting and Best themselves had had a taste of such failure in December – and in fact became almost the norm among other people trying to make insulin for the first time. There were so many variables in the isolation process that no amount of record-keeping could have guaranteed against failure. Best later discovered, for example, that variable water pressure in the medical building was causing inconsistencies in the vacuum-distilling process by which the alcohol was removed, creating significant variations in temperature, distilling time, and the strength of the resulting extract.[24] Best, Macleod, and Collip all made important contributions to the gradual recovery of a way of making insulin, based on Collip's original method. One of the results of this three months of frustration, however, was a decision to get more help with the problem of large-scale manufacturing than the Connaught Laboratories, at that time still a very small operation lacking both money and manpower, could supply. The result was a formal collaboration between the University of Toronto and the very large, very interested firm of Eli Lilly and Company.

The quarrels with Banting and then the difficulties of making insulin dissolved whatever negotiations took place about Collip staying permanently with the University of Toronto group. At the end of May 1922, the researchers read six short papers on their work to the annual meeting of the Royal Society of Canada. Two of these contained the recipes for making insulin developed by

Banting and Best on the one hand ("The Preparation of the Earlier Extracts"), and Collip ("The Preparation of the Extracts as Used in the First Clinical Cases") on the other.[25] Best and Collip went to Indianapolis to tell the Lilly chemists all they knew about making insulin. His sabbatical in Toronto having ended, Collip went back to his job at the University of Alberta. Only small quantities of insulin were produced in Toronto and Indianapolis during the next several months. When Lilly chemists, simultaneously with other American researchers, discovered how to precipitate insulin out of solution by adjusting the acid-base balance as indicated by the iso-electric point, the problem of large-scale production disappeared.

Collip left Toronto just as the discovery of insulin began to get wide publicity and diabetics began to descend on the city in search of the magic hormone. Banting had forced Macleod and Graham to recognize that as a licensed physician he was qualified to give insulin clinically; in the summer and fall of 1922 he was strategically placed to become the physician whom diabetics, diabetologists, and the general public looked to as the discoverer of insulin. He made a point of sharing credit with Best, who had replaced Collip in charge of Toronto's insulin manufacture. Neither of them felt that Collip deserved more than token credit. In Banting and Best's view, Collip had come on the scene only after the essential discovery had been made. Such work as he had done was a contribution to the development of insulin, not its discovery. As well, while there was a general conspiracy among those who knew the inside story to cover up the undignified quarrelling of the winter of 1922, the fight had led to lasting resentments. "With regard to Dr. Collip," Banting wrote in the spring of 1923, "Charles and I both feel that although he did contribute splendidly to the work, the manner in which he made his contribution has lost for him any personal gratitude from us."[26]

Banting's other enemy, of course, was Macleod, with whom relations did not improve either. Through much of 1923, Banting's many friends in the city's medical community, aided by Banting himself, carried on a complex struggle to make sure that honours for the discovery of insulin went primarily to Banting, not Macleod or Collip (or, for many of Banting's friends, to Best, who they assumed was little more than a student helper.) They were largely successful in convincing the Canadian and Ontario governments and the lay public that Banting, the man who had had the idea, ought to be given the honours. To a lesser extent Best also shared the limelight.[27]

In Edmonton, where he was directing continuing experimental work relating to insulin, Collip was considerably embittered at not being recognized as a co-discoverer. While he never revealed the inner history of the discovery period at Toronto, perhaps because the confrontation with Banting was embarrassing to everyone involved, in 1923 he summarized his relations with those people to a friend:

> There are some people in Toronto who felt that I had no business to do physiological work. Against this I would say that when I entered the collaborating group early in December 1921 it was with a view of putting my whole effort into the pushing forward of the research irrespective of any water-tight compartments. The result was that when I made a definite discovery my confreres instead of being pleased were quite frankly provoked that I had had the good fortune to conceive the experiment and to carry it out. My own feelings now in the matter are that the whole research with its aftermath has been a disgusting business.[28]

Collip also made several lists of his contributions to the research, wrote an important history of the discovery, and urged Macleod to speak out on his behalf. His contribution to the discovery was well known at the University of Alberta, where he was one of the most illustrious members of the faculty. There was strong feeling among Albertans that Collip was being unfairly neglected by the medical establishment in Toronto and by the eastern press. Everything in Canada, even the discovery of insulin, becomes grist for the mill of regionalism.[29]

In the spring of 1923 Collip briefly received international publicity when he announced that he had discovered a new hormone, present in yeast, onions, barley roots, sprouted grains, green wheat leaves, beet tops, lettuce, and probably all other plants, which was just as essential to the metabolism of sugar in the plant as insulin is in the animal. Collip named his hormone *glucokinin*, and announced that "there can be little doubt" of its usefulness in the treatment of diabetes. It might even be better than insulin. "Green Onion Tops to Cure Diabetes" ran the headlines in newspaper accounts of Collip's work.[30]

The more Collip published on glucokinin – and he published a great deal very quickly, making sure he was not denied credit this time – the more qualifications and doubts crept into his work. Finally he lapsed into silence, having apparently realized that the vegetable extracts he was working with were actually far less effective and probably much more toxic than insulin. The whole gluco-kinin affair became an embarrassment, a near-perfect example of the heat of discovery and bitter competition for priority leading to scientific error, poor judgement, and unsustainable claims. The most experienced member of the Toronto group, Macleod, sensed what was happening and was critical of Collip's precipitate rush to publication. "If every discovery entails as much squabbling over priority etc. as this one has," Macleod wrote privately, "it will put the job of trying to make them out of fashion."[31]

His errors and the bitterness of the discovery period notwith-standing, Collip received important, if unpublicized, recognition as a discoverer of insulin. The basic insulin patent – from one point of view a clear, formal recognition of priority in discovery – was applied for and granted in the names of Banting, Best, and Collip. The three discoverers then assigned their rights to the University of Toronto; they shared equally in that portion of the insulin royalties set aside by the university to support research under their direc-tion.[32] J. J. R. Macleod's published and unpublished accounts of the discovery always stressed Collip's role, arguing that while Bant-ing and Best had made the first essential step in the discovery process, Collip had been instrumental in several of the succeeding steps.[33] When the Danish physiologist, August Krogh, himself a recent Nobel laureate, nominated Banting and Macleod for a Nobel Prize after visiting Toronto in the autumn of 1922, the only third person he thought deserved consideration was Collip, for his work on purification and manufacture of the extract.[34] Whether or not Macleod would have divided his half of the prize had not Banting taken the lead cannot be determined. He did divide it, however, and wrote to a friend a few months later: "I think I have succeeded in getting people to realize that his [Collip's] contribution to the work as a whole was not incommensurate with that of Banting. It is of course sad that it should require such drastic methods to persuade people of this fact . . . "[35]

Collip went on from glucokinin to do very important pioneering work on the isolation of the parathyroid hormone. Moving to McGill University in 1928, he spent the next decade generating a whirlwind of endocrinological research. He and his students were in the forefront of the isolation and study of the ovarian and gona-dotrophic and adenocorticotrophic hormones. Deeply influenced by his experience with insulin, Collip always hoped he could isolate another magic hormone. In collaboration with drug companies he produced a long succession of new products – parathormone,

Emmenin, Premarin, and brands of ACTH (Adrenocorticotrophic hormone) – with a wide variety of uses. None of them came close to insulin, of course, but in trying so hard and so variously (and, it must be added, with a high failure rate and a number of premature claims, resulting from his eagerness and from methods he later described as "bathtub chemistry") Collip made himself by far the dominant figure in the history of endocrinology in Canada, indeed a pioneer in endocrinology. He became something of a legendary figure in Canadian medical research, the "jack-of-all-glands," restlessly, endlessly tinkering with his hormonal concoctions, his conversational style so quick and disconnected that people sometimes had trouble understanding him, the restlessness carried into his personal life in the marathon automobile trips he would take back and forth across North America. In 1947 he became Dean of Medicine and Head of the Department of Medical Research at the University of Western Ontario, carrying on in the latter capacity after his deanship ended in 1961. J. B. Collip died in 1965 at age seventy-two. In the late 1920s, Collip and Banting, both of whom matured noticeably after the insulin period, decided that their fighting had been all a misunderstanding. They eventually became close friends, to the point where they could reminisce together about the night when Fred had Bert down and was banging his head against the floor. Perhaps if Banting had not died in an airplane crash in 1941 (six years after J. J. R. Macleod had died in Scotland) he would have rewritten his accounts of the discovery of insulin to give Collip more credit. Without realizing it, he had underlined the importance of Collip's research by implication in his most important published history of the discovery when he admitted that at the time of clinical testing his and Best's results "were not as encouraging as those obtained by Zuelzer in 1908."[36]

More generosity might have ensued, as well, had Banting ever realized that his original idea of getting to the internal secretion of the pancreas by causing it to atrophy through duct ligation actually played no important part in the discovery. Banting's and Best's working hypotheses were largely incorrect, and their readings of their experimental results often questionable. Their work was not particularly well received at the New Haven meeting in 1921 because it was neither very well done nor any more impressive than that of several predecessors.[37] The one vital contribution Banting and Best made was in convincing the skeptical Macleod that there really was a potent anti-diabetic agent somewhere in pancreatic extracts. As Best wrote in 1922, Macleod gave the two researchers "the opportunity to conclusively prove the efficiency of our extract upon diabetic animals, and patients before the other members of the Physiological staff participated in this work."[38] Fortunately for the University of Toronto, its resources were such that when additional expertise was needed, Macleod was able to supply it by adding a trained biochemist, Collip, to the insulin team. In solving the purification problem, Collip made the leap forward that had been baffling experimenters for years.[39] Given the record of difficulties and failures in Banting's and Best's notebooks, as well as the failure of the first clinical tests; given also the inadequate training and limited experience possessed by Banting and Best, it is a fair speculation that without Collip's work insulin might well have been isolated somewhere else, probably in the United States.

The discovery of insulin was an excellent example of progress made possible by collaborative research. Unfortunately the collaborating group fell apart so thoroughly, its members literally at each other's throats on virtually the day of insulin's discovery, that the popular history of the discovery came to reinforce older, more romantic images of medical research being done by misunderstood geniuses with great ideas. Through the 1950s and early 1960s when there were seemingly endless occasions honouring Banting's and Best's discovery of insulin, Collip was often urged to tell his side of the story. He always refused, saying that it would be found in the literature after his death if people looked carefully enough.

6

From Salvarsan to Penicillin: Medical Science and VD Control in Canada

Janice Dickin McGinnis

By the time white settlement of Canada began, the two major venereal diseases had established themselves among the populations of Europe. No matter which theory one accepts regarding the origins of syphilis,[1] it certainly was a fact of western European life by the early sixteenth century. The origins of gonorrhea are more ancient, possibly dating back to biblical times. It is probable that both diseases entered Canada with, or soon after, the earliest white settlement and a virulent, if somewhat anomalous, epidemic of syphilis is documented for Quebec in the late eighteenth century.[2] Still, in Canada as elsewhere, venereal disease did not become the subject of a widespread public health campaign until the early twentieth century. For centuries, medicine had been searching for a cure and sufferers had undergone unsuccessful treatment with various substances but, as has been pointed out for tuberculosis and as is likely to prove true for cancer, intelligent assault on a disease cannot really take place until that disease has been scientifically defined and its cause discovered.[3] The diagnosis of gonorrhea was placed on a scientific basis in 1879 with the identification of the causal organism, the gonococcus, but it was not until the same was true for syphilis that anti-VD campaigns got under way. Although gonorrhea would be swept along in the campaign and despite the fact that it was by far the more prevalent of the two diseases, it was neither as debilitating nor as feared. It was syphilis – the maimer of the innocent as well as punisher of the guilty – that would receive the most attention.

Both gonorrhea and syphilis were, and can still be, serious threats to personal and public health. Gonorrhea can cause considerable pain and may lead to sterility. It can predispose the body to arthritis and, in women, due to their open reproductive tract, it can penetrate to produce pelvic abscess and peritonitis. Sufferers can be infectious for years, making them not only dangerous to sex partners but, again in the case of women, to their children. The newborn child of a gonorrhea sufferer can be blinded through contact with gonococci in the birth canal. Syphilitics can also unwittingly damage their children: the fetuses of infected women are subject to increased risks of miscarriage, stillbirth, and physical and mental defects. Congenital syphilitics who escape these direct effects still frequently suffer from ill-health and premature death. Sufferers who are directly infected face a whole range of symptoms, the most debilitating of which are unsightly skin lesions, paralysis, and insanity.[4] In an era when the diseases went untreated, infection with either could prevent Canadians from actively shouldering their economic and social responsibilities and those made blind or insane could become direct drains on the public coffers.

The active campaign against both diseases came in Canada at the end of the First World War. Several factors converged to spur action at this time. Perhaps the main motivating force was the surprisingly high VD rate among all soldiers of the Great War. It is unlikely that the recruits were any more immoral than their predecessors had been; it is simply that they were the first large group of people ever to undergo effective scientific testing for syphilis and gonorrhea.[5] Canada feared the return home of these young men who had fought for her freedom. It was not just the sickness she feared but the deleterious effects that that sickness would have on the country's birth rate: in the past four years alone, the nation had lost some fifty thousand lives in war casualties, another forty to fifty thousand to tuberculosis (which had long been endemic in the population), and, finally, fifty to seventy thousand from the influenza epidemic of 1918–19. Canada emerged from the war eager to increase and strengthen its population.[6] Any disease was a direct threat to such an ambition, and, immediately after the war, Canada, like many other western nations, set up its first national Department of Health to engender and safeguard the well-being of Canadians.

Among the department's most important tasks was the overseeing of a string of 102 VD treatment clinics established with federal and provincial funds in all provinces but Prince Edward Island. A large part of the departmental budget was poured into these clinics to treat syphilis, gonorrhea, and chancroid (one of the dozen or so minor venereal diseases). Existing in a symbiotic relationship with the clinics was a system of medical research. Canadian doctors and scientists experimented continually throughout the period of the campaign. Patients were the organisms on which drugs and methods of application were perfected; equally, patients benefited from the adaptation of the available medications to Canadian conditions. The resulting combination of medical skills used in the development of treatments and of public health expertise in getting those treatments to the population put Canada at the forefront of the anti-VD campaign. As Gordon Bates, head of the Canadian Social Hygiene Council, would boast in 1937, "Canada led the world in the field of venereal disease control."[7] Where Canada would excel was in turning specific medical discoveries produced by the scientific revolution occurring in Germany just after the turn of the century to use in a quintessentially Canadian campaign: compulsory, paternalistically authoritarian, but at the same time as decent and dignified as possible. The marriage of German science to Canadian public health philosophy can be traced by following the discussions of the treatment of syphilis and gonorrhea in Canadian medical periodicals, most importantly the *Canadian Medical Association Journal (CMAJ)*. This paper will look at the application in Canada of the latest anti-VD technology medical science had to offer between the two world wars.

The scientific groundwork for the Canadian public health campaign against venereal disease was laid just before the Great War by August von Wassermann and Paul Ehrlich. Wassermann is instantly recognized as the developer of the test that still bears his name. His work was of general importance for medical science; after the zoologist Fritz Schaudinn (another German) discovered the causal organism of syphilis – the spirochete – in 1905, Wassermann set out to discover a universal blood-serum test for the antibody produced by infected persons. In so doing, he helped extend basic tenets of immunology to diagnosis. Ehrlich's work is less popularly well-known but had at least equally important implications for medical research. These were immediately grasped by the Canadian medical profession. The very first issue of the *CMAJ* carried a detailed and intelligent article on the topic by J. G. Fitzgerald, lecturer in bacteriology at the University of Toronto. The paper, published in January 1911, had originally been read before the Medical Section of the Academy of Medicine, Toronto, on November 8, 1910.[8] Ehrlich had only released his results in February of that year. Fitzgerald's article was part of the world-wide flood of literature on the topic that followed that release and would be only the first of many published in the *CMAJ*. A good number of these papers would be read prior to publication before medical societies from Halifax to the Fraser Valley and (during the war) before physicians posted in Great Britain with the Canadian Army Medical Corps.

Clearly much of the interest was due to the simple fact that Ehrlich and his assistant, Sahachiro Hata, had, after 605 disappointing experiments, come up with an effective treatment – called salvarsan or 606 – for a deadly disease. The fascination can also be partly explained by the fact that the cure was potentially as deadly as the disease; salvarsan was a preparation of arsenic. But the excitement was also due to the way Ehrlich had gone about his work. In the past, chemists had merely suggested the possible use of various chemicals to doctors. Ehrlich broke ground in that he sought out a specific solution to a specific medical problem. Drawing on the work of others who had previously tried to adapt arsenic for use against spirochetes, he set out to find what he called "the magic bullet."[9]

Ehrlich held that, rather than the scatter-gun tactics of treatments like mercury, which, it was to be hoped, killed the parasite before killing the host, chemists should aim substances directly at the offending parasite and hurt the host as little as possible. He thought he had found this with 606. He originally claimed that his *"therapia sterilisans magna"* provided not only a one-shot cure for syphilis but produced some sort of antibody against the disease. Both claims were confronted by early and unfavourable press in Germany and the United States.[10] The truth of the matter was that one treatment of salvarsan did often produce a negative reading on the Wassermann test. However, the result could return to positive, without re-infection, after as little as six months.[11] A good scientist, Ehrlich admitted the problems and soon recommended at least one follow-up injection.[12] Gradually this would shift to administration of salvarsan over an extended period, its effect regularly checked by the Wassermann test.[13] It would take several years for this to become established on a systematic basis. In the meantime, belief in 606 would range all the way from claims of a complete cure in one dose to assertions that no amount of it could ever cure.[14] Some medical men felt that search for a cure was only muddying the issue – that syphilis, like tuberculosis, should be accepted as an incurable disease. Once this was faced, doctors could settle down to helping syphilitics, like tuberculars, live as long and as usefully as possible.[15] Others agreed that 606 was no cure but, rather than abandon hope for cure, turned their attention to remedies based on metals other than arsenic.[16]

What was at issue was salvarsan's ability to cure, not its ability to treat. Its early results in the field of treatment could be spectacular. Before salvarsan, the only effective preparations available had been mercury and potassium iodide. The latter seemed to take some part in breaking down the gummatous tumours of late syphilis, the former in attacking skin lesions more directly. But potassium iodide had no effect on the Wassermann reaction whatsoever and mercury, after as much as three years' treatment, had very little.[17] This meant that though both ameliorated the condition, neither significantly threatened the hold syphilis had over the body. As long as spirochetes were hidden underground, symptoms could return at any time. The fact that salvarsan rendered the Wassermann negative, even if only for a time, meant that it was getting at the underlying cause. It also beat mercury and potassium iodide at the game they played best – within weeks, facially disfigured people treated with salvarsan would see their skin lesions clear.[18] By 1935, the two most disfiguring symptoms of syphilis – bone necrosis and gummata – had virtually disappeared due to early dosing with salvarsan.[19] In fact, skin manifestations became so rare that the place of syphilis in the medical scheme of things was upset. Now syphilis had been driven underground, internists were fighting to have it moved from dermatology into their own specialty.[20]

The success of salvarsan also had implications for the field of psychiatry. *Dementia paralytica* was first defined as a separate disease in 1822 and was recognized as having not a psychological but a pathological basis. As syphilis came to be better understood, *dementia paralytica* was realized to be a manifestation of the spirochete's attack on the cerebro-spinal system. Still, some medical men found it difficult to divorce themselves from a psychological explanation, one theory being that at least some cases of *dementia paralytica* were due to latent psychoses which the effect of syphilitic infection had caused to surface.[21] There also existed a related designation – parasyphilis – whose sufferers displayed symptoms akin to those of cerebro-spinal syphilis but who were not considered to be syphilitic. Salvarsan put an end to all this. Not only did cerebrospinal syphilitics often respond immediately and remarkably to treatment – one hemiplegic being able to carry one hundred pounds of coal up three flights of stairs within eight months of treatment[22]

– so did so-called parasyphilitics.[23] By 1918, parasyphilitic diseases were no longer spoken of; by 1929, they were declared non-existent.[24]

It should not be thought that Canadian doctors simply sat back and monitored work being done abroad in this field. If such were the case there would be little reason to write a paper on VD treatment in Canada. Nor would the *CMAJ* be a very useful source for research if all it printed were synopses from other journals or descriptions of foreign methods of research and application. The Canadian medical profession involved itself actively in the salvarsan revolution as soon as Ehrlich's results became known. Indeed, the Genito-Urinary Clinic of the Montreal General Hospital began its tests in late 1910, thanks to a supply of 606 made available to it partly due to the generosity of Ehrlich himself and obtained through the good offices of the eminent pathologist and bacteriologist, Simon Flexner, of the Rockefeller Foundation.[25] Shortly thereafter, Canada, along with all its allies, would be forced to come to grips with the problem of manufacturing its own arsenical preparations, German supplies being cut off at the declaration of war.[26] In addition, Canadian labs had to become proficient at all tests used in VD treatment. Ontario provided such work free to all physicians by 1919.[27] Canadian physicians also experimented on animals.[28]

All research work was aimed at finding a way to make sure salvarsan was used to its best advantage. As one writer would point out in 1942, the means to control syphilis was made available early in the century; the problem ever since then had been one of application.[29] One thing was obvious very early and that was that Ehrlich's dream of a magic bullet had eluded him – salvarsan would not deal out instant death to the spirochete. Instead, warfare would have to be waged over an extended time and that had implications for doctors and patients alike.

There are problems with long-term treatment in any disease. A great amount of onus is placed on the patient to continue treatment faithfully even after such time as he/she may be feeling better. Obviously, the shorter the term of treatment and the pleasanter and less risky the cure the easier it is to obtain the patient's commitment. Unfortunately, in the case of salvarsan, treatment was very long-term, unpleasant, and risky in a social as well as a physical sense. It was also expensive and required an up-grading in medical training in both diagnosis and application. Much emphasis would be placed in *CMAJ* articles on solving the doctors' side of the dilemma – how to make treatment as effective and painless as possible. There is also some discussion of the problem of ensuring that patients maintained treatment until cured but this – the closest that most professionals came to discussing the patients' side of the issue – is covered in far more detail in the *Canadian Public Health Journal*.[30] This was known as case-holding and really involved social welfare and public health rather than medical techniques and has been dealt with elsewhere.[31] It is mentioned in this paper only with an eye to its implications for treatment. What will follow instead is an assessment of how Canadian doctors went about fulfilling their part of the bargain.

Just how long-term was syphilis treatment? By 1920, trial and error had led to the establishment of an active treatment period of at least two years, followed by another three to five years of regular observation. During the first two years, patients were dosed weekly with preparations of arsenic and one or more of mercury, potassium iodide, and bismuth.[32] This would change little over the next two decades. By 1938, a typical series was three doses of preparations of arsenic the first week, followed by eight weekly injections of preparations of arsenic, eight of bismuth, and then eight of mercury. The rotation was repeated over the next two years.[33] It was the availability of large numbers of accessible syphilitics among the troops of all nations in the Great War that allowed the experimentation necessary to settle on the longer course of treatment.

One syphilologist stated that he had expected to leave the subject behind when he went into the war.[34] He soon recognized his mistake. Among Canadian troops alone, syphilis and gonorrhea together accounted for 12 per cent of all sickness, exclusive of wounds.[35] The tendency at first was to treat these men until they got back on their feet and then to send them back to the lines. Change in this policy came for two reasons. The first was that many of these soldiers soon broke down again, either dying or requiring another, longer, period of care. In strict accounting terms it paid off to dose them thoroughly the first time.[36] But the second reason had to do with the concern for civilian society in the postwar period. Although the army argued that the majority of its cases were due to previous infection in civilian life,[37] civilian reformers were not convinced. Demonstrating the siege mentality so prevalent during wartime, Jennie E. Smillie, convener of the public health committee of the National Council of Women, summed up the concern: "We must be prepared for the end of the war, when the return of the army will inevitably increase the danger of contagion from venereal diseases."[38] Fortunately, this defensive attitude on the part of civilian reformers found its ally in the militaristic attitude of the army doctors. Together they would wage war on the

> assailants who go over the top without any preliminary bombardment, dig themselves in unobtrusively, fight silently and insidiously, and when finally in at the death may even then be unrecognized by the stretcher bearers present.[39]

The war was to be waged by the proper use of the methods military doctors had been able to polish during the war:[40] the injection of arsenicals, comparable to "a barrage of shrapnel from field guns which quickly destroys all troops in the open," and the application of mercury, comparable to "the bombers and bayonet men who follow up the barrage and proceed to 'mop up' the trenches and dug-outs."[41] These means were to be applied by use of trained personnel coming home from Europe, in a series of clinics, some already in service and the rest shortly to be established with much-demanded funding from the provincial and federal governments.[42]

Once it was decided that an assault on the venereal diseases was imperative, government clinics became inevitable. Although the Canadian medical profession has never been happy about relinquishing any aspect of treatment to government agencies,[43] VD simply could not be handled by private practitioners. The reasons for this had to do with expense to the patient, lack of professional expertise, and legality. The 1917 fee schedule for the Alberta Medical Association recommended that the flat rate for one injection of salvarsan be fifty dollars.[44] Perhaps the price was inflated by war-time scarcity; perhaps doctors felt a high price had some preventive worth, discouraging the sufferer from chancing reinfection. At any rate, although a syphilitic might be able to afford one injection, he/she certainly would have to be well-to-do to fund the long-term treatment accepted as necessary by the end of the war. Although some syphilitics certainly opted for the pricey but private care of the personal physician, most turned to the clinics where government subsidization made the treatment free. In Ontario, each clinic was given a free supply of salvarsan and one thousand dollars to assemble the proper equipment, and allowed fifty cents for each syphilis or gonorrhea treatment administered.[45]

Why did the governments not simply spread this largesse among doctors rather than establish such clinics? This was done in locales where the population was too small to justify a clinic, however, the results were not happy: doctors were untrained in this work and their technique was often inept.[46] Specialists worried over the harm that could come to a syphilitic in the hands of an untrained and ignorant general practitioner.[47] Some argued that certain preparations should simply be kept out of the hands of non-specialists.[48] Some pressed for better training of medical students before they were "thrown upon the public."[49] Others gave papers before local medical associations in order to educate those already in practice.[50] Even in the care of experts, patients were not entirely safe. One specialist made the interesting admission that one patient had undergone a severe chill after treatment with a mixture of left-over arsenical products: "Being Scotch, I thought it best to use up these odds and ends."[51] One woman at one of Canada's most important research clinics was so badly hurt during her first serological examination that she refused to undergo another lumbar puncture.[52]

By the late thirties, one of Canada's foremost writers on the topic cited such cavalier treatment as one of the reasons people succumbed to a neurosis he called "syphilophobia" – fear of contracting and/or failing to recover from syphilis. Although he admitted that, were syphilis eradicated, some of those phobics would turn their attention to another disease, he felt that some of the fear was well-founded in a realistic apprehension regarding treatment.

> The use of large-bore, dulled needles, and a fitful, jabbing, and hacking venipuncture technique, soon renders the weekly treatment session a veritable torture, causes frequent lapses, and consequent fear of a relapsing infection.[53]

To be fair, arsenic is not the easiest thing to introduce safely into the human body and even the most careful preparation and application were fraught with danger.

Although the term *salvarsan* will be used throughout this paper, it is not generic. *Salvarsan* was a word coined by Ehrlich from the Latin for "save" to apply specifically to the product of his experiment number 606. It was unstable and difficult to prepare and dangerous to use. Due to the search for a safer product, but also due to the need to replace German supplies curtailed by the war, other arsenical drugs were soon concocted: 914, arsenobenzol, neosalvarsan, atarsenol, arsphenamine, neoarsphenamine, tryparsamide, etc. Each had its champions. Year after year, the federal health department tried to get the provinces to settle on one, at most two, brands to be used by all so that ordering of supplies donated by the Dominion to the provinces could be done more economically and efficiently. Year after year, the provincial health officers failed to reach an agreement. Finally the federal department gave up, admitting that as all arsenicals were dangerous, it could not really ask any province to use a product of which it disapproved.[54]

In order to prepare the arsenicals for injection, delicate procedures and elaborate apparata were needed.[55] Clearly these could best be provided for in a clinic properly equipped and staffed. Even then, side-effects were frequent and sometimes nasty. Ehrlich's work was early accused of causing death from renal failure and the *CMAJ* is full of warnings about what precautions the physician should take and what other problems he should be on the look-out for. Some were very serious: besides kidney failure, side-effects could include severe dermatitis, optic nerve atrophy, haemorrhage, and even medical shock. One hundred and fifty deaths had been laid at the door of 606 before 1912 and it was estimated by 1935 that there were eight hundred deaths annually in the United States as a result of pulmonary embolism following arsenical injections. Damage to the liver was a particular problem.The Toronto General Hospital alone reported fifty-eight cases of jaundice, including eight deaths, resulting from 606 by 1920. Attempts were made to counteract this – all syphilitics under treatment were put on a heavy carbohydrate diet and some clinics ran tests on the liver at every second treatment in order to forestall acute yellow atrophy.[56]

Far more frequently, patients felt only some degree of discomfort after an injection; typically one or more of: a feeling of fullness in the stomach, a bursting sensation in the head, intense flushing, dilated pupils, skin eruptions, dry throat, constipation or diarrhoea, and difficulties in breathing. These usually soon passed although quite severe nausea might follow for one or two days.[57] These were all side-effects of the arsenic itself and in general the reactions could be divided into three groups: acute poisoning, idiosyncrasy (i.e., reaction peculiar to the individual patient), and chronic cumulative effects.[58] Little could be done to counteract these except to monitor all patients more closely. In the early days, it was suggested that arsenicals not be used in certain cases where the patient was weak or too far gone to make the risk worthwhile,[59] but this was soon rejected. The decision to treat virtually all syphilitics was probably made easier by the fact that, as time went by, the patients seen were suffering from infections of much shorter duration and were therefore in better shape.But it also had to do with a conviction that the disease was worse than the cure and that, especially when syphilitics were thought to be almost constantly infectious, risks had to be taken on the part of the individual in order to guarantee the public health.[60]

But the risks involved in treatment were never taken lightly. Constant experimentation went on to make the treatments less dangerous and, perhaps more important to the average patient, less uncomfortable. Faulty preparation was early recognized as a cause of trouble. Problems could come from so simple a factor as a toxic agent contained in new rubber tubing through which the preparation passed.[61] Since arsenic in its pure form was not capable of being injected, it had to be combined with something. What that something was made a difference. Arsenobenzol (914), introduced to by-pass some of the side-effects apparent in 606, could lead to fatal benzol poisoning.[62] Although Canada lagged behind both the United States and Great Britain in formulating standards and testing for toxicity, it did have access to the hygiene laboratory in Washington, D.C., which actively sought samples of toxic arsenicals accompanied by information on body weight, age of patient, dose and dilution of drug given, symptoms, and results (i.e., fatal or not).[63]

Problems of application could sometimes be explained by ineptness but also had to do with uncertainty as to the best method – in terms of effectiveness as well as comfort – for administering drugs. Originally, it was thought that injection into a muscle was necessary to allow the arsenic to stay long enough in the body to do its work. Intravenous application was thought to allow the arsenic to be excreted too fast and was also blamed for a sharp exacerbation of symptoms called Jarisch-Herxheimer reaction. Ehrlich recommended intravenous injection only where immediate results were desired, especially in the case of severe or obstinate cases.[64] However, intramuscular injection, usually into the buttocks, had a side-effect, not fatal but terribly important to the patient and, in the long run, important to professionals who wanted to hold their cases: it caused pain to the point where patients required morphia.[65] One patient in the Montreal General Hospital could not move about in bed for four weeks due to pain and another could not cross his legs even after ten months.[66] Attempts to combine arsenicals with local anaesthetics proved unsatisfactory.[67]

Some of the pain could be countered by extremely careful preparation of the arsenic with sodium hydrate, to make the combination as neutral as possible. Distilled water used in the product was also checked for sterility. (Dissolved in water alone, 606 yielded a clear solution too acidic to inject without causing unbearable pain.)[68] By 1912, with the growing acceptance of serial rather than single injections, acceptance of intravenous injection became possible and necessary. With several treatments, doses were reduced, therefore reducing the likelihood of Jarisch-Herxheimer reaction. Also with several injections, patients could not be expected to suffer too much with each. Fortunately, with growing familiarity it was found that arsenic was not excreted as fast as formerly thought. Ehrlich himself came to the conclusion that 606 should only be injected intravenously.[69]

There was still pain and destruction of tissue but there also was no choice. Attempts to treat syphilitics with arsenicals enclosed in capsules to be swallowed or introduced into the rectum failed because the drug lost its curative power.[70] Doctors simply had to settle into a regular routine of checking their patients regularly for side-effects and of taking special care during injections. As any heroin addict can testify, repeated injections can cause veins to collapse. Syphilologists found this to be a particular problem with women, whose veins were often small, and infants, whose only suitable veins were in the neck.[71] In short, it was once again demonstrated that the true heroes of medicine are the patients. It was admitted at the Mayo Clinic that: "Many patients have declared that they would rather have the disease than the cure."[72] This brings us to the legal side of the question.

By the end of the Great War, compulsory treatment for VD was law in most Canadian provinces.[73] It had already become apparent by this time that, although private practitioners might be able to count on fairly regular attendance by their patients, public dispensaries could not.[74] With the turn to set courses of treatment, regularity was very important – lapsed patients could not simply just take up where they left off. For most people, fear was held for their own well-being, for their prospective children, and for the society that might have to support them should they become debilitated by VD. It was hoped that a law would make such individuals more conscientious, would impress on their minds the importance of treatment, and would allow some leverage when it came to convincing them to return. As is obvious from the fact that complaints regarding the difficulty of holding cases were still being written far into the Second World War,[75] the laws were not applied in any wholesale manner. As a rule, little was done to force those no longer infectious to continue treatment.[76] The laws were, however, applied when considered necessary against "those who are spreading the disease."[77] These could be designated the guilty infected as opposed to the innocent infected, a body constituted of those who had contracted the diseases from towels, dishes, etc. (still considered by the time of the Second World War to account for a large number of "respectable" cases); congenital syphilitics; spouses (usually wives) infected by partners who had contracted the disease; and nice young people who had had their morals temporarily disrupted by the temptations and stresses of urban industrial society. The guilty, on the other hand, were those suspected of having contracted syphilis or gonorrhea during the pursuit of money or pleasure: prostitutes, "loose women" (also called clandestine prostitutes), immigrants, or anyone with a criminal record. Such people could be and were forced to attend clinics regularly for treatment, sought out by police if they lapsed and kept or put in gaol until declared non-infectious. Considering the possibly debilitating consequences of such treatment, the legal implications are obvious. By 1926, some of the United States had already had to face the possibility of legal action.[78] Perhaps awareness of the legal touchiness of compulsory treatment partly accounted for lack of serious case-following among "respectable" Canadians.

The legal side of the question would no doubt have been much easier to deal with were diagnosis for syphilis an exact science. It was not. Although the Wassermann test was a wonderful breakthrough and was not displaced by other tests developed subsequently, it was prone to error.[79] It was capable of giving both false negative – for example, in the case of cerebro-spinal syphilis – and false positive results – especially for persons with histories of yaws, leprosy, or rat-bite fever.[80] Sometimes two different labs would come up with opposite readings for the identical sample[81] and an especially irritating problem was caused by "floppers," people whose Wassermann would keep going from positive to negative and back without any evidence of re-infection.[82] The All American Conference on Venereal Diseases held in Washington, D.C., in December 1920 unanimously concluded that the Wassermann should be relied upon only if supported by a general clinical examination.[83]

Although constituting a double check, diagnosis of syphilis on clinical grounds was confused by the vast variety of symptoms the disease could display. The conditions causing various patients to seek help give some idea of how varied responses to infection could be: failing vision, dizziness, stomach complaints, and flu symptoms. One man had been under treatment for psoriasis and others misdiagnosed as having tuberculosis of the bone or skin. Congenital syphilitics were brought in for a variety of reasons and only one-fifth of those checked at the Hospital for Sick Children in Toronto had severe enough symptoms to compel their parents to seek treatment for them during the early stage. The syphilis clinic at the Toronto General Hospital regularly had more patients referred to it from other specialties than it had patients who sought aid directly for syphilis.[84] To help them make such referrals, general practitioners were addressed by articles specifically designed to help them diagnose the disease.[85] Other types of professionals were sometimes more knowledgeable. One Vancouver brothel-keeper correctly diagnosed one of her employees by the young woman's persistent headache and a dinginess about the chin and neck. The doctor consulted remarked admiringly: "Experience had given this woman a knowing eye."[86]

Given the subtlety of correct clinical diagnosis, it is not surprising that many syphilitics failed to recognize the primary signs on their own bodies. It would seem that as the treatment campaign began to clear up the more grossly affected, the patients it did encounter were less and less aware of the truth of their condition. In 1918, one report stated that 53 of 71 syphilitics in one group admitted being infected one or more times; the other 18 denied all knowledge of infection. In another group of 255 reported in 1924, fully 41 per cent were not aware of ever having had any venereal infection. There are obvious problems in drawing a very solid conclusion from the scanty data represented by these two studies but there is evidence that venereologists were beginning to accept that symptomless syphilis was not necessarily due to deliberate deceit or poor memory: by 1935, it had been proven with the use of lab animals that syphilis need demonstrate no obvious signs in the early stages.[87]

Failure to obtain a history of infection from a patient must also have been due partially to other difficulties. One was the tendency of doctors and patients to talk a different language. For a large number of lay people, VD was known only by the vague term used in quack advertisements: "blood trouble." For others, only cruder terms rang a bell and one doctor suggested his colleagues adopt the use of a more "Rabelaisian vocabulary."[88] Patients also tended to try to protect themselves from moralizing, and for this reason, one doctor emphasized that male patients could only be questioned effectively in private, not before students or in a public ward, and that women should not be questioned at all! Another reported that, in one sample, only 23 per cent of women as compared to 81.6 per cent of men could give any historical detail aiding in diagnosis.[89] Women may have been more ignorant about VD, more trusting of their sex partners, or simply more shy before their doctors.

Patients may also have failed to be explicit in an attempt to protect others. Case-tracing has long remained a controversial side of VD control. Obviously, in a disease so difficult to diagnose and so potentially dangerous as syphilis, it is to the sufferer's advantage to be sought out and treated. Also obviously, in a disease so condemned, there are considerable social disadvantages attendant upon discovery. Attempts to trace contacts and family members became part of the campaign very early and remained a regular part of the diagnosis.[90] This rather imperfect system was, however, about as official as case-finding got. Aside from routine blood checks should one check into an institution such as a general hospital or a prison, the only chance one had of being diagnosed without being reported was through the compulsory pre-marital blood tests introduced in many western countries after the Great War.[91] It should further be remarked that, although preventive depots offering condoms and disinfectants had been employed successfully in some allied armies during the First World War and would be again in the Second, such things were never seriously considered for the civilian population. The only acceptable form of prevention was abstinence outside and sometimes even within marriage.[92]

The original VD campaign had, of course, been launched on a ticket of prevention as well as of cure. If prevention – to be accomplished through propaganda – failed to fulfill its promise of a higher morality, cure must be assessed as a success. Despite difficulties of case-finding, case-holding, and side-effects (in short, the problems of application), Ehrlich's concoction successfully treated thousands of people until it was rendered outmoded by a new wonder drug a third of a century later. Earlier hopes held out for its efficacy were too confident but in the long run it proved its worth. The CMAJ is full of material attesting to this fact – not just the congenitally syphilitic child improved to the point of unrecognizability within three days of treatment, but infirmaries and clinics full of people finding help where none had existed before. Because of difficulties of keeping in touch with cured cases, little data exists regarding these people's health in later life but what does exist is heartening.[93]

Plagued though it was by difficulties of preparation and application, arsenic was not surpassed within this period. Its major competitor was, not surprisingly, the old and beneficial stand-by for skin problems, mercury. Ehrlich had never advised the abandonment of mercury, and, despite arguments that because it was toxic in its own right it only added an extra burden to the body, it remained a part of most courses of treatment into the 1940s when it began to be replaced by bismuth. Some doctors, tied to the old ways, continued for some time to use it in place of arsenic, a practice roundly condemned by one expert as attempting "to kill a lion with birdshot." Furthermore, it was more toxic, took longer to ameliorate symptoms, and was considered by some to cause the disease to run an atypical course, thereby leading to more serious developments. Attempts to develop more effective preparations of mercury were not successful.[94]

Potassium iodide was never more than an adjunct treatment to help dissolve gummata, but bismuth, although it never displaced arsenic, grew in popularity. First used against syphilis in 1889, it underwent rigorous testing in the 1920s, during which time it was even fleetingly considered as a prophylactic against the disease. By the late 1930s, it had found its place as a back-up to arsenic. In the young and robust, the two drugs were sometimes combined in the same preparation, but more often, due to bismuth's own set of uncomfortable side-effects (inflammation of the mouth, headache, joint pains, dermatitis), they were administered alternately.[95] There was, however, one treatment that would displace the arsenicals in the treatment of one form of syphilis.

Despite early hopes and some success, salvarsan did not seem to cure cerebro-spinal syphilis permanently, even when administered intensively. In fact, it often increased the pains of tabetics – those affected in the spinal cord – and was accused of sending the spirochetes farther underground, into the brain, and thereby increasing the incidence of *dementia paralytica*.[96] Mercury was no help against neurosyphilis either.[97] For a while in the mid-1920s, a special preparation of arsenic, tryparsamide, seemed to hold out hope. Developed by the United States Army in 1915 while it looked for a substitute for German arsenicals, tryparsamide was early rejected as a treatment for primary and secondary syphilis because it was not powerful enough. However, it also proved to be less toxic, less irritating, and, most importantly, more penetrating. As salvarsan's inability to wipe out neurosyphilis became apparent, tryparsamide was turned to because it could follow the spirochetes far into the recesses of human tissue and kill them. It certainly proved to be a better solution than other arsenical products – some paretics (those suffering from general paresis of the insane or *dementia paralytica*) experienced marvellous remissions – but the statistical results were not heartening. Of one group in the Ontario Hospital at Whitby, Ontario, only 40 per cent showed marked or maintained improvement. These were far better results than the Mayo Clinic was getting at about the same time. Only 12 per cent of its paretics showed definite remissions after treatment with tryparsamide, mercury, and bismuth. Still, it was worth a try: the alternatives were death within three to four years or a longer life of insanity on a grand and spectacular scale. And the problem was not a small one. Of one group of 425 cases examined at Toronto General Hospital's VD clinic, 41 per cent showed evidence of involvement of the nervous system.[98] Seemingly, arsenic could not be expected to take in this final affliction; neither were other chemical answers forthcoming. What finally was put to work successfully against syphilitic insanity was another disease – malaria.

Once again syphilitics owed their salvation to German medicine, this time to Julius Wagner von Jauregg, a Viennese psychiatrist and neurologist who first noticed in 1887 the beneficial effect high fevers could have upon his insane patients. After experiments with other fever-provoking diseases and preparations, he had settled, by 1917, upon tertian malaria as the most effective treatment. It produced regularly a fever high enough to kill spirochetes (about 104 to 106 degrees Fahrenheit); it was easy to control with quinine; it could be almost totally controlled after eight to fourteen bouts of fever, taking between two weeks and two months, had done their work; and it was safer and quicker than tryparsamide. Wagner von Jauregg's discovery had implications not just for syphilology but for psychiatry, constituting as it did the first example of shock therapy. It earned him the 1927 Nobel Prize for Physiology or Medicine. Ironically, malarial therapy also led, over the years, to a better understanding of malaria itself.

Heroic as it seems, the medical concepts behind malarial therapy were quite old and well-accepted, thought to depend upon stimulation of the body's natural resistive forces. It was beginning to be used widely in European asylums by the early 1920s, and Alberta's chief VD control officer, Dr. Harold Orr, imported its use into Canada in 1924 when he returned from a two-year study tour of Europe. Malaria had its drawbacks; some patients suffered ruptured spleens or died of exhaustion. Patients needed careful nursing. In the early days, wards were screened for fear that patients would come into contact with mosquitoes which would then cause an epidemic among the general population. This practice was stopped when it became obvious that, after years of being injected directly, the malarial strain used had mutated to the point of no longer being capable of transmission via its traditional insect vector.[99]

Malarial therapy was used because it worked. To give only one of numerous examples discussed in the *CMAJ*, a man who formerly suffered marked incontinence of urine and feces, who could only walk with the aid of a cane and a crutch, and who could only wash his face if he were propped up in a corner, took a job as a freight handler after only eight chills.[100] True, most patients were farther gone than this man; the largest clientele for malarial therapy was to be found within the walls of insane asylums. Wagner von Jauregg's own results from injecting thousands of inmates yielded only 20 to 25 per cent who recovered and returned to their former vocations; 15 to 20 per cent showed no change and 5 to 10 per cent died of malaria. This does not seem like glowing success until one considers that the remaining 55 to 60 per cent, although never well enough to live without institutional or private care, had the disease arrested and lived much longer and less demented lives than they could otherwise have expected. Canadian results closely followed these, the most effective and intensive tests being carried on at the Verdun Protestant Hospital in Verdun, Quebec, which started the cycle by sending a patient to New York City in 1925 to be inoculated directly from a paretic patient there.[101] Malarial therapy, like the arsenicals, would be put out of business by a new medical breakthrough.

The new miracle was penicillin. It was effective not only against syphilis but gonorrhea, a disease neglected not only in this paper but, not coincidentally, by Canadian medical science. During the three decades of fascination with syphilis, remedies for gonorrhea stayed pretty well within the realm of local applications of disinfectants. Still, gonorrhea treatment in Canada was not without its heroic moments. In 1924, Dr. H. E. Young, head of VD control in British Columbia, reported to the Dominion Council of Health that B.C. clinics used X-rays on women who had not responded to other treatment. The idea was to stop menstruation, thereby supposedly giving the body time to heal itself. The dose was 200,000 volts filtered through copper and aluminum, given at a distance of fifty centimetres for sixty to seventy-five minutes each over the pelvis, anterior and posterior. A second, increased, dose followed. No protection was used. Not surprisingly, all the women stopped menstruating. More surprisingly, five out of the eight had resumed menses by the time of Young's report and a sixth had become pregnant. All but two of the eight were considered cured of gonorrhea.[102]

One Toronto doctor reported on his use of a technique imported from Chicago. Obviously inspired by the success of malarial treatment in syphilis, Professor Clarence A. Neymann of Northwestern University had started research in the field of hyperpyrexia: he sought to raise patients' temperatures by external means. This was done by placing the patient in a cabinet, raising his/her temperature over two and a half hours to between 106 and 107 degrees Fahrenheit and keeping it there for seven hours. Throughout this period a nurse administered salt solution and ice-cold drinks and made sure that no part of the patient's body touched another – contact could cause severe burns. This was all done in the doctor's office and after two or three hours' sleep there the patient went home. If the patient's urine was found free of gonococci, he/she was considered cured and could return to work in one or two days. When reporting on his use of hyperpyrexia on five patients in 1937, Dr. W. H. Avery confessed to allowing one patient's temperature to rise to 109.6 degrees Fahrenheit. When the accident was discovered, Avery cooled him immediately with wet blankets, sponge baths, and an ice-cold enema. No untoward results were reported.[103]

Perhaps fortunately for gonorrhea sufferers, local rather than systemic treatment remained the favoured method. Salves and irrigations continued in use even after yet another German scientist and Nobel prize-winner, Gerhard Domagk of I. G. Farben Laboratories, discovered sulfa drugs in 1932. By 1937, the sulfonamides had been proven to cure 80 per cent of gonorrhea cases within one week.[104] Still, Canadian doctors found it difficult to detach their gaze from the region of the body through which the infecting organism entered. One of the very few articles devoted to gonorrhea published in the *CMAJ* counselled against sulfa because it worked too fast, especially in stopping discharge. This, argued the author, was deleterious to the whole treatment because: "It is of the greatest benefit to the patient to feel himself a sick man and conduct himself accordingly."[105] As late as 1941, women being treated by sulfa were likewise advised to eschew sexual excitement and its supposedly frequent companion, alcohol, and, again showing medical belief in the debilitating effects of the normal female cycle, to take bed rest during menstruation.[106] The argument was all made more or less academic by the introduction of penicillin. The *CMAJ* made the first reference to the use of penicillin against gonorrhea in 1944, reporting by 1945 that penicillin could wipe out the disease with a single injection.[107] Such a quick and effective cure would revolutionize Canadian VD treatment.

Although discovered by Alexander Fleming (another Nobel winner, but British) in 1926, penicillin had to wait until 1939 before work by others led to its isolation, purification, testing, and quantity production. Its antibiotic properties were of obvious advantage to any nation involved in war. In early 1943, the National Research Council introduced production into Canada and by August three plants in Toronto and Montreal were operating under the direction of the federal government. By May 1945, production was such that general distribution could be permitted.[108]

Venereal disease would be a concern in the Second World War just as it had been in the First. The first item on the agenda of the first meeting of the Dominion Council of Health after the outbreak of war was "Wartime measures for VD control." The provinces and the armed services carried on the work until the federal government administered an injection of funds in 1943, re-establishing the VD-control division of the Department of Pensions and National Health, making grants to the provincial programs and liaising with the armed forces. The ultimate aim was to destroy syphilis and gonorrhea through use of a "four-sector Canadian front," comprised of health, welfare, legal, and moral components. In this way, Canada would not only ensure for itself a healthier army but also a healthier industrial work-force. Treatment centres expanded and improved their service to both the military and civilian populations and faster methods were sought. By 1942, a five-month intensive treatment of arsenicals was being heralded as very effective, its danger seemingly tempered by close observation of the patient's condition and reactions. But this method was never really developed on a large scale – penicillin stepped in to change everything.

Like gonorrhea, syphilis could be cured by one shot but it would take some time before the entire medical profession accepted this fact. For those who grasped it immediately the implications were obvious.[109] Other types of professionals also realized that the introduction of a simple, safe cure was bound to change societal attitudes towards the diseases. As one theologian fretted, "there is a grave danger that we shall regard the problem almost solely as a medical problem and not in its sociological and moral implications."[110] The truth was that with penicillin the social side to VD control became much less important. With penicillin, syphilis and gonorrhea could be cured quickly and painlessly as many times as one might become infected. Pregnant women could be cured before confinement, their children born untainted. Case-holding became a thing of the past and sufferers did not face the possibility of having their regular attendance at a clinic discovered. Failure to trace cases also became less of an evil as the disease was easily curable no matter at what stage the unsuspecting sufferer might be diagnosed.

Penicillin helped VD become established as a disease of the body rather than as a disease of the society. In doing so it built on the advances in this direction already made by salvarsan. When first introduced, Ehrlich's discovery was greeted by outcry on the part of some segments of the public on the grounds that it would undermine standards of morality, that syphilis was God's punishment for promiscuity. It is said that Ehrlich replied that God would simply have to find another way to punish people. This rather glib response strikes directly at the issue of how a society assimilates its technological advances into its system of values. The system of VD clinics Canada established after the Great War depended for its medical efficacy on advances in diagnosis and treatment but the way in which it utilized these was deeply influenced by Canadian concepts of shame, privacy, and the tension between individual freedom and civic responsibility.

The extent to which morality affected the way in which the VD treatments were administered to the population is immediately thrown into the light by contrasting the anti-VD campaign with that waged against tuberculosis immediately after the Second World War.[111] At that time anti-microbial drugs became available for treatment of what had formerly been a disease largely immune to chemical intervention. Just as for VD, the availability of an effective treatment sparked a public campaign. Like the anti-VD campaign, it offered propaganda as well as dosing. But unlike the anti-VD campaign, it set out to discover every Canadian tubercular. The entire Canadian population was X-rayed, identified tuberculars were openly and actively treated, and, as a result, Canadian sanatoria were virtually emptied within fifteen years. No similar attempt has ever been made to diagnose Canadian sufferers from syphilis and gonorrhea, perfectly possible though such a national check-up has been since shortly after the turn of the century. The reason for this is that while TB by 1945 had come to be perceived almost exclusively as a disease of the body, VD was – and still is – largely perceived as being in addition a disease of the society.

Although it removed much of the danger from treatment, the

introduction of penicillin would not succeed in eradicating this perception. Some argument can be made, however, that the availability of penicillin has had, as predicted, some effect on the degree of promiscuity in this society: more recent demonstrations of the nexus between medical technology and attitudes towards sexual morality are available in the "sexual revolution" following the introduction of the birth control pill in the 1960s and in the effect that AIDS is currently having upon changes in sexual habits among the North American homosexual community. But if penicillin could not manage to change social attitudes enough to make an anti-TB style campaign possible, it did alter sharply approaches to the purely medical aspects of its treatment. Doctors no longer felt a need to discuss sexual abstinence: this preliminary form of prevention no longer had a vital place in medical treatment. Discussions of how to relieve patients of all unnecessary pain and embarrassment also became things of the past. Penicillin could cure and did cure and did so relatively painlessly and safely. It also did so without entailing long-term contact between the doctor and patient. The Canadian medical profession need no longer trouble itself with such things and Canadian medical science, as evidenced by the shift in emphasis away from VD in post-Second-World-War medical journals, could go on to other things.

The Search for the
Decline of Maternal Mortality:
The Place of Hospital Records

Suzann Buckley

It is heartening to consider the surprise with which today's younger students greet the news that it was once quite common for Canadian women to die in childbirth. Since childbirth is no longer particularly dangerous for the prospective mother, most students next ask what happened to account for this change. Unfortunately, the only sources they can be guided to at this point in an effort to answer that question are American and European.[1] If that was the only problem with using these sources perhaps it would be legitimate to leave the Canadian history of maternal mortality largely unexplained and simply to rely on analogies. However, the two main sources – Edward Shorter's *A History of Women's Bodies*[2] and Joyce Antler's and David Fox's joint study of the New York Academy's report on maternal mortality in New York City for 1931–32[3] – emphasize the introduction of sulfonamides, used for the treatment of bacterial infections contracted during the birth process, as the major factor in the rapid decline of maternal mortality after 1936. Shorter is more single-minded in his belief in the unilateral curative effects of chemicals than are Antler and Fox. While Shorter puts the decline down almost solely to the application of the discoveries of medical science – not just sulfa drugs but also the introduction after 1867 of antiseptic conditions for childbirth, which marked the beginning of a preliminary period of slow decline in maternal mortality – Antler and Fox look more broadly at better obstetrical training for doctors; the institutionalization of obstetrics as a medical specialization; the establishment of medical review committees of doctors, conducting continuous investigations of obstetric practices; and improved hospital facilities for antiseptic treatment of maternity cases.

But no matter how effective new medical procedures may be, their introduction and application are affected by the society in which they must function. Even if we accept the theses of Shorter and Antler and Fox, we must find out whether their explanations hold true for Canadian society. To do that, we must look at a broader range of social and environmental factors than those authors have. Thus, we will not only discover if the analysis *can* be parachuted in to explain the Canadian situation, but we will also be able to assess how much medical solutions are affected in general by social and environmental factors. One source that brings both sides of the question together and makes their comparison possible is hospital records. In them we find much data regarding a woman's social status and health history as well as a record of diagnosis and treatment. Here, I will refer to the records of two Ottawa hospitals, the Ottawa Maternity Hospital and the Ottawa Civic Hospital. First the information that can be found in such files will be outlined, and then it will be placed against the backdrop of socio-medical studies being proposed in the inter-war period in Canada regarding the causes and, of course, the proposed solutions, of maternal mortality. Only by looking at all available sources can we conduct a thorough search for the cause of the decline of maternal mortality in Canada and provide interested students with a solid explanation.

The Ottawa Maternity Hospital was in existence from 1895 to 1924. It was established by Lady Aberdeen, wife of the Governor General and a reformer in her own right, as part of an effort to reduce maternal mortality by providing medical attendance for poor women in childbirth. As outlined by its founder, the hospital had three special objectives: (1) to afford to married women for a small remuneration (or, if necessary, no remuneration) proper accommodation, medical attendance, and experienced nursing during their confinement; (2) to give to unwed pregnant women a home where they would receive medical attendance and proper care; and (3) to afford aid and experienced nursing at their own homes to poor women during their confinement. In effect, Lady Aberdeen linked maternal mortality for all poor women to lack of medical care. For poor married women, she also linked it to overwork on domestic chores.[4]

The hospital had its own charter and was independent of any

other hospital in the city. Its annual report of 1911 boasted that it was "managed wholly by women for women."[5] In its early years most of its patients were unmarried mothers or poor married women, but within five years married women able to pay full fees became the majority. By 1920 so numerous were the full-fee patients that Ella Bronson, the president of the hospital board of trustees, felt impelled to correct an "erroneous impression . . . that no charity work is done in the institution."[6]

Thus, for the years 1895–1924, the approximately 5,000 patients at Ottawa Maternity ranged in socio-economic status from charity cases to those who could pay full fees. As such, they represent a socio-economic cross-section of the society of that city and its surrounding area. Because of this, a study of the causes of death of the fifty-seven patients who died in childbirth during that period offers an excellent opportunity to assess whether Shorter's and Antler and Fox's assertions regarding causes of the decline of maternal mortality apply to the Canadian experience.

Two sources inform us about the deaths at the Ottawa Maternity. For the period 1895–1924 there exists a complete set of annual reports which usually indicate the cause of death. In addition, for the period 1896–1917, there are patient and medical registers. Between 1903 and 1916 these sometimes give particulars such as age, number of pregnancies, hours of labour, and cause of death.[7] Both sets of records show only two deaths diagnosed as due definitely to puerperal septicemia, the symptoms of which include high fever, chills, and rapid pulse and breathing. It is a condition associated with failure to take adequate antiseptic precautions during delivery. The Ottawa Maternity's low rate of so-called childbed fever suggests that its personnel were fully aware of the need for antisepsis. This impression is supported by the annual reports which reveal the superintendent's awareness of the seriousness of infection and the need to take precautions to prevent its spread. Also, a revision of the by-laws in 1915 included a requirement that attending physicians isolate any patient suspected of having puerperal septicemia. This evidence from a Canadian hospital would seem to support Shorter's and Antler and Fox's arguments regarding the positive effect of antisepsis on the decline of maternal mortality.

If the old demon of puerperal fever had been quelled, what major threats to the lives of women giving birth at that time at the Ottawa Maternity remained? There were two: eclampsia (a condition caused by the presence of toxic products formed within the body and distinguished by high blood pressure, retention of water, excessive protein in the urine, convulsions, and finally coma and death) and placenta previa (a condition wherein the placenta precedes the expulsion of the fetus from the womb, causing severe bleeding). Of the fifty-seven deaths at Ottawa Maternity, fourteen can be attributed to eclampsia and seven to placenta previa. The other notable causes were post-partum haemorrhage (five) and pneumonia (nine, of which four were associated with the influenza epidemic of 1918).

Although there were sufficient data available to allow hospital officials to assess what we now know to be high-risk pregnancy cases – the indigent, the multiparous (having had several pregnancies), and those past age thirty-five – there seems to have been little attempt to prevent childbirth complications other than that of infection arising at the time of birth. This was prevention at the last minute, using antiseptics to avoid adding more problems to a mother's condition. But what of problems of longer standing which she brought into the delivery room with her? The hospital was not totally ignorant of these more preliminary problems and there was at least one attempt to prevent complications arising from them: in 1920 a prenatal clinic was established at the hospital for public ward patients. This clinic, alleged to be one of the first of its kind in Canada, enabled doctors to determine if a woman was a candidate for problems either at delivery or earlier in the pregnancy. For instance, in 1921, several cases of mild toxemia (a condition similar to eclampsia, but stopping short of convulsions) were diagnosed and courses of treatment in the form of bed rest and proper diet were prescribed. But the focus of the doctors at the clinic was clearly (and perhaps understandably) fixed upon prevention and treatment (largely of syphilitics whose condition posed a threat to their babies) rather than on conducting clinically based research studies (no matter how possible these may have been) or on applying the results to more general and preliminary types of prevention.[8]

Such studies were, however, beginning to be made by others in Canada. One of the first attempts at a systematic study of maternal mortality was undertaken by Dr. Helen MacMurchy,[9] head of the Child Welfare Division of the Department of Health. Dr. MacMurchy's study was spurred by the fact that, in 1925, Canada's maternal mortality rate was 5.6 per thousand, the highest of the fourteen countries polled. MacMurchy's enquiry entailed an examination of about eleven thousand official reports of the deaths of all women between the ages of fifteen and fifty years who had died between July 1925 and July 1926. The preliminary reports indicated a total of 1,202 deaths from puerperal causes. MacMurchy then asked the physicians who had signed the individual death certificates to fill out a form on each of the 1,202 deaths. Questions were asked about prenatal care and the pregnancy, labour, and delivery. Suggestions were requested regarding how each death might have been prevented. About 92 per cent of the physicians replied, providing data on 1,105 cases. In addition to cases of obvious maternal mortality, MacMurchy also sought information on women whose death certificates indicated that they *might* have died from puerperal causes. She again contacted the physicians who had signed these certificates and asked for similar data. To ensure that these deaths were relevant to the survey, the doctor was asked if the patient had been pregnant and if the pregnancy had contributed to the death. In 330 instances the response was in the affirmative, bringing the total number of cases to 1,532 for a maternal mortality rate of approximately 6 per 1000 live births.[10]

One of MacMurchy's chief goals in undertaking the enquiry had been to document the existence of a problem. She intended to use this documentation to convince physicians to take maternal mortality seriously and to educate the public to regard pregnancy as a pathological condition with risks that might be reduced by medical care, especially prenatal supervision. It was not an easy task. Many within the profession never saw an obstetrical case and some of those who did rarely lost a patient. It therefore made it difficult for the profession as a group to be seized with the importance of a solution to a problem which they did not perceive as existing.[11] For most doctors, "the maternal mortality rate [was] so comparatively low [in relation] to the surgical mortality rate and other mortality rates that they were lulled into a sense of safety of the so-called normal physiological process."[12] On the other side of the coin was a populace which failed to demand better prenatal care from doctors. Many could simply not have afforded it anyway and those who could were as ignorant of its importance as were their doctors.[13]

In 1928, MacMurchy presented a version of her final report about maternal mortality to the annual meeting of the Canadian Medical Association. It focused on two questions: why did mothers die and how might their deaths have been prevented? The first question centred on a very brief description of the mother's health and concluded that of the 1,532 deaths under study, 795 had shown evidence of the following complicating factors:

No. of deaths	Complicating factor
68	very poor, even to the point of destitution
153	general poor health
226	cardiac disease
132	influenza and/or pneumonia
96	tuberculosis
67	exhaustion from domestic chores
27	lack of sleep
26	too frequent pregnancies.

Despite the fact that her data clearly showed that non-medical factors played a role in maternal mortality, MacMurchy did not expand upon the likelihood of relationships between such factors as destitution and prenatal complications caused by malnutrition. Although acknowledging that at least 10 per cent of the women had died because of poverty or causes associated with poverty, Mac-Murchy's medical training led her to stress medical solutions rather than socio-economic ones. Proper prenatal, nursing, and medical services, she maintained, could do much to reduce maternal mortality. In preparation for her argument for more and better services, MacMurchy spoke specifically to the question of the major "medical" causes of maternal deaths.

MacMurchy concentrated on three. Puerperal sepsis accounted for 33 per cent of the deaths reported in the survey. Haemorrhage, a copious discharge of blood occurring during labour or following delivery, accounted for 23 per cent. The third cause was toxemia, accounting along with eclampsia for 22 per cent of the deaths. According to MacMurchy, all of these conditions were preventable. Sepsis, she implied, might be prevented by strict adherence to sanitation during delivery, the others by proper prenatal care. She did not expand on any of these points. Upon consideration, this is hardly surprising with respect to haemorrhage and toxemia since there was little that could be done prenatally to prevent either. At best, the conditions could be identified and treated by therapeutic abortion, salt-free diet, or bed rest.

But MacMurchy was not really concerned with how accessible recommended methods of prevention and treatment were to pregnant women. For instance, she did not deal with the fact that so simple a solution as bed rest might be out of the question for many women, especially those with several children and extensive domestic responsibilities. Neither did she address the fact that not all women requiring prenatal care could get it. Rather, MacMurchy's message was medical advice for medical men: employ better aseptic techniques and learn to regard pregnancy as a condition requiring medical supervision.

MacMurchy produced similar literature to get a matching message across to women. Educational materials disseminated widely by the Child Welfare Division of the federal Department of Health drove home to women MacMurchy's belief that it was the responsibility of a pregnant woman to give herself over to medical care and advice. She envisioned a simple world wherein doctors fulfilled their responsibilities by taking charge and pregnant women fulfilled their responsibilities by taking orders. "Doctors and nurses must be able and willing to give advice acceptably and mothers must be ready and anxious to receive it." Again, she did not address the fact that many women in need of care might have to forgo it due to cost.

A logical extension of MacMurchy's definition of pregnancy as a pathological condition was belief in the necessity of hospitalization at childbirth. MacMurchy expressed distress that as many as twenty to thirty thousand women annually went unattended in childbirth and that others were attended only by untrained midwives. For those in isolated areas she had no immediate solution. Although recognizing that "lack of medical care in the outposts is a serious problem," she preferred to leave the resolution of that problem to the Canadian Medical Association. She concentrated instead on more urbanized areas. She spoke in favour of the centralization of all types of medical care into hospitals, stating that it was wasteful that only 16 per cent of births took place in hospitals whereas those institutions were capable of accommodating 40 per cent. MacMurchy clearly felt that in settled areas institutionalization for childbirth was the solution to the problem of maternal mortality. Again, she failed to deal directly with the fact that many were unable to bear the cost of hospital care.

MacMurchy's call for medical solutions to maternal mortality found acceptance not only with the Canadian Medical Association and local medical groups but with several lay organizations. Many groups set up maternal mortality committees. The Canadian Medical Association's committee was headed by Dr. W. B. Hendry, professor in obstetrics and gynecology at the University of Toronto.

Hendry's committee found that a major contributing factor in maternal mortality was poor obstetrics. Some doctors were remiss in not adhering to asepsis, premature in their use of forceps, and ignorant of recent changes in obstetrical practice. The committee made several recommendations which it hoped would correct this situation. Medical schools were encouraged to develop postgraduate and refresher courses in obstetrics, and medical associations to devote one meeting per year to the issue of maternal mortality. The committee also proposed that the Hospital Committee of the Canadian Medical Association gather information about the provincial inspection of maternity homes and lying-in hospitals, presumably to check if doctors and institutions were observing strict rules of hygiene. A list of suggestions for the management of the maternity patient was drawn up by the committee and distributed by the federal Department of Health to all practitioners. In addition to these attempts to educate doctors and make them aware of the need for increased accountability, the committee recommended that an obstetrics specialist be made available in each district for general practitioners to consult when difficulties arose during a delivery.[14]

Apparently anticipating opposition to these proposals from their colleagues, the committee proposed using women's groups to generate public pressure that would force the profession to make efforts to reduce maternal mortality. The committee was not recommending a return to the situation of the 1890s when women's groups led the campaign for safe maternity. Rather, it envisioned women's groups playing a secondary role to doctors championing that very same cause. "The female laity,"[15] as it was disparagingly called by some doctors, was expected to support obediently any solutions proposed by the professionals. It is true that on some issues this presented no difficulty because the same views were shared by both groups. For example, as early as 1928 the United Farm Women of Ontario passed a resolution calling on the government to subsidize health care for pregnant women and to recognize the connection between maternal mortality and poverty and the lack of medical care in remote areas. The organization also called for recognition by medical colleges of "the great need for more scientific and intensive training of medical students in obstetrics and a great need of experience before they are allowed to practice."[16]

Neither did the National Council of Women of Canada go against the proposals of the professionals on the issue of improvement in obstetrical training. On the advice of Dr. Charles Hastings, the Medical Officer of Health for Toronto, and on the initiative of the

Canadian Nurses Association, the propaganda efforts of the Council about maternal mortality had changed since the days of its support for midwives. Although the Council retained an interest in midwives, its efforts were now directed towards having the public and medical professionals recognize the responsibility of the medical profession for safe maternity.[17] Accordingly, when Mrs. H. P. Plumptre, convenor of the Council's annual meeting in 1930, posed the question of the possibility of organizing a system of midwives in Canada, she herself responded by asking another question. Perhaps Canada might continue the direction already taken by employing in public health work "only fully trained doctors and nurses with the addition of thorough obstetrical training?"[18] In short, competent doctors and graduate nurse-midwives might be preferable to trained midwives. Rather than recommending such a proposal, however, Plumptre and members of her committee resolved that members of the Council and the Canadian Medical Association should confer on the question of midwives. The decision as to midwives, graduate nurse-midwives, or neither thus rested finally with doctors.

At most, only a handful of doctors and nurses were sympathetic to the idea of midwives. Writing in 1935 to Dr. John Puddicombe, an active proponent of the need to reduce maternal mortality, Dr. Bengee Atlee, the chief of obstetrics and gynecology at Dalhousie University, recommended that if Puddicombe was convinced that the low maternal mortality rates for countries with a system of midwives (for instance, the Scandinavian countries), were valid,

> it would seem a reasonable thing to consider the question of introducing the well-trained midwife into Canada . . . I have long felt that it is better for the average woman to be confined by someone who perforce cannot use the more rigorous methods of getting the passenger through the Pubic Strait, than by a practitioner who is permitted, and often only too willing in order to save himself time, to use everything in his armamentarium whether it is indicated or not.[19]

Puddicombe expressed no comment on the matter in subsequent correspondence and apparently did not pursue it.

By and large, most doctors and nurses opposed the idea of midwives for the same economic and professional reasons that had been presented in the 1890s. Many nurses, unemployed as a result of the Depression, may have feared midwives would compete with them for nursing jobs;[20] some doctors definitely were apprehensive about their competition. As Dr. McCullough, the Ontario representative on the Dominion Council of Health remarked in 1924, "the midwives are seeking to earn a living in this work, so that they will necessarily remain where there will be work for them – in the large cities – and will not be inclined to go out to remote parts of the provinces any more than a physician will be."[21]

Economic arguments aside, some professionals were opposed to midwives not so much because they feared inroads into their own practice but because they wanted to make inroads into midwifery. These were those nurses and doctors working to change obstetrics. Together, they were moving toward the idea of a graduate nurse-midwife. By obtaining a greater specialization in midwifery, the graduate nurse could improve her status within the profession.[22] From a doctor's perspective, the idea of having a graduate nurse-midwife as an assistant was very appealing. As one doctor pointed out, "trained obstetrical nurses cooperating with a doctor [would] give the busy practitioner conditions approaching those enjoyed by the hospital obstetrician but also enable him to maintain the standard of obstetrics at a higher level than hitherto possible."[23]

There were several advantages to this arrangement. The presence of another well-trained professional would help to streamline the childbirth process. Much of the time-consuming work of establishing and maintaining a sanitary environment and supervising labour would be handled by the graduate nurse-midwife, thus leaving the doctor more time for other patients and enabling him to make obstetrics cost-effective. Also, the presence of a graduate nurse-midwife would aid the doctor in keeping the patient's family and friends at bay during a home birth, thereby taking the pressure off doctors to use forceps or other means to hasten the delivery.[24] Such measures would in turn help reduce the rate of maternal mortality.

In addition to the studies by doctors, public health officials in Ontario and Manitoba surveyed maternal mortality reports and discerned five common variables among those women who survived childbirth. First, most were between the ages of twenty and twenty-nine, suggesting an optimum range during which time the woman was old enough to withstand the stress of childbirth but not too old to be debilitated by it. The second variable was the order of the pregnancy. Second and third pregnancies carried less risk than first or fourth and subsequent births. The third factor was the successful birth of a live child: many women who gave birth to stillborns died themselves as a result of the birth. Giving birth in spring or summer, when the incidence of puerperal sepsis was lower (allegedly because resistance to streptococcal infections was higher than in fall or winter) was the fourth factor. Finally, survival of childbirth by the mother was more likely if she were neither impoverished nor exhausted.[25] One effect of this patient profile was to indicate the need for research into the biological, sociological, pathological, and obstetrical factors in maternal mortality. Those who wished to make obstetrics a specialization urged that such research be done.[26] Once again, as with the physicians and MacMurchy, the trend was towards medicalization of maternal mortality.

Were the proposed solutions, especially the push for better obstetrics, merely self-interest on the part of their proponents or were poor obstetrical practices a significant factor in maternal mortality?

With this question in mind, I examined the records of maternal deaths from 1934 to 1939 at the second hospital, the Ottawa Civic. This institution had earlier absorbed the Ottawa Maternity Hospital and its staff included some of the physicians most active in pushing for a reduction in maternal mortality. From 1934 to 1939, the number of live births at the Civic was approximately 5,951, with 36 maternal deaths. On an average, the Civic accounted for 6 of the 15 puerperal deaths annually at institutions in Ottawa during those years. Its rate of 6 per 1,000 live births was higher than the average national (4.3) and provincial (4.8) rates and the rate for home births (2.3) in Ontario. Its rate was lower than the average of 8 per 1,000 for similar institutions in Ontario.[27] Of the 36 deaths, 8 were diagnosed as being due to toxemia (including eclampsia), 7 as being due to puerperal sepsis, 3 as being due to haemorrhage, and the other 18 as being due to a variety of conditions. The Civic thus follows the pattern of the various maternal mortality surveys by demonstrating a significant number of deaths attributed to the same three main causes and by showing a higher percentage of maternal mortality for hospital births than was the norm for home births.

I have divided the cases into two groups, based on the most significant contributing factor in the patient's death. The first group consists of nineteen patients whose health, because of a temporary illness, long-standing medical condition, or failure to seek treatment quickly, created complications which could not be overcome. For example, one patient, aged thirty-five, died of a heart attack on December 10, 1935, after twenty-three hours of apparently normal labour. The determination of death was cardiac dilation (enlarged heart). Nothing was done to retrieve the fetus.[28] Another woman, the mother of four children aged from fifteen months to four and a half years, had had a complete physical examination during which nothing was found to be wrong. Nevertheless, she was admitted for observation because following an earlier delivery she had experienced pain in her hands, feet, and legs. Once in the hospital she was found to be suffering from bacterial endocarditis (inflammation of the inner lining of the heart, linked to a streptococcal infection). Those predisposed to this condition are often in poor health. She became paralyzed and died on August 8, 1935, from glomerular nephritis (a kidney condition usually secondary to an infection, especially streptococcal).[29]

The causes of death for the other seventeen patients are as follows:

No. of deaths	Cause of death
1	post-partum haemorrhage
1	pulmonary edema (fluid in the lungs) and tuberculosis of the spine
1	mitral stenosis (obstruction of the flow of blood through the mitral valve of the heart) and actual fibrillation (grossly irregular heartbeat)
2	pneumonia
1	cerebral embolism (obstruction of a cerebral artery) and chronic endocarditis
1	chronic endocarditis
1	chronic nephritis and paralytic ileus (intestinal obstruction)
2	eclampsia
1	toxemia
1	eclampsia and chronic nephritis
2	eclampsia with endocarditis and uremia (severe nephritis)
1	myocarditis (inflammation of the muscle tissue of the heart)
1	post-partum haemorrhage and haemophilia*
1	pre-eclampsia and placenta previa[30]

* Clearly not what we now know as classic haemophilia, a disease limited to males.

The second category involved patients whose deaths could be linked to a specific obstetrical practice, such as apparent lack of asepsis, a doctor's error, or his/her inability in handling a complication (for instance, a retained placenta). Seventeen patients fall into this group. One woman began labour on January 11, 1934. The doctor attempted a high forceps delivery and version (that is, turning the fetus) twice without success. Twelve hours later the woman was admitted to the hospital in severe shock. A craniotomy (decompression of the fetal head in preparation for removal) was performed, but the patient died at 4:00 A.M. on January 14 from puerperal septicemia.[31] Another patient, aged thirty-four, gave birth on July 31, 1936, and became ill two days later. She grew worse and was admitted to the Civic on August 8. She was given blood transfusions, presumably to reverse the effects of earlier haemorrhage, but to no avail. She died on August 13 of puerperal septicemia.[32] The remaining fifteen deaths were as follows:

No. of deaths	Cause of death
1	post-partum haemorrhage (no blood transfusions given)
1	ruptured ectopic gestation (development of the fetus within the fallopian tube which subsequently ruptures and haemorrhages)*
2	puerperal septicemia
1	contracted pelvis (misshapen pelvis due to malnutrition during childhood) and a breech (buttocks first) birth unsuccessfully completed
1	cerebral embolism and contracted pelvis accompanied by a "rough" Caesarean section
1	acute myocarditis, contracted pelvis, and late Caesarean section due to incorrect reading of X-rays
1	obstructed trachea (windpipe)
1	shock after forty-six hours of labour
1	post-partum haemorrhage
1	pleurisy (inflammation of the membrane surrounding the lungs) with septicemia
1	retained placenta
1	adherent placenta
1	pulmonary embolism with pneumonia and puerperal septicemia
1	endocarditis with pulmonary tuberculosis and puerperal septicemia[33]

* This woman had been given a clean bill of health the morning of her death.

While it is true that some of these women could have been saved through better obstetrical intervention, as MacMurchy and others argued, medical approaches alone would not have been sufficient to save some of these lives. Some patients died while others, similarly diagnosed, lived. A closer study of individual patients within similarly diagnosed groups indicates that, all medical factors being fairly equal, a patient in generally poor health or suffering temporary or chronic disease was at greater risk than one in good health.

This indicates that there were environmental factors at play here, in addition to the medical ones. The records of the Ottawa Maternity Hospital, MacMurchy's report, and the various studies all point to a link between poor health and poverty. Inferences drawn from these sources alone are not substantive enough to allow a convincing argument that poor health caused by poverty did in fact cause women to die in childbirth. When taken in context with a more direct clinical study done on maternal mortality in 1940, however, these inferences can be seen as important pieces in the puzzle.

Three doctors from the Department of Pediatrics and Obstetrics at the University of Toronto – J. H. Ebbs, F. F. Tisdall, and W. A. Scott – evaluated, over the course of a year, prenatal diets of 400 women from low-income homes. The control group consumed an inadequate diet low in protein, calcium, and vitamins B^1 and C. The second group had their diet supplemented by adequate amounts of protein, calcium, and vitamins during the last three or four months of pregnancy. The third group already had moderately adequate diets but were taught how to make improvements through the application of knowledge about nutrition. The researchers concluded that pregnant women on an inadequate diet had poorer health and more complications than those on adequate diets. These women also were worse obstetrical risks and were more likely to experience miscarriage, stillbirth, or premature labour.[34]

The nutrition study and the other records examined thus suggest that women who died in childbirth did so because of socio-economic conditions as well as medical ones. This hardly seems startling in an era where we have begun to realize that medical problems are part of the whole cloth of society. We now accept readily that people become ill not simply because some external factor known as "disease" makes them ill, but because some combination of factors comes to play that reduces a person's well-being below a level we have come to regard as "healthy." It is true that this reduction sometimes is accomplished dramatically and acutely by invasion of the body by a disease-causing external organism (infectious disease) or chemical (environmental disease) but how well bodies withstand such invasions – and sometimes whether they feel their effects at all – often depends upon their individual strength and level of fitness. The fact that such a holistic idea of human health was not universally accepted during the first part of this century is indicated by the very fact that such studies were taking place and that their results were considered worthy of publication. What would seem more surprising to us is that scholars such as Shorter and Antler and Fox should still be susceptible to the old, strictly medical view of health and the related belief that the treatment of disease by medical means alone could cause such a reduction in maternal mortality that our younger generation of students should have come to regard childbirth as virtually a no-risk venture. While sulfonamides were a great breakthough in battling bacterial infections of all types, not just those associated with childbirth, the range of causes of death given by records such as those at the Ottawa Maternity and Civic hospitals points to a broader range of health problems beyond the reach of purely medical solutions such as the application of chemicals.

But simply to state that one cannot be satisfied with sulfa drugs as an answer for the general reduction of maternal mortality is facile. If we are to insist that there were also important socio-economic factors at play we must be ready to identify and assess them. In particular, we must be able to determine the exact connection between poverty and risk. One way of getting at the problem is to look at more available hospital records and to look at them more closely. In addition to facts about the patient's social and economic status, we must also look for evidence of types of medication used, including sulfonamides, and use of and changes in various obstetrical techniques. We must also balance any conclusions we come to against the medical literature of the time. For example, how do we deal with an article in the *Canadian Medical Journal* of 1940 which curiously suggests that the use of sulfonamides may have contributed to rather than reduced maternal deaths? This seeming contradiction must be addressed. A good example of a successful attempt by historians to place maternal mortality in the context of socio-economic issues is W. Peter Ward and Patricia Ward's article on "Infant Birth Weight and Nutrition in Industrializing Montreal."[35]

Among the facts historians must weigh when trying to determine why the decline occurred when it did is that by 1938 some of the severity of the Depression had waned and the subsequent years were marked by increasing prosperity. More prosperity may have resulted in a decrease in malnutrition or in other conditions that lowered resistance to the infections that contributed both directly and indirectly to maternal mortality. We must also consider whether the decrease in maternal mortality was just part of an overall decrease in mortality. Was there a general reduction in the number and severity of epidemics such as that of influenza and its frequent companion, pneumonia, in 1936?

After the 1930s could women of child-bearing years have been reaping the benefits of earlier complex medical and socio-economic changes, thereby being less likely to have tuberculosis, a contracted pelvis, or other conditions which made childbirth risky? Greater availability of contraceptive devices might also have enabled some women to avoid the strain of too many pregnancies and their attendant risks. Finally, increased immunity to infections or decreased virulence of some organisms may have contributed to a general decline in the mortality rate.[36]

Hospital records such as those held at the Ottawa Maternity and Civic hospitals are one vital resource for such research. Access to such records in the past has not always been easy for historians to attain – that is, assuming the records even exist: many have been destroyed, some quite recently. Let us hope that more of these collections are kept extant and that their keepers make them available to historians seeking a full and accurate explanation for the fortunate tendency on the part of Canadian women to survive childbirth in significantly greater numbers after the mid-1930s.

Notes

Introduction

1. For a discussion of the situation in the United States see Gerald Grob, "The Social History of Medicine and Diseases in America: Problems and Possibilities," *Journal of Social History*, 10, 4(Summer 1977): 391–409.
2. Thomas McKeown, *The Modern Rise of Population* (New York, 1976), 162.
3. Thomas McKeown, "A Sociological Approach to the History of Medicine," *Medical History*, 14(October 1970): 342–51.
4. Caroline Whitbeck, "Women and Medicine: An Introduction," *Journal of Medicine and Philosophy*, 7, 2(May 1982): 120.
5. Eliot Freidson, *The Profession of Medicine* (New York, 1972), 318.
6. Janice Dickin McGinnis, "From Health to Public Welfare, 1919–1945," Ph.D. thesis (University of Alberta, 1980), 8.
7. Thomas McKeown, *Medicine in Modern Society* (New York, 1966), 21–58; McKeown, "A Sociological Approach," 346.
8. F. B. Smith, *The People's Health, 1830–1910* (London, 1979), 9.
9. David Flaherty, "Privacy and Confidentiality," *Review in American History*, (September 1980): 419.
10. Suzann Buckley, "Ladies or Midwives? Efforts to Reduce Infant and Maternal Mortality" in Linda Kealey (ed.), *A Not Unreasonable Claim: Women and Reform in Canada, 1880–1920* (Toronto, 1979), 131–50; Angus McLaren, "Birth Control and Abortion in Canada, 1870–1920," *Canadian Historical Review*, 59, 3(September 1978): 319–40; Special issue of *Ontario History*, 75, 1(March 1983) on midwifery; W. Mitchinson, "Historical Attitudes Toward Women and Childbirth," *Atlantis*, 4, 2, part 2 (1979), 57–75.
11. Tom Brown in his article "Shell Shock in the Canadian Expeditionary Force, 1914–1918: Canadian Psychiatry in the Great War," in Charles Roland (ed.), *Health, Disease and Medicine in Canadian History* (Toronto, 1984), 308–32, has traced how treatment of soldiers varied with class and rank.
12. H. E. MacDermot, *History of the Canadian Medical Association, 1867–1921* (Toronto, 1975), 1.
13. William Canniff, *The Medical Profession in Upper Canada, 1783–1850* (Toronto, 1984), 20.
14. The most recent work in this vein is Ronald Hamowy's *Canadian Medicine: A Study in Restricted Entry* (Vancouver, 1984).
15. See particularly Ivan Illich, *Limits to Medicine: Medical Nemesis: The Expropriation of Health* (London, 1976). Literature on the insane asylum particularly has been influenced by social control. See Rainer Baehre, "Victorian Psychiatry and Canadian Motherhood," *Canadian Women's Studies*, 2, 1(1980): 44–46; Cheryl Krasnick, "In Charge of the Loons: A Portrait of

the London, Ontario, Asylum for the Insane in the Nineteenth Century," *Ontario History*, 74, 3(September 1982): 138–84; W. Mitchinson, "R. M. Bucke; Asylum Superintendent," *Ontario History*, 73, 4(December 1981): 239–54; Henry Stalwick, "A History of Asylum Administration in Pre-Confederation Canada," Ph.D. thesis (University of London, 1969); T. E. Brown, "Living with God's Afflicted: A History of the Provincial Lunatic Asylum at Toronto, 1830–1911," Ph.D. thesis (Queen's University, 1982); Michael Katz, *The Social Organization of Early Industrial Capitalism* (Cambridge, 1982), 349–92.

16. McKeown, "A Sociological Approach," 350.

17. Feminist historians in the United States have been particularly vehement about the degree of medical intervention in childbirth. There is beginning to be some recognition that patients often demanded certain interventionist techniques, viewing them as the latest and safest way to ensure a successful birth. See Judith Walzer Leavitt, "Birthing and Anesthesia: The Debate Over Twilight Sleep," *Signs*, 6(Autumn 1980): 147–67 and Margarete Sandelowski *Pain, Pleasure and American Childbirth: From the Twilight Sleep to the Read Method, 1914–1960* (Westport, Conn., 1984). For an example of this turning away in Canadian literature, see David Coburn, *et al.*, "Medical Dominance in Canada in Historical Perspective: The Rise and Fall of Medicine?" *International Journal of Health Services*, 13, 3(1983): 407–32. Hamowy's *Restricted Entry* is an anomaly in this respect.

The City of Wealth and Death: Urban Mortality in Montreal 1821–1872

I would like to thank my colleagues Jean-Paul Bernard, Joanne Burgess, Louise Dechêne, and Normand Seguin for their comments on the original draft written in 1982. I also wish to acknowledge the help of Lise St-Georges for the parish registers.

1. This reflection was, at the same time, rooted in the class structure; therefore it is not surprising to find middle-class values put forward as social objectives by those doctors and reformers. For an analysis of the social and political involvement of doctors see: Claudine Pierre-Deschênes, "Santé publique et organisation de la profession médicale au Québec, 1870–1918," *Revue d'histoire l'Amérique française*, 35, 3(décembre 1981): 355–75; Martin Tétreault, "L'inégalité sociale devant la mort et la perception de la santé chez les contemporains à Montréal pendant la seconde moitié du XIXe siècle ou le discours sur la santé publique comme discours idéologique," *Nouvelles recherches québécoises*, 1, 2(1978): 59–81.

2. The major work is Terry Copp, *The Anatomy of Poverty: The Conditions of the Working Class in Montreal, 1897–1929* (Toronto, 1974). On the subject of late-nineteenth-century mortality, see Martin Tétreault, *L'état de santé des Montréalais, 1890–1914*. MA thesis, Université de Montréal, 1979.

3. Jean-Claude Perrot, *Genèse d'une ville modern. Caen au XVIIIe siècle* (Paris, 1975), Vol. II, 939. My translation.

4. E. A. Wrigley, *Société et population* (Paris, 1969), 174. Originally published in English under the title *Population and History* (London, 1969).

5. *Provincial Statutes of Lower Canada*, 6 George IV Chapter VIII, "An Act for Ascertaining the Annual Increase of the Population of the Province."

6. In the appendices of the journals of the House of Assembly. Until 1837 see *Journal of the House of Assembly of Lower Canada*, and after 1841, the *Journal of the Legislative Assembly of the Province of Canada*.

7. C. Glackmeyer, *Charte et règlements de la Cité de Montréal* (Montréal, 1865), Capitre X, "Règlement concernant les enterrements," 275–77.

8. For an evaluation for Montreal see Jean-Claude Robert, *Montréal, 1821–1871. Aspects de l'urbanisation*. Thesis for a doctorate in history, Paris, École des Hautes Études en sciences sociales/Université de Paris I, 1977, 53–75

9. Yolande Lavoie, *L'émigration des Canadiens aux États-Unis avant 1930* (Montréal, 1972), 25.

10. See the introduction to the *Census of Canada 1870–71*, Vols. I, X, and XII.

11. J. Henripin and Y. Peron, "La transition démographique de la province de Québec," H. Charbonneau (ed.) *La population du Québec: études rétrospectives* (Montréal, 1973), 26–28; F.-A. Angers et P. Allen, "Evolution de la structure des emplois au Canada," *L'Actualité économique*, 29, 1(avril/juin 1953): 78.

12. *Provincial Statutes of Lower Canada*, 5 George IV, Chapter VII.

13. P.-A. Linteau et J.-C. Robert, "Un recensement et son recenseur: le cas de Montréal en 1825," *Archives*, 8, 2(septembre 1976): 29–36.

14. As noted before, no series were found in the city archives and I have not attempted to reconstruct the series from the various papers.

15. For a good introduction to the literature, see H. Charbonneau (ed.) *La population du Québec: études rétrospectives* (Montreal, 1973), 5–22.

16. They appear in the first volume of *Annuaire statisque du Québec*, (1914): 88.

17. Fernand Ouellet, *Histoire économique et sociale du Québec, 1760–1850* (Montréal, 1966), 346, 468. Published in English under the title: *Economic and Social History of Quebec, 1760–1850* (Toronto, 1980).

18. J. Henripin et Y. Peron, "La transition démographique," 43.

19. *Census of Canada 1870–71*, Vol. V. Note that, contrary to what appears in Table III, 173–265, of the Census, figures are not for the city only but for the whole parish.

20. A. F. Weber, *The Growth of Cities in the Nineteenth Century* (1899). (Reissued, Ithaca, 1963), 318–65.

21. At this point, the causes for the peaks in the 1860s are unknown. There was a mild epidemic of scarlet fever in 1864 and in 1868 the parish priest noted that there was a heavy mortality among infants.

22. W. Kelly, "On the Medical Statistics of Lower Canada," *Transactions of the Literary and Historical Society of Quebec*, III (1833–37): 192–221.

23. "On Bills of Mortality," *The British American Journal of Medical and Physical Science* (hereafter, *Br. Amer. J. Med. & Phys. Sc.*) (15 July 1845): 109–10.

24. Kelly was careful enough to include an estimate for migrants temporarily living in the city and also for sailors and soldiers. If he had failed to do so his rates would have been higher still.

25. Even if there are still some deficiencies in the registration – for instance, in the early fifties one cemetery warden refused to file reports unless he was paid – those figures can be used to evaluate the under-registration of burials. P. P. Carpenter figured that for the period 1855–65 there were 34,687 burials (Catholic and Protestant) in the cemeteries but only 32,553 according to parish registers. This difference of 6.2 per cent is not all under-registration; part of it must have been caused by burials of out-of-towners in the city's cemeteries. But we have no way of figuring those out at the moment. Carpenter also compared the figures appearing in the census of 1861 and he found that they were lower by more than a third than the registered burials. See P. P. Carpenter, "On the Vital Statistics of Montreal," *The Canadian Naturalist and Geologist* (hereafter, *Can. Nat. & Geol.*), (1867) 3, 147.

26. A. Hall, "Observations on the Mortality of the City of Montreal, for the Year 1846," *Br. Amer. J. Med. & Phys. Sc.*, III (October 1847), 141–44.

27. P. P. Carpenter, "On the Vital Statistics of Montreal," 147.

28. P. P. Carpenter, "On Some of the Causes of the Excessive Mortality of Young Children in the City of Montreal," *Can. Nat. & Geol.*, IV (1869): 203.

29. In my estimates I made no allowance for the floating population.

30. W. Kelly, "On the Medical Statistics," 210–12, 221.

31. P. P. Carpenter, "On the Relative Value of Human Life in Different Parts of Canada," *Can. Nat. & Geol.*, (1859): 175–77.

32. This is also related to the place of the child in the family. See the classic by Philippe Ariès, *L'enfant et la vie familiale sous l'ancien régime* (Paris, 1960); and for a recent discussion, Elisabeth Badinter, *L'amour en plus. Histoire de l'amour maternel XVIIe–XXe siècles* (Paris, 1980); Jean-Louis Flandrin, *Familles* (Paris, 1976).

33. W. Kelly, "On the Medical Statistics," 220

34. Louise Dechêne et Jean-Claude Robert, "Le choléra de 1832 dans le Bas-Canada: mesure des inégalités devant la mort," dans H. Charbonneau et A. Larose (eds.) *The Great Mortalities: Methodological Studies of Demographic Crises in the Past. Les grandes mortalités: étude méthodologique des crises demographiques du passé* (Liege, 1979), 229–56.

35. This is comparable to data for eighteenth-century France and New France. See Marcel Reinhard, André Armengaud, and Jacques Dupaquier, *Histoire générale de la population mondiale* (Paris, 1968), 189–90; Jacques Henripin, *La population canadienne au début du XVIIIe siècle*, Cahiers de l'INED (Paris, 1954), 106. It is interesting to note also that infant mortality was about the same level, if not higher, in Quebec City, for the same period. André L'espérance, *La mortalité à Québec de 1771 à 1870*. Thesis MA (démographie), Montréal, Université de Montréal, 1970.

36. A. Hall, "Observations on the Mortality," 141–44.

37. George E. Fenwick, "The Medical Statistics of the City of Montreal," *Br. Amer. J. Med. & Phys. Sc.*, II (1861): 390–94, 439–42, 489–93; III (1862), 33–37.

38. P. P. Carpenter, "On Some of the Causes of the Excessive Mortality of Young Children," 195.

39. Archives du séminaire Saint-Sulpice de Montréal, dossier statistique, "Extrait des Registres des Baptêmes, Mariages et Sépultures," 16 juillet 1869. My translation.

40. On 14 January 1871, *Le Nouveau Monde* published an abstract of mortality since 1855 and mentioned that of the 56,515 deaths recorded, 40,094 or 70.9 per cent, were those of children under fifteen years of age.

41. P. P. Carpenter, "On Infantile Mortality in Large Cities," *The Year Book and Almanac of Canada for 1871, 1872, 1873 and 1874*, 171-74.

42. G. Grenier, *Quelques considérations sur les causes de la mortalité des enfants contenant des conseils aux mères sur les soins à donner aux enfants* (Montréal, 1871).

43. "They are visited once a month by the Sister in charge. There they remain until they are about two years old, when they are brought back to the Asylum and maintained and educated, until they arrive at an age capable of earning their own living at service." G. E. Fenwick, "The Medical Statistics of the City of Montreal," *Br. Amer. J. Med. & Phys. Sc.*, III (1862), 36.

44. The reports are printed in the appendices of the *Journal of the House of Assembly of Lower Canada*. They do not appear after 1837.

45. P. P. Carpenter, "On Some of the Causes of the Excessive Mortality of Young Children," 188-206.

46. Ibid., 203.

47. City of Montreal. *Rapport des officiers de santé de la cité de Montreal pour l'année 1868*, 5.

48. Not only is there uncertainty about the origins of the foundlings (Carpenter shows a little more than one-third from out of town and Fenwick argues for more than three-quarters), but also we do not have many figures. However, we can get an idea from the data of 1875. That year, if we include foundlings in the calculation, the proportion of deaths of children under one year is 45 per cent; if we do not include them, the proportion is 39 per cent. City of Montreal, *Report of the Medical Officers of Health of the City of Montreal for the Year ending 31st December 1875* (Montreal, 1876).

49. Jacques Henripin, "L'inégalité sociale devant la mort: la mortinatalité et la mortalité infantile à Montréal," *Recherches sociographiques*, 11, 1(janvier/mars 1961): 3-34.

50. P. P. Carpenter, "On Infantile Mortality in Large Cities," 172.

51. J. Henripin, "L'inégalité sociale," 32.

52. *Report of the Commission appointed by the Sanitary Board of the City councils to visit Canada, for the investigation of the epidemic cholera prevailing in Montreal and Quebec* (Philadelphia, 1832).

53. Many travellers comment on the smallness of French Canadians and one wrote, "The French Canadians, however, except for very light work, were almost useless. They have not physical strength for anything like heavy work," A. Helps, *Life and Labours of Mr. Brassey 1805-1870* (London, 1872).

54. A recent study of mortality for Paris and the Seine Department shows a

somewhat high rate of infant mortality (190 to 200 per thousand) which is lower than the Montreal figure. However, the authors point out that if the mortality of the age group one to four years can be easily linked to sanitary conditions, the mortality of infants less than one year old seems to have been caused more by poor care. Etienne Van de Walle et Samuel H. Preston, "Mortalité de l'enfance au XIXe siècle à Paris et dans le département de la Seine," *Population*, XXIX (1974): 89–108.

55. "In all ordinary cities of the old world, it is the winter which kills-off the largest number of victims: in Montreal it is exactly the reverse. Our infants can stand the extreme severity of the external cold; they seem not to be injuriously affected by being taken to church shortly after birth, with the thermometer below zero; for then nature has mercifully frozen up and covered with snow, the deadly corruptions of our yards and streets." P. P. Carpenter, "On Infantile Mortality in Large Cities," 172.

56. See Claudine Pierre-Deschênes, "Santé publique et organisation de la profession médicale au Québec, 1870–1918," *Revue d'histoire de l'Amérique française*, 35, 3(décembre 1981): 355–75.

57. The cholera epidemic is a good example. See Geoffrey Bilson, *A Darkened House. Cholera in Nineteenth-Century Canada* (Toronto, 1980).

58. There are 2,500 cholera deaths out of a total population of 34,000.

59. There were, however, some quarantine regulations. See J. J. Heagerty, *Four Centuries of Medical History in Canada*, 1, 193; Maude E. Abbott, "Medicine and Surgery in the Province of Quebec," in W. Wood, (ed.), *The Storied Province of Quebec*, II, 1121.

60. The expression is from the diary of Romuald Trudeau, nineteenth-century apothecary, Archives Nationales du Québec à Montréal, Romuald Trudeau, *Mes tablettes*, No. 11.

61. R. E. McGrew, "The First Cholera Epidemic and Social History," *Bulletin of the History of Medicine*, XXIV, (1950); 67.

62. My translation. The original read: "Les autres objets qui me paraissent en ce moment mériter le plus ton attention sont: le meurtre de nos Canadiens le 21 mai, approuvé depuis officiellement par le gouverneur; et l'envahissement de nos terres incultes par l'émigration britannique qui menace de nous chasser de notre payes et de le dépeupler de Canadiens périodiquement et chaque année par la maladie." J.-J. Lartigue à Denis-Benjamin Viger, le 22 octobre 1832, *Rapport de l'Archiviste de la Province de Québec 1942–43*, 165.

63. It was published as late as 1861 in the *Br. Amer. J. Med. & Phys. Sc.* II (1861): 60–66, 104–109.

64. Ibid. 61–62.

65. See Note 52.

66. Canada, *Sessional Papers 1867–68*, no. 3, "Report of the Medical Conference on Cholera"; U.S. Congress Papers, *The Cholera Epidemic of 1873 in the United States*, Chap. IV, "Cholera Epidemic of 1832, 1833 and 1834, in North America"; Robert Nelson, *Asiatic Cholera. Its Origin and Spread in Asia, Africa and Europe. Introduced in America through Canada* (New York, 1866).

67. My translation. The original reads "classes pauvres et malpropres et adon-

nées à l'intempérance, les classes ouvrières exposées aux grandes chaleurs et à des travaux excessifs." *La Minerve*, 18 juin 1832.

68. Louise Dechêne et Jean-Claude Robert, "Le choléra," 229–56.
69. This was done through name counts in the parish registers.
70. W. Kelly, "On the Medical Statistics."
71. See Charles G. Roland and Paul Potter, *An Annotated Bibliography of Canadian Medical Periodicals, 1826–1975*, (Toronto, 1979).
72. *Dictionary of Canadian Biography*, Vol. x.
73. Russell Lant Carpenter, *Memoirs of the Life and Work of Philip Pearsall Carpenter, B.A., London, Ph.D., New York, Chiefly Derived from his Letters* (London, 1880), second edition, 284 pages.
74. J. D. Borthwick, *History and Biographical Gazetteer of Montreal to the year 1892* (Montreal, 1892), 456.
75. *First Annual Report of the Montreal Sanitary Association.*
76. *Fifth Annual report of the Montreal Sanitary Association.*
77. E. Gagnon, "Notes on the Early History and Evolution of the Department of Health of Montreal," *Canadian Public Health Journal*, 29, 5(May 1938): 216–17.
78. One of his specialties was waterworks.
79. T. C. Keefer, "Montreal and the Ottawa," *Philosophy of Railroads* (Reissued Toronto, 1972), 85.
80. P. P. Carpenter, "On the Relative Value of Human Life in Different Parts of Canada," *Can. Nat. & Geol.*, (1859): 178.

Poor Relief and Health Care in Halifax, 1827–1849

1. Public Archives of Nova Scotia (hereafter PANS), RG1, Vol. 214 1/2C, Minutes of the Executive Council, 29 June 1827, 94.
2. PANS, RG1, Vol. 214 1/2C, Minutes of the Executive Council, 2 July 1827.
3. Nova Scotia House of Assembly, 1828, *Journals* (hereafter, *Journals*), 21 February 1828, 26. See also M. Grant, "Historical Sketches of Old Hospitals and Alms Houses in Halifax, Nova Scotia, 1749 to 1859," *Nova Scotia Medical Bulletin*, 27(June 1937): 491–512.
4. PANS, RG34-312, P10, Halifax, Minutes of Special Sessions. The doctors who took part in the investigation were S. Head, R. Hume, W. B. Almon, M. Hoffmann, W. Grigor, W. Sterling, J. Avery, and Joseph Prescott.
5. *Acadian Recorder*, 29 May 1831, 4 June 1831. The dispensary vaccinated 461 children. For a discussion of vaccination practices in England see C. W. Dixon, *Smallpox* (London, 1962), 282–95.
6. R. J. Morris, *Cholera, 1832: The Social Response to an Epidemic* (New York, 1976), 81–83; F. B. Smith, *The People's Health, 1830–1910* (New York, 1979), 65–69, 316–23; Dixon, *Smallpox*, 344–45.
7. PANS, RG1, Vol. 214 1/2C, Minutes of the Executive Council, 21 December 1827, 109–11; *Journals*, 11 February 1828, 20 and 22 February 1828, 227.
8. *Journals*, 13 February 1832, 170–71 and 11 April 1832, 303. An account for hospital expenses of £83/17/0 was also submitted. For one reference to a scale of fees see *Novascotian*, 22 August 1833, "Fair Play" to the editor. The

scale in Yarmouth was 5/- for a visit to a residence, travel costs under five miles were 5/-, and over five miles 1/- per mile. Medicines were an additional charge.

9. *Journals*, 17 March 1829, 457; *Journals*, 11 March 1830, 654; *Journals*, 18 December 1830, 73; PANS, RG5, Vol. xcii, Petition of T. E. Jeans, Health Officer, Sydney, 1831.

10. Paul Starr, *The Social Transformation of American Medicine*, (New York, 1982), 60–78.

11. For a discussion of attitudes toward the poor see Judith Fingard, "The Relief of the Unemployed: The Poor in Saint John, Halifax and St. John's, 1815–1860," *Acadiensis*, v, 1(Autumn 1975); 32–53, and G. E. Hart, "The Halifax Poor Man's Friend Society, 1820–27, An Early Social Experiment," *Canadian Historical Review*, xxxiv, 2(June 1953): 109–24.

12. PANS, RG25, Series C, Vol. v, Minutes of the Commissioners of the Poor, 7 May 1831.

13. In 1830 there were 267 men, 106 women, and 109 children admitted as transients compared with 59 men, 90 women, and 111 children from the town. Twenty of the inmates were classified as lunatics. PANS, RG25, Series C, Vol. v, Return of Persons, 1 January 1830 to 7 November 1830.

14. *Journals*, 29 December 1831, 90, and Appendix No. 29; *Novascotian*, 11 January 1832, 18 January 1832, "Christopher Crabtree" to the editor.

15. *Novascotian*, 27 July 1831. For information on dispensaries see Michael M. Davis, *Clinics, Hospitals and Health Centers* (New York, 1927): Michael M. Davis and Andrew W. Warner, *Dispensaries: Their Management and Development* (New York, 1918); Charles Rosenberg, "Social Class and Medical Care in Nineteenth-Century America: The Rise and Fall of the Dispensary," *Journal of the History of Medicine and Other Sciences*, xxix (January 1974): 32–54; Smith, *The People's Health, 1830–1910*, 32–33.

16. In 1832, two-thirds of the 2,612 admitted to the dispensary were transients, mostly Irish. PANS, RG5, Series P, Vol. lxxx, Petition of Sterling and Grigor, 1833.

17. *Novascotian*, 5 April 1832, Synoptic Debates of the Assembly, 1-26 March 1832; *Journals*, 1832, Appendix No. 50.

18. *Novascotian*, 15 February 1832, "Anglus" to the editor. For information concerning the medical profession in Nova Scotia see A. E. Marble, "A History of Medicine in Nova Scotia, 1784–1854," *Nova Scotia Historical Society*, *Collections*, xli (1982): 73–101.

19. *Novascotian*, 22 March 1832, "A" to the editor.

20. *Novascotian*, 18 January 1832.

21. *Journals*, 29 December 1830, 90, and Appendix No. 29; PANS, RG34–312, P10, Halifax, Minutes of Special Sessions, 5 January 1831; RG34–312, P13, Halifax, Minutes of Sessions, 5 January 1831; RG34–312, P13, Halifax, Grand Jury, December Term, 1831.

22. PANS, RG1, Vol. 214 1/2C, Minutes of the Executive Council, 24 August 1831, 352–58. Dr. C. Wallace, who had also served as health officer since 1827, had resigned and had become the provincial treasurer in the place of his father.

23. PANS, RG34–312, P10, Halifax, Minutes of Special Sessions, 5 February 1832.

24. PANS, RG34–312, P13, Halifax, Minutes of Grand Jury, 12 March 1832, 19 March 1832. Support for a new hospital also came from the magistrates.

25. *Journals*, 9 April 1832, 291; 13 April 1832, 311, and Appendix No. 49. The Executive Council appointed Enos Collins, H. H. Cogswell, and Joseph Allison to investigate the subject.

26. *Novascotian*, 5 April 1832, 12 April 1832, Synoptic Debates of the Assembly, 30 March 1832.

27. Margaret Pelling, *Cholera, Fever and English Medicine 1832–1865* (Oxford, 1978), 14–33; J. C. Macdonald, "History of Quarantine in Britain During the Nineteenth Century," *Bulletin of the History of Medicine*, 19, 1(1951): 23–44; Morris, *Cholera 1832*, 136–39.

28. Ralph Chester Williams, *The United States Public Health Service, 1798–1950* (Washington, 1951), 73; Pelling, *Cholera, Fever and English Medicine* 24–30.

29. PANS, RG1, Vol. 214 1/2C, Minutes of the Executive Council, 26 June 1832, 447–81. Dr. Shoreland, surgeon of the 96th Regiment, also served on the twelve-person board. The non-medical members were George P. Lawson and Michael Tobin, who were both Commissioners of the Poor, and the Attorney-General and the Solicitor-General.

30. PANS, RG1, Vol. 214 1/2C, Minutes of the Executive Council, 31 July 1832, 493–94. Other hospitals in the city included the private hospital operated since 1813 by Dr. S. Head, the ordnance hospital, and the garrison hospital. In addition, in 1832 the navy rented a building to serve as a general hospital. Admiralty 1, Vol. 3446, Articles of Agreement, 5 September 1832; Geoffrey Bilson, *A Darkened House* (Toronto, 1980), 92–93.

31. *Novascotian*, 26 September 1832, Dr. Alexander F. Sawers to the editors.

32. *Journals*, 1833, Appendix No. 62, and PANS, RG25, Series C, Vol. II, 17 April 1833.

33. PANS, RG1, Vol. 214 1/2C, Minutes of the Executive Council, 5 September 1832, 509.

34. PANS, RG1, Vol. 214, 1/2D, 18 June 1833, 29–30. Some two hundred immigrants had been sent to Halifax in 1833 from Sydney.

35. Bilson, *A Darkened House*, 96.

36. *Novascotian*, 17 September 1834.

37. PANS, RG1, Vol. 214 1/2C, Minutes of the Executive Council, 6 September 1834, 95–96; *Novascotian*, 10 September 1834.

38. Morris, *Cholera, 1832*, 104–106

39. Charles E. Rosenberg, *The Cholera Years: The United States in 1832, 1849 and 1866* (Chicago, 1962), 33; Morris, *Cholera, 1832*, 108–17.

40. *Novascotian*, 27 August 1834.

41. PANS, RG25, Series C, Vol. V, Minutes of the Commissioners of the Poor, 9 August 1834, 102–103.

42. Ibid., 15 August 1834, 104–105; 20 August 1845, 106–107.

43. Bilson, *A Darkened House*, 98–99.

44. Public Record Office, Colonial Office, 217/156, Campbell to Spring Rice, 30 September 1834, 863–69.

45. PANS, RG1, Vol. CXLIX, Rupert D. George to Lewis M. Wilkens, 11 September 1834, 49.

46. Anthony S. Wohl, *Endangered Lives: Public Health in Victorian England* (Cambridge, Mass., 1983), 166–73.

47. PANS, RG25, Series C, Vol. V, Minutes of the Commissioners of the Poor, 7 March 1835, 115–20.

48. PANS, RG1, Vol. 214 1/2D, Minutes of the Executive Council, 7 July 1835, 152.

49. PANS, RG25, Series C, Vol. V, Minutes of the Commissioners of the Poor, 16 February 1839, 221; Pelling, *Cholera, Fever and English Medicine*, 35–43; Wohl, *Endangered Lives*, 6–7, 117–41.

50. PANS, RG25, Series C, Vol. V, Minutes of the Commissioners of the Poor, 16 November 1835, 144–45.

51. Ibid., 20 September 1837, 194.

52. PANS, RG1, Vol. 214 1/2D, Minutes of the Executive Council, 29 July 1837, 203–204. Vessels with illness on board were occasionally allowed to leave port; RG34–312, P12, Halifax, Special Sessions, 8 October 1836.

53. Nova Scotia *Statutes*, 2 Victoria, Chapter XLVI.

54. PANS, RG1, Vol. 214 1/2D, Minutes of the Executive Council, 12 June 1840, 320–21; 322–24, Memorial of John Sutherland. The government finally agreed to accept a bond of £100 to cover medical expenses.

55. Ibid., 320–21.

56. PANS, RG25, Series C, Vol. V, Minutes of the Commissioners of the Poor, 8 November 1841, 7 February 1842, 7 February 1846; RG1, Vol. 214 1/2D, Minutes of the Executive Council, 4 April 1841, 433.

57. PANS, RG25, Series C, Vol. II, M. Hoffmann, surgeon, to Rupert D. George, 2 November 1840. For a review of Hoffmann's career see K. C. Pryke, "Matthias Hoffmann," *Dictionary of Canadian Biography* (Toronto, 1985), Vol. V, 398–400.

58. PANS, RG25, Series C, Vol. II, Rupert D. George to George H. Russell, 15 January 1841.

59. PANS, RG25, Series C, Vol. II, Accounts to Waterloo Hospital, 1841; William Lawson Jr. to J. Whedden, 9 February 1842.

60. PANS, RG25, Series C, Vol. V, Minutes of the Commissioners of the Poor, 17 February 1842, 53–54; 7 April 1842, 55; 7 September 1842, 63–64; 7 December 1842, 64–65.

61. *Journals*, 1838, 354. A grant of £50 was denied in 1838, although the legislature had approved a similar amount in 1837.

62. PANS, RG25, Series C, Vol. V, Minutes of the Commissioners of the Poor, 7 December 1837, 197–200.

63. *Novascotian*, 13 August 1840.

64. *Journals*, 1830–40, Appendix No. 22.

65. *Novascotian*, 4 November 1844. See also *Nova Scotian Medical Society*, VIII, 157.

66. Nova Scotia *Statutes*, 4 Victoria, Chapter LV. The newly established city council was empowered to act as a Local Board of Health.

67. "The Medical Society of Nova Scotia," *Nova Scotia Medical Bulletin*, 6, 3(March 1927): 21–22.

68. *Journals*, 1846, Appendix No. 42. Memorial of the Medical Society of Halifax and the Commissioners of the Poor; PANS, RG5, Series P, Vol. XLIV, Misc. B, 29 January 1846.

69. PANS, RG5, Series P, Vol. XLIV, Misc. B, Petition of the Undersigned Members of the Halifax Medical Society, 1846; RG35, 102–28, A1, Halifax, Minutes of the Board of Health, 7 December 1849, 40–75; Starr, *The Social Transformation of American Medicine*, 20–21.

70. Neville Goodman, "Medical Attendance on Royalty: The Diary of Dr. Sieveking," in *Medicine and Science in the 1860s*, F. N. L. Poynter (ed.) (London, 1968), 134–36. For a brief review of the discussion concerning paternalism see Greg Marquis, "The Contours of Canadian Urban Justice, 1830–1875," *Urban History*, XV, 3 (February 1987): 269–73.

71. Judith Fingard, *Jack in Port* (Toronto, 1982), 117–26. For information on marine hospitals in the United States, see Williams, *The United States Public Health Service*.

72. Starr, *The Social Transformation of American Medicine*, 147–53.

73. Colin D. Howell, "Elite Doctors and the Development of Scientific Medicine: The Halifax Medical Establishment and 19th Century Medical Professionalism," in Charles G. Roland (ed.), *Health, Disease and Medicine: Essays in Canadian History* (Toronto, 1984), 112–13; see also his "Reform and the Monopolistic Impulse: The Professionalization of Medicine in the Maritimes," *Acadiensis*, XI 1(Autumn 1981): 3–22 and "William Grigor," *Dictionary of Canadian Biography*, VIII, 348.

74. *Novascotian*, 24 May 1847; *Acadian Recorder*, 29 May 1847; PANS, RG24, Series C, Vol. V, Minutes of the Commissioners of the Poor, May 1847, 148–50; RG7, Vol. XVI, Clarke to Rupert D. George, 7 October 1847; Vol. 214 1/2F, Minutes of the Executive Council, 28 October 1847. During a two-week period in May 1847, 870 emigrants, many of whom were ill, landed in Halifax. The city soon established a lazaretto in a damp, dirty shack in Richmond. Later this lazaretto was moved to Melville Island where it remained open until October 2. Of those admitted, 30 died.

75. PANS, RG25, Series C, Vol. V, Minutes of the Commissioners of the Poor, 7 January 1848, 16. Of those admitted in 1847, 64 were sent to Waterloo Hospital. See also *Acadian Recorder*, 19 February 1848, for Synoptic Debates of the Assembly for 16 February 1848.

76. *Novascotian*, 2 April 1849, Synoptic Reports of the Assembly, 19 March 1849; PANS, RG7, Vol. XVI, William Denison (Newport) to Ichabod Dimock, 23 February 1848.

77. PANS, RG7, Vol. XX, Dr. E. Jennings to Joseph Howe, 8 February 1849; RG35, 102–28, A1, Halifax, Minutes of the Board of Health, 8 March 1848, 3–6.

78. The Halifax Board of Health, unable to rent a house in the city, opened up a lazaretto in a house in Dartmouth, and then a few weeks later, moved to a

new site on the Dartmouth commons. This provoked a considerable outcry in Dartmouth, especially after typhus appeared in the town. The lazaretto was eventually closed and a few remaining patients moved into the Halifax poor asylum. Typhus soon broke out in the asylum and then in the city. PANS, RG1, Vol. 214 1/2F, Minutes of the Executive Council, 3 March 1848, 117; RG35, 102–28, A1, Halifax Minutes of the Board of Health, 7 April 1848, 12–14; 3 May 1848, 18; *Journals*, 8 April 1848, 186, 187, 191.

79. *Acadian Recorder*, 15 April 1848, Synoptic Reports of the Assembly, 10 April 1848.

80. PANS, RG5, Series P, Vol. XI, No. 6, Report of John Naylor to the Subscribers of the Small Pox Hospital, 21 January 1850.

81. PANS, RG35, 102–28, A1, Halifax, Minutes of the Board of Health, 7 December 1849, 40–75.

82. Dan Francis, "The Development of the Lunatic Asylum in the Maritime Provinces," *Acadiensis*, VI, 2(Spring 1977): 23–38.

83. S. E. Finer, "The Transmission of Benthamite Ideas, 1820–1856," in G. Sutherland (ed.), *Studies in the Growth of Nineteenth Century Ideas* (London 1972), 11–32; Wohl, *Endangered Lives*, 142–43; Pelling, *Cholera, Fever and English Medicine*, 10–11; Smith, *The People's Health*, 349–52.

84. One example of awareness and support for developments in England was that the Provincial Secretary, Joseph Howe, ordered a report on cholera issued by the London General Board of Health on 5 October 1848 be printed and distributed throughout the province. Furthermore, the *Novascotian* reprinted the "Report on Quarantine" also issued by the board. See *Novascotian*, 2 July 1849, 16 July 1849, 23 July 1849. For a discussion of this report see Pelling, *Cholera, Fever and English Medicine*, 63–70 and R. A. Lewis, *Edwin Chadwick and the Public Health Movement, 1823–1854* (London, 1952), 346–49.

Public Health and the "Sanitary Idea" in Toronto, 1866–1890

I would very much like to thank my University of Toronto colleague, Roger Riendeau, for his helpful criticism and expert editorial advice.

1. For a more thorough discussion of this theme see my article "Epidemics and the Environment: The Early Development of Public Health in Toronto, 1832–72," in R. A. Jarell and A. E. Roos (eds.), *Critical Issues in the History of Canadian Science, Technology and Medicine/Problemes cruciaux dans l'histoire de la science, de la technologie et de la médecine canadiennes* (Toronto, 1983), 135–51.

2. George Nader, *Cities of Canada*, Vol. II (Toronto, 1976), 198.

3. *Canadian Freeman*, 18 May 1865; *Globe*, 6 September 1865.

4. Edwin Chadwick, *Report on the Sanitary Conditions of the Labouring Population of Great Britain*, 1842, M. W. Flinn (ed.), (Edinburgh, 1965) 62–71; R. A. Lewis, *Edwin Chadwick and the Public Health Movement, 1832–1854* (London, 1952), offers a very thorough assessment and explanation of Chadwick's career as a sanitarian.

5. W. M. Frazer, *A History of English Public Health, 1834-1934* (London, 1950), 69.

6. Ibid.; see also Howard D. Kramer, "The Germ Theory and the Early Public Health Program in the United States," *Bulletin of the History of Medicine*, 22, 3(May/June 1948): 233-47; Phyllis Allen Richmond, "Some Variant Theories in Opposition to the Germ Theory of Disease," *Journal of the History of Medicine*, 9(July 1954): 290-300; Richmond, "American Attitudes Toward the Germ Theory of Disease (1860-1880)," in Gert H. Breiger (ed.), *Theory and Practice in American Medicine: Historical Studies from the Journal of the History of Medicine and Allied Sciences* (New York, 1976), 58-84; W. R. Rothstein, *American Physicians in the Nineteenth Century: From Sects to Science* (Baltimore, 1972), 261-81.

7. Although Sir Joseph Lister developed antisepsis as a means of preventing post-operative infection, the impact of his work on sanitarians in Britain, the United States, and Canada was limited because they were seeking means to prevent rather than cure on a city-wide or country-wide rather than individual scale.

8. John Eyler, *Victorian Social Medicine: The Ideas and Methods of William Farr* (Baltimore, 1979); Eyler, "Mortality Statistics and Victorian Health Policy: Program and Criticism," *Bulletin of the History of Medicine*, 50, 1(Fall 1976): 335-55.

9. Edwin Chadwick pioneered the investigative approach and his work was emulated by Lemuel Shattuck in his *Report on the Sanitary Condition of Massachusetts* (Boston, 1850), Sir John Simon in his reports to the Privy Council, and Stephen Smith, New York City's first effective Medical Officer, 1866-75. For a graphic description of the quality of life in New York City in the 1860s see S. Smith, *The City That Was* (New York, 1911), and John Duffy, *A History of Public Health in New York City*, Vol. 1 (1625-1866), Vol. 2 (1866-1966), (New York, 1968, 1974).

10. M. W. Flinn, *Public Health Reform in Britain* (London, 1968), 30-32.

11. C. Fraser Brockington, *Public Health in the Nineteenth Century* (Edinburgh, 1965), 177-84; R. J. Lambert, *Sir John Simon (1816-1904) and English Social Administration* (London, 1963) presents the most interesting discussion of the challenges of both municipal and central health officership.

12. *Globe*, 5, 6, 13, 15, 18, 23, 27 September and 6, 26 October 1865; *Leader*, 4, 5, 6 September 1865.

13. *Leader*, 4, 6 November 1865.

14. *Globe*, 7, 10 November 1865; *Leader*, 15 November 1865.

15. *Leader*, 15 November 1865.

16. *Leader*, 10 January 1866; *Globe*, 9 January 1866.

17. *Globe*, 14 February 1866.

18. Ibid.

19. *Leader*, 12 May 1866.

20. *Globe*, 14 February 1866.

21. Ibid., 15 February 1866.

22. Ibid., 3 March 1866; *Leader*, 5 March 1866.

23. During the 1849 cholera epidemic, Dr. John Snow, a London anesthetist with an interest in epidemiology, deduced that cholera was a water-borne ailment. When the disease broke out again in 1854, he informed civic authorities that if they removed the handle of the Broad Street pump in Golden Square, the disease would cease. Much to their surprise, Snow's suggestion worked. Snow had arrived at his conclusion by comparing mortality rates of those who subscribed to the Southwark and Vauxhall Waterworks with those who derived their water from the Lambeth Waterworks. By 1854, the latter company had moved its intake pipe further up the Thames and thus supplied a purer product. Since the pump in Broad Street was serviced by the former, the water it supplied was highly contaminated with cholera vibrios. Snow made his findings public in *Snow on Cholera*, intro. Wade Hampton Frost (New York, 1936; London, 1855). See also Lambert, *Sir John Simon*, 248, and Sir John Simon, *English Sanitary Institutions* (London, 1897), 262–63. Like John Snow, William Budd was engaged in independent research and, in 1854 he too concluded that cholera was water-borne. Although doctors and health officers paid more attention to the quality of water supplies as a result of the findings of Budd and Snow, the cholera vibrio was not clearly delineated until 1883. Thus, from 1854 to 1883, a variety of theories was used to explain the etiology and mode of transmission of cholera and most authorities therefore took a variety of sanitary measures to combat the disease. During the discussions in Toronto in February 1866, Alderman Harman made a direct reference to the Broad Street pump incident when he told his fellow citizens that "It was to the bad state of one well of water in London, that over 700 cases of cholera were attributed." *Globe*, 15 February 1866.

24. *Globe*, 3 March 1866.

25. Ibid.; *Leader*, 5 March 1866.

26. Ibid.

27. See Lewis, *Edwin Chadwick*, 341; Lambert, *Sir John Simon*, Chapter 10; Nancy R. Bernstein, *The First One Hundred Years: Essays on the History of the American Public Health Association* (Washington, 1972), 9–11.

28. Dr. John King had provided curative services to the city in 1834 and had been unable to obtain his promised salary of £200. Dr. George Grasett, the medical officer in 1847, died of typhus, and in 1849 citizens burned down the cholera shed which the Board of Health had erected. During the 1854 epidemic, Alderman Joseph Rowell directed the city's efforts with curative assistance from two junior staff members of the Toronto General Hospital who were given commendations and new sets of instruments for their pains. See Toronto, *Council Minutes*, 1834, 1847, 1849, 1854.

29. *Globe*, 3 March 1866; *Leader*, 5 March 1866.

30. Ibid., 15 March, 11, 12, April 1866.

31. Toronto, *Council Minutes*, 1866, Appendix, 1–15 in the section following the Health Officer's Report.

32. See Eric Jarvis, "Mid-Victorian Toronto: Panic, Policy and Public Response, 1857–1873," Ph.D. thesis (University of Western Ontario, 1978).

33. *Globe*, 11 April 1866.

34. Ibid., 16 April 1866.
35. *Leader*, 19 April 1866; see also *Leader*, 10, 13, 16 April 1866.
36. *Leader*, 9 May 1866.
37. *Leader*, 18 April 1866.
38. *Globe*, 8 May 1866; Jarvis, "Mid-Victorian Toronto," 245–52.
39. *Globe*, 3 March, 14 May 1866; William Canniff, *The Medical Profession of Upper Canada, 1783–1850* (reprint edition, Toronto, 1980), 649; *City of Toronto Directory, 1867–68* (Toronto, 1867), 452, 460.
40. Toronto, *Council Minutes*, 1866, pp. 206–209. See also *Globe*, 14 May 1866.
41. Toronto, *Council Minutes*, 1866, Appendix, 207.
42. Ibid., 208–12.
43. Jarvis, "Mid-Victorian Toronto," 255.
44. *Leader*, 25 June 1867; *Globe*, 3 July 1867.
45. Under Section 92 of the British North America Act, jurisdiction over and financing of hospitals was assigned to the provinces. Since the Sandfield Macdonald government did not make immediate provisions for continuing the provincial government grant to Toronto General, the institution found itself so short of funds that it was unable to continue to provide service after August 1, 1867. It appealed for municipal aid but Toronto's Council declined funding because of suspicions of mismanagement by the trustees. As a result, the city's health officers had to supply curative services to the indigent poor until the hospital reopened in 1868. See *Leader*, 12 March, 18, 25, June, 15 October 1867, and 17 August 1868.
46. *Globe*, 9, 16 July 1867. Aldermen Boulton and Medcalf were long-time enemies. Boulton had claimed that Medcalf engaged in profiteering when selling a scow to the city in 1863.
47. Ibid., 12, 19 May 1868; *Leader*, 22 June 1868.
48. Toronto, *Council Minutes*, 1869, Appendix, 113; *Globe*, 16 February 1869.
49. *Globe*, 2, 23 March, 16, 20, 26 April 1869; Toronto, *Council Minutes*, 1869, Appendix, 113.
50. *Leader*, 12 April 1869.
51. *Telegraph*, 5 April 1869.
52. Ibid., 7 April 1869.
53. Ibid.; *Globe*, 20 April 1869. At the stormy council meeting which the *Globe* reporter covered, Alderman Hynes charged that the health officers were exaggerating the number of smallpox cases; Alderman Manning claimed that they were frauds who had done nothing but "bury 16 cats and empty a few pails of slops into the sewers to wash away an imaginary epidemic." Alderman Medcalf charged that they were merely "electioneering agents," and Alderman Sheard felt that one good man was preferable to three (the two health officers and the jail physician). Only Alderman Dickey briefly defended them.
54. *Telegraph*, 19 April 1866.
55. Toronto, *Council Minutes*, 1869, 113–14.
56. Jarvis, "Mid-Victorian Toronto," 259–62.
57. Lambert, *Sir John Simon*, 221–416; Derek Fraser, *Power and Authority in*

the Victorian City (Oxford, 1979), 151–73. See also the most recent and comprehensive examination of public health in Britain in A. S. Wohl, *Endangered Lives: Public Health in Victorian Britain* (Cambridge, Mass., 1983).

58. Brockington, *Public Health*, 177–84; Lewis, *Edwin Chadwick*, 173, 194–95, 305.

59. Toronto, *Council Minutes*, 1868, Appendix, 10.

60. *Leader*, 23 February 1869.

61. Nader, *Cities of Canada*, 203.

62. Ontario *Statutes*, 37 Victoria, Chapter 43, 1873.

63. *The Canada Lancet*, 7(October 1874): 31–33, 9(September 1876): 13; 9(October 1876): 59; 10(October 1877); 53; 13(August 1880): 369–70; 14(September 1881): 392. John Ferguson, *The Ontario Medical Association, 1880–1930* (Toronto, 1930), 5–8.

64. *The Canada Lancet*, 15(October 1882): 33–37; John J. Heagerty, *Four Centuries of Medical History in Canada*, Vol. 1 (Toronto, 1928), 44–45.

65. Toronto, *Council Minutes,* 1871, By-law 524, "To Provide for the appointment of a Public Officer to be called The City Commissioner," 7 July 1871, 111–15.

66. *Telegraph*, 29, 30 August, 17 October, 7 November, 19 December 1871, 9 January 1872.

67. *Globe*, 16, 18, 24 January 1872; *Telegraph*, 23, 24 January, 6, 13 February 1872.

68. Special Board of Commissioners, *By-laws of the City of Toronto* (Toronto, 1870), No. 502, "A By-law relative to the Public Health of the City of Toronto," 138.

69. Toronto, *Council Minutes* 1872, 6–7, 46–47; *Telegraph*, 17 April 1872.

70. *Telegraph*, 3 April 1872.

71. *Globe*, 23, 24 January, 19 March 1872; *Telegraph*, 24 January, 13 February, 10, 11, 14 May 1872.

72. Toronto, *Council Minutes*, 1874, 40, 398; 1877, 201; 1878, 212, 264; 1879, 771.

73. *Globe*, 16, 18 January 1872; *Telegraph*, 24 January 1872.

74. Dr. Riddell was appointed as the superintendant of the smallpox hospital in 1872 and carried out his duties there until 1874 when the hospital was burned down by citizens who disliked the thought of living in such close quarters with a virulent disease. Toronto, *Council Minutes*, 27 May 1872; 12 October 1874. Riddell continued his part-time curative activities until 1883 when he asked council's permission to resign to concentrate on his private practice. *Mail*, 20 February 1883.

75. Toronto, *Council Minutes*, 29 January 1877; 18 February 1878.

76. *Toronto Daily Mail*, 10 April 1872.

77. Toronto, *Council Minutes*, 1881, Appendix, 155.

78. The *Mail* contained articles on milk adulteration on 24 May, 25 October, 4 December 1878, 7 January, 25 February, 25 March, 12 September 1879, and 17 December 1880. It dealt with meat supplies on 10 March, 12, 21, 23 November, 2, 8, 9, 15, 20, 22, 24, 31 December 1881. The water supply received extended coverage on 8 April 1878, 21, 24 June, 3 July, 6, 27

August, 3 September 1879, 28 May, 8 July 1880, 28, 29, 30 September, 16, 21 November 1881. Waste-removal controversies were discussed 16 March, 12 May, 10, 18 August 1880, 6, 7 April, and 12 May 1881.

79. Toronto, *Council Minutes*, 1879, Appendix, 772; 1880, Appendix, 761–62; 1881, Appendix, 926; 1882, Appendix, 1060; Appendix, 601.

80. Toronto, *Council Minutes*, 1880, Appendix, 762.

81. Ontario, Report of the Select Committee on Public Health, *Journal of the Legislative Assembly*, 1878, Appendix 2.

82. Ontario *Statutes*, 45 Victoria, Chapter 29, 1882.

83. Heagerty, *Four Centuries*, 44–45.

84. *News*, 6, 13, 20, 21 February 1883; see also *The Canada Lancet*, 15(February 1883): 188.

85. Toronto, *Council Minutes*, 1883, Appendix, 123–24.

86. Archives of Ontario (hereafter AO), Canniff Papers, Package 7, Envelope 2; Charles G. D. Roberts and A. L. Tunnell (eds.), *A Standard Dictionary of Canadian Biography*, Vol. 1 (Toronto, 1934), 93–94; United States National Archives, RG 94, Records of the Adjutant General's Office, 1780s–1917, Medical Officers and Physicians of All Classes, William Caniff. For Canniff's views on disease causation see his *Principles of Surgery* (Philadelphia, 1866) and an interview that he gave to the *News* on February 24, 1884. See *The Canada Lancet*, 15(April 1883): 254–55; *Canadian Practitioner*, 8(April 1883): 128 for the medical profession's reaction to Canniff's appointment.

87. Toronto, *Council Minutes*, 1883, Appendix, 536.

88. Ibid., 537; Ninth Annual Report of the Provincial Board of Health, 1890, *Ontario Sessional Papers* (hereafter OSP), No. 72, 1891, Appendix, 25.

89. *Revised Statutes of Ontario*, 1887 (Toronto, 1887), Chapter 205, 2286–93; Toronto, *Council Minutes*, 28 April 1884.

90. Medical Health Officer's *Annual Report* (hereafter MHO *Ann. Rep.*), 1886, (Toronto, 1887), 22; Ninth Annual Report of the Provincial Board of Health, 1890, OSP, No. 72, 1891, Appendix, 24; MHO *Ann. Rep.*, 1886 (Toronto, 1887), 21; MHO *Ann. Rep.*, 1887 (Toronto, 1888), 809; *News*, 7 January 1885; MHO *Ann. Rep.*, 1887 (Toronto, 1888), 11.

91. *News*, 3 December 1883; 27 February 1884; 2, 4, 5, 8, 14, 18, 26 September, 10 November, 10, 21 December 1885.

92. Ninth Annual Report of the Provincial Board of Health, OSP, No. 50, 1890, Appendix, 21–22.

93. *Globe*, 25 September, 2, 4, 6, 8 October, 3, 5 November 1886.

94. *Canadian Practitioner*, 12 (July 1887): 250.

95. *Mail*, 18 February 1881; *News*, 25 November 1884; *Canadian Practitioner*, 9(August 1884): 249.

96. *News*, 25 November 1884. The TSA was formed for the purpose of lobbying in favour of sanitation projects and its membership included doctors, architects, builders, plumbers, philanthropists, and politicians.

97. *News*, 5–8 October 1886; *Globe*, 5–8 October 1886.

98. Canniff, *The Medical Profession*, 314.

99. Sixth Annual Report of the Provincial Board of Health, 1887, OSP, No. 14,

1888, Appendix, 147–48; *News*, 25 June, 9 July, 1886; Toronto, *Council Minutes*, 1886, Appendix, 1879–81.

100. *News*, 20, 23 September 1884.

101. Desmond Morton, *Mayor Howland: The Citizens' Candidate* (Toronto, 1973), 59, 102–103.

102. LBH *Ann. Rep.*, 1887, Appendix, 39.

103. Ninth Annual Report of the Provincial Board of Health, 1890, OSP, No. 72, 1891, Appendix, 20; Heather MacDougall, "Public Health in Toronto's Municipal Politics: The Canniff Years, 1883–1890," *Bulletin of the History of Medicine*, 55, 2(Summer 1981): 186–202.

104. *News*, 30 April 1885; Fifth Annual Report of the Provincial Board of Health, 1886, OSP, No. 74, 1887, Appendix, 162–63.

105. MHO *Ann. Rep.*, 1888 (Toronto, 1889), 13; R. Wilson, *A Retrospect, Being a review of the steps taken in sanitation to transform the town of Muddy York, into the Metropolitan City of Toronto of to-day, the Queen City of the West*, (Toronto, 1934), 30; *Toronto City Directory* for 1890 (Toronto, 1890), 1519.

106. *News*, 19, 23, 24 September 1890; *Globe*, 19 September 1890; Toronto, *Council Minutes*, 1890, Appendix 1121, 1959–60, 2467–81.

Reasons for Committal to a Mid-Nineteenth-Century Ontario Insane Asylum: The Case of Toronto

I would like to thank the University of Windsor and the Hannah Institute for the History of Medicine for providing funding for this research and Barbara Craig of the Archives of Ontario for her assistance. Also thanks to Dr. S. E. D. Shortt for reading an early draft of the paper.

1. This amounted to $2.3 million for the united Canadas between 1852 and 1867. Harvey Stalwick, "A History of Asylum Administration in Pre-Confederation Canada," Ph.D. thesis (University of London, 1969), 203–204, 313.

2. Annual Report of the Inspector of Asylums, Prisons for the Province of Ontario (hereafter ARIA), 1874, Ontario Sessional Papers (hereafter OSP) No. 2, 1874 (second session), 3.

3. ARIA, 1874, OSP No. 2, 1874 (second session), 6–7.

4. T. J. W. Burgess, "A Historical Sketch of Our Canadian Institutions for the Insane," *Transactions of the Royal Society of Canada*, Section IV (1898): 4; Gifford Price, "A History of the Toronto Hospital for the Insane," MSW thesis (University of Toronto, 1950); Henry Hurd, *The Institutional Care of the Insane in the United States and Canada* (Baltimore, 1917).

5. Michel Foucault, *Madness and Civilization: A History of Insanity in the Age of Reason* (New York, 1965), 246–47.

6. David Rothman, *The Discovery of the Asylum: Social Order and Disorder in the New Republic* (New York, 1971), xviii.

7. Christopher Lasch, "Origins of the Asylum," in C. Lasch (ed.), *The World of Nations* (New York, 1974), 16–17.

8. Andrew Scull, *Museums of Madness: The Social Organization of Insanity in the 19th Century* (London, 1979), 220.

9. The literature on the asylum influenced by the social control debate is extensive. See Stanley Cohen and Andrew Scull (eds.), *Social Control and the State* (New York, 1983); K. Doerner, *Madmen and the Bourgeoisie: A Social History of Insanity and Psychiatry* (Oxford, 1981): Richard Fox, *So Far Disordered in Mind: Insanity in California, 1870-1930* (Berkeley, 1978); Richard Fox, "Beyond 'Social Control': Institutions and Disorder in Bourgeois Society," *History of Education Quarterly* 16(Summer 1976): 203-207; Gerald Grob, *Mental Institutions in America; Social Policy to 1875* (New York, 1973); Kathleen Jones, *Mental Health and Social Policy 1845-1959* (London, 1967); Michael Macdonald, *Mystical Bedlam: Madness, Anxiety and Healing in Seventeenth-Century England* (New York, 1983); W. A. Muraskin, "The Social-Control Theory in American History: A Critique," *Journal of Social History* (hereafter, *J. Soc. Hist.*) 19, 4 (1976): 559-69; Andrew Scull (ed.), *Madhouses, Mad-Doctors, Madmen: The Social History of Psychiatry in the Victorian Era* (Philadelphia, 1981); Andrew Scull, "The Domestication of Madness," *Medical History*, 27(1983): 233-48; Vieda Skultans, *English Madness: Ideas on Insanity 1580-1890* (London, 1979); Thomas Szasz, *Law, Liberty and Psychiatry: An Inquiry into the Social Uses of Mental Health Practices* (London, 1974); Nancy Tomes, *A Generous Confidence: Thomas Story Kirkbridge and the Art of Asylum-Keeping, 1840-1883* (London, 1984); John Walton, "Lunacy in the Industrial Revolution: A Study of Asylum Admissions in Lancashire, 1848-1850," *J. Soc. Hist.*, 13, 1(Fall 1979): 1-22; J. Zainaldin and P. Tyor, "Asylums and Society: An Approach to Industrial Change," *J. Soc. Hist.*, 13, 1(Fall 1979): 23-48; Thomas E. Brown, "Foucault Plus Twenty: On Writing the History of Canadian Psychiatry in the 1980s," *Canadian Bulletin of Medical History*, 2, 1(Summer 1985): 23-50; Harvey G. Simmons, "The New Marxist Orthodoxy," *Canadian Bulletin of Medical History*, 2, 1(Summer 1985): 96-114.

10. Gerald Grob, "The State Mental Hospital in Mid-Nineteenth Century America: A Social Analysis," *American Psychology*, 21(1966): 511.

11. Michael Katz, Michael Doucet, and Mark Stein, *The Social Organization of Early Industrial Capitalism* (Cambridge, Mass., 1982), 364-67.

12. Katz seems to suggest that the social control perspective is too rigid. Institutions were created to fill a real need in society and not just an imagined one. Katz, *Social Organization*, 367-68.

13. Grouping different people together in gaols was simple incarceration. Classifying them into specialized institutions was the first step towards cure.

14. See Tomes, *A Generous Confidence*; Fox, *So Far Disordered in Mind*; Constance McGovern, "The Myths of Social Control and Custodial Oppression: Patterns of Psychiatric Medicine in Late-Nineteenth-Century Institutions," *J. Soc. Hist.*, 20, 1(Fall 1986): 3-24.

15. *The Canada Lancet*, 5, 6(February 1873): 269.

16. The sources used were the Questionnaires for Patients Proposed for Admission to the Asylum; the Admission/Discharge Warrants and Histories; the

Casefiles; Discharges/Deaths files; the Casebooks; the Registers; and the General Register. Most of the casebooks are missing and none exist after 1850. The description of the insanity was usually made on the certificates of insanity filled out by committing physicians who were usually local practitioners, representing a good cross-section of the medical profession. The various committal forms contained information on the patient in the hopes that this might help identify the cause of the person's insanity. The data consisted of the usual vital statistics: name, age, sex, religion, marital status, and place of birth. The forms also asked whether the present attack of insanity was the first. Did the patient suffer from epilepsy? Was the patient suicidal or dangerous? Was there an hereditary element in the insanity? Had the health of the patient changed? Was the insanity decreasing, remaining steady, or increasing? Did the patient rave on one subject or more than one and what were these subjects? Was the insanity connected with pregnancy? Had the patient's head been injured? Before admission to the asylum had the patient undergone any treatment? Had the patient been in an asylum before? Eliciting such data not only emphasized their importance in the diagnosis of insanity but also provided information on the care and treatment the patient would need when admitted to the asylum. The forms also provided insight into the perceived symptoms of insanity and the reasons for committal.

17. Hurd, *The Institutional Care of the Insane*, IV, 121-22; J. Workman, "Operations on Insanity," *Canada Medical Journal* (hereafter, *Can. Med. J.*) 1(1864): 401.

18. Annual Report of the Medical Superintendent of the Toronto Asylum (ARMS), 1870-71, OSP No. 4, 1871-72, 124.

19. Ranier Baehre, "Joseph Workman (1805-1894) and Lunacy Reform: Humanitarian or Moral Entrepreneur?" paper presented to the annual meeting of the Canadian Historical Association, June 1980, 24.

20. Joseph Workman, "Asylums for the Chronic Insane in Upper Canada," *American Journal of Insanity*, 24(1867): 44.

21. Harvey Simmons, *From Asylum to Welfare* (Downsview, Ontario, 1982), 8. Andrew Scull has argued that by accepting the incurable, superintendents provided themselves with a ready excuse for a low cure rate. Scull, *Museums*, 189-90.

22. Joseph Workman, "Asylums for the Chronic Insane in Upper Canada," *American Journal of Insanity*, 24(1867): 44-45, 49; T. H. W. Burgess, "Presidential Address: The Insane in Canada," *Montreal Medical Journal*, 34(1905): 403, 412.

23. Joseph Workman, "Operations on Insanity," *Can. Med. J.*, 1(1864): 401.

24. ARMS, Toronto 1870-71, OSP No. 4, 1871-72, 124.

25. ARIA, 1874, OSP No. 4, 1875/76, 210. This even division was a forced one since equal numbers of beds had been set aside for each sex.

26. ARMS, Toronto 1875, OSP No. 4, 1875, 213.

27. *Can. Med. J.*, 1(1864): 406-407.

28. ARMS, Toronto 1873, OSP No. 2, 1874, 160.

29. This is especially true when the number of immigrants is considered.

30.

Patients Admitted 1841 – 30 September 1875
Counties of Residence

	Prior to This Year	This Year 1875	Total
Durham	152	3	155
Halton	108	1	109
Lincoln	140	2	142
Middlesex	100	–	100
Northumberland	143	7	150
Ontario	133	5	138
Peel	126	5	131
Simcoe	143	11	154
Wellington	176	11	187
Wentworth	141	5	146
York	357	11	368
City of Toronto	775	44	819
Hamilton	173	9	182

SOURCE: ARMS, Toronto 1875, OSP No. 4, 1875/76, 211–12. These represent the counties from which more than 100 patients came between 1841–74.

31.

Occupations of Patients in Asylum, 1841–1876*

	Men
Labourers	592
Carpenters	100
Farmers	647
Tailors	50
Shoemakers	68
Merchants	54
Clerks	79
No Occupation	83
Occupations Not Stated	203

	Women
Domestics	847
Housekeepers	190
Seamstresses	60
Spinsters	56
No Occupation	149
Wives	431
Occupations Not Stated	246

* Only those occupations which had fifty or more patients engaged in them were listed.

Total number of male patients was 2,332 and female was 2,069.

SOURCE: ARMS, Toronto 1876, OSP No. 2, 1877, 224–25.

32. ARMS, Toronto 1842, *Journal of the Legislative Assembly of the Province of Canada* (hereafter *JLA*) (1842): Appendix U.

33. *Can. Med. J.*, 1(1864): 411.

34. Baehre, "Joseph Workman and Lunacy Reform," 23.

35. ARMS, Toronto 1875, OSP No. 4, 1875/76, 212.

36. ARMS, Toronto 1867, *Journal of the Legislative Assembly of Ontario*, I, 1867–68.

37. Mania meant abnormal excitement, melancholia referred to depression, and dementia described a situation where the mind seemed almost obliterated. In the 1841–75 period, the asylum believed more than 70 per cent of the asylum's patients suffered from mania. Under the classification of mania there existed different forms, one of which was chronic. It referred to those people whose insanity was incurable and not to the type of insanity they had. However, unless the person had been insane for a long time, the chronic aspect of the insanity would not reveal itself until after committal and after moral treatment had been tried and had failed.

38. See Simmons, *From Asylum* Part I for a discussion of idiots being sent to asylums.

39. Under excitement I included singing, dancing, swearing, incoherency, and restlessness. The estimates for this category are conservative because of lack of detail in the records and because often epilepsy was seen as a sign of mania and abnormal excitement, although it was not included under excitement for the purpose of this analysis.

40. The dangerous symptoms could have disappeared once the patient was in the controlled atmosphere of the asylum and separated from the pressures and problems which had precipitated his/her insanity.

41. Hurd, *Institutional Care of the Insane*, 122.

42. Stalwick, "A History of Asylum Administration," 186–87.

43. D. Tuke and H. K. Lewis, *The Insane in the United States and Canada* (London, 1885), 210.

44. Stalwick, "A History of Asylum Administration," 199. ARMS, Toronto OSP No. 4, 1869, 49. Unfortunately, in the early period the records do not indicate how a patient was committed, that is, whether the patient entered under warrant or from the request of his/her family. Thus it is impossible to make a linkage between dangerous cases and warrant cases. Warrant procedure was also popular because superintendents had to accept warrant patients. Simmons, *From Asylum*, 40. The 1873 Act to Make Further Provisions as to the Custody of Insane Persons required three medical certificates of insanity, signed and witnessed, saying that each physician had examined the patient separately. Ontario *Statutes*, 36 Victoria, Chapter 31, 1873, 102–103.

45. Modern statistics have indicated that women are more prone to attempt suicide than are men. One study concluded that 69 per cent of attempted suicides in the United States were made by women. Phyllis Chesler, *Women and Madness* (New York, 1972), 48. Assuming that this was true also for the nineteenth century there may be several reasons why it was not reflected in asylum patients. Asylums, like that in Toronto, were built to house equal numbers of males and females and thus there may not have been enough

beds in the asylum for the female attempted suicides. Since women were less violent than men in any case, it was probably easier to control a woman with a disposition to suicide at home than it was a man and thus many females with a tendency to suicide may never have become part of asylum statistics.

46. People suffering from depression or melancholy would have been less likely to attract the attention of the authorities and would thus not be sent to the asylum through the use of warrants.

47. ARMS, Toronto 1842, *JLA*, 1842, Appendix U.

48. This computes to a rate of somewhat less than 10 per cent of the entire asylum population. ARIA, 1874, OSP No. 2, 1874 (2nd session), 11.

49. This should be remembered by social control historians who have suggested care for the insane at home as an alternative to the asylum in the nineteenth century.

50. It is possible that some of the patients were upset by asylum care and died as a consequence of it.

51. Ann B.'s death was caused by a symptom associated with tuberculosis. Since tuberculosis is often accompanied by a high fever, this may have been the source of her delusions.

52. The number of people entering the asylum after a long illness is a very conservative estimate since the records are not always accurate. Often many people suffered from recurrent mania for years but for each admission to the asylum, only the most recent attack and its duration was listed.

53. The 17 per cent is a very low estimate since it represents only those patients whose re-admissions were picked up by looking at every tenth patient.

J.B. Collip: A Forgotten Member of the Insulin Team

1. This essay draws upon material presented in more detail in my book, *The Discovery of Insulin* (Toronto: McClelland and Stewart, 1982). I am grateful to the Connaught Fund of the University of Toronto and to the Social Sciences and Humanities Research Council for financial support of this research. The most widely circulated secondary accounts of the discovery of insulin have been Lloyd Stevenson, *Sir Frederick Banting* (Toronto, 1946); Seale Harris, *Banting's Miracle* (Philadelphia, Montreal, 1946); and G. A. Wrenshall, G. Hetenyi, and W. R. Feasby, *The Story of Insulin* (Toronto, 1962). The one reconsideration of the "Banting and Best" view is Joseph H. Pratt, "A Reappraisal of Researches Leading to the Discovery of Insulin," in *Journal of the History of Medicine* (hereafter *J. Hist. Med.*) 9(1954): 281–89. It was responded to by W. R. Feasby, "The Discovery of Insulin," *J. Hist. Med.*, 13(1958): 68–84. The most balanced history of the discovery, erring only on the matter of the first clinical test, is the "Report of the Special Committee set up to present a written summary of work leading up to the discovery of insulin," *News Bulletin of the International Diabetes Federation*, 16, 2(1971), 29–40.

2. Biographical material on Collip is contained in M. L. Barr and R. J. Rossiter, "James Bertram Collip, 1892–1965," in *Biographical Memories of Fel-*

lows of the Royal Society, 19(December 1973): 235–67; R. L. Noble, "Memories of James Bertram Collip," in *Canadian Medical Association Journal* (hereafter, *CMAJ*), 93(December 1965): 1356–64; R. J. Rossiter, "James Bertram Collip," *Proceedings of the Royal Society of Canada* (1966): 73–82; D. L. Thomson, "Dr. James Bertram Collip," in *Canadian Journal of Biochemistry and Physiology*, 35(1957).

3. J. B. Collip, "Internal Secretions," *CMAJ*, 6(December 1916).

4. Academy of Medicine, Toronto, Banting Notebook; J. J. R. Macleod, "History of the Researches Leading to the Discovery of Insulin," *Bulletin of the History of Medicine*, 52, 3(Fall 1978): 295–312 (written September 1922).

5. Fisher Rare Books Library, University of Toronto, F. G. Banting papers, "The Story of Insulin," unpublished manuscript 1940 (hereafter, Banting 1940), typescript, 46; ibid., manuscript account of the discovery of insulin written in September 1922 (hereafter, Banting 1922).

6. Macleod, "History"; Banting 1922; Banting 1940.

7. Banting Papers, Insulin Notebooks, December 1922; Macleod "History"; Canadian Diabetes Association, W. R. Feasby Papers, C. H. Best, "A Report of the Discovery and the Development of the Knowledge of the Properties of Insulin" manuscript written in September 1922 (hereafter, Best 1922).

8. There are some hints in the sources that Collip believed his method of doing this predated Banting's and Best's. Whether this was so cannot be determined. Banting and Best got their first result with whole pancreas on December 11. The first date Collip is known to have been at work was December 12. He may have been at work earlier and may have made effective extracts of whole beef pancreas simultaneously with or even before Banting and Best, although the latter's notebooks suggest to me that they reached this stage on their own. For Collip's work see Note 9.

9. This and subsequent accounts of Collip's work have been pieced together from the following: Collip, "The History of the Discovery of Insulin," *Northwest Medicine*, 22(1923): 267–73; Collip, "Some Recent Advances in Endocrinology," *CMAJ*, 14(1924): 812–20; Faculty of Medicine Library, University of Western Ontario, London, Ontario, J. B. Collip papers, an undated signed statement, "The Contribution Made by J. B. Collip to the Development of Insulin While he Was in Toronto 1921–22"; Biochemistry Department, University of Western Ontario, stored Collip files, undated second page of a letter written by Collip in 1923; Collip papers privately held (by Dr. Barbara and Dr. C. J. Wyatt, Rome, Georgia), undated second page of another Collip letter written in 1923.

10. Macleod, "History"; Banting 1922; Banting 1940; Banting Papers, Insulin Notebooks, December 1922.

11. Banting 1922; Banting 1940; Macleod "History."

12. University of Alberta, H. M. Tory Papers, File 504–509, Collip to Tory, January 8, 1922.

13. Banting 1922.

14. F. G. Banting, C. H. Best, J. B. Collip, W. R. Campbell, and A. A. Fletcher, "Pancreatic Extracts in the Treatment of Diabetes Mellitus. Preliminary

Report," *CMAJ*, 12(March 1922): 141–46; Banting 1940, 52–53.

15. See, for example, Banting, *Diabetes and Insulin*, Nobel Lecture delivered at Stockholm on September 15, 1925 (Stockholm, 1925).

16. Banting, Best, Collip, Campbell, and Fletcher, "Pancreatic Extracts"; Collip, "History"; Macleod "History."

17. Macleod, "History."

18. Collip's accounts present this as an independent discovery, but if he had been reading the literature he would have seen an earlier account of the hypoglycaemic reaction by F. C. Mann and T. B. Magath.

19. Collip's various accounts discuss the development of his method and, on a close reading, its relation to Banting's and Best's. The best comparisons of the two methods are in Banting, Best, Collip, and Macleod, "The Preparation of Pancreatic Extracts containing Insulin," *Transactions of the Royal Society of Canada*, Sec. v, 1922; Collip Papers, Georgia, also Collip Papers, Special Collections Library, University of Western Ontario, Collip to Dr. C. F. Martin, November 23, 1949; Banting, Best, Collip, Campbell, and Fletcher, "Pancreatic Extracts."

20. Banting 1940, 54; Feasby Papers, C. H. Best to H. H. Dale, February 22, 1954.

21. Banting Papers, Scrapbook (Vol. 48), copy of the Connaught agreement; Macleod "History."

22. Macleod, "History"; Banting 1922; Banting 1940; Best "History"; C. H. Best and D. A. Scott, "The Preparation of Insulin," *Journal of Biological Chemistry* (hereafter, *J. Biol. Chem.*), 57, 3(October 19, 1923): 709–23.

23. Banting 1922.

24. Best, "History."

25. Banting, Best, Collip, and Macleod, "The Preparation of Pancreatic Extracts."

26. Banting Papers, 1, Banting to Lillian Hallam, March 13, 1923.

27. For the details of the struggle for honours see *The Discovery of Insulin*, Chapter 9.

28. Biochemistry Department, University of Western Ontario, stored Collip files, undated second page of a Collip letter written in 1923.

29. Calgary *Herald*, May 30, 1923; Public Archives of Canada, W. L. M. King Papers, JI,80795–6, C. A. Stuart (Chancellor of the University of Alberta) to King, June 27, 1923. For Collip's statements of his contributions see Note 9.

30. University of Toronto, records of the Insulin Committee, clippings file; Collip, "The demonstration of a hormone in plant tissue to be known as 'glucokinin,'" *Proceedings of the Society for Experimental Biology and Medicine*, 20(1923): 321–23; Collip, "Glucokinin; a new hormone present in plant tissue," *J. Biol. Chem.*, 56(1923): 513–43; Collip, "Effects of plant extracts on blood sugar," *Nature*, III(1923): 571; Collip, "Glucokinin. Second paper," *J. Biol. Chem.*, 57(1923): 65–78; Collip, "Glucokinin," *Proceedings and Transactions of the Royal Society of Canada*, 17, Sect. v, (1923): 39–43; Collip, "Glucokinin; report of work in progress," *Transactions*

of the Section on Pharmacology and Therapeutics, American Medical Association, (1923): 41–42; Collip, "Glucokinin; an apparent synthesis in the normal animal of the hypoglycaemic producing principle; animal passage of the principle," *J. Biol. Chem.*, 58(1924): 163–208.

31. Best Institute, University of Toronto, J. J. R. Macleod Papers, Macleod to H. H. Dale, May 15, 1923.
32. Records of the Insulin Committee, Patents United States file; University of Toronto Archives, Sir Robert Falconer Papers, case 81, memorandum regarding insulin royalties, January 23, 1923.
33. Macleod, "History"; Macleod, "Insulin," Lecture to the Eleventh International Physiological Congress, July 1923, *British Medical Journal*, (August 4, 1923): 165–72; Macleod, *Carbohydrate Metabolism and Insulin* (London, New York, Toronto, 1926); Macleod and W. R. Campbell, *Insulin: Its Use in the Treatment of Diabetes* (Baltimore, 1925).
34. Nobel archive, Caroline Institute, Stockholm, Nominations 1923, August Krogh to the Nobel Committee, January 31, 1922.
35. Best Institute, Macleod Papers, folder 342, Macleod to B. P. Watson, January 3, 1924.
36. Banting, "The History of Insulin," *Edinburgh Medical Journal* (The Cameron Prize Lecture), (January 1929): 1–18.
37. The most important published studies discussing the problems with Banting's and Best's experiments are Pratt, "Reappraisal," and F. Roberts, "Insulin," *British Medical Journal*, (December 16, 1922): 1193–94.
38. Best, "History."
39. Collip confused the matter somewhat by writing in his last published statement on the discovery that he had done only what any well-trained biochemist would have done. He wrote this in the context of his profound grief at the death of Banting.

From Salvarsan to Penicillin: Medical Science and VD Control in Canada

1. The two basic theories are the Columbian which posits that Columbus's men brought syphilis back with them from the New World, and the Unitarian which argues that changing social conditions, climate, and personal habits caused a yaws-like disease long prevalent in Europe to mutate. For discussion see R. S. Morton, *Venereal Diseases* (Harmondsworth, 1966), 24–28. A similar argument was current in Canada in the 1920s. See "The Origin of Syphilis," *Canadian Medical Association Journal* (hereafter *CMAJ*), 17(February 1927): 252, for speculations regarding the shape of Socrates' nose.
2. J. J. Heagerty, *Four Centuries of Medical History in Canada*, Vol. I (Toronto, 1928), 131–60.
3. See Susan Sontag's angry essay, *Illness as Metaphor* (New York, 1978).
4. The lay person can find a straightforward discussion of the characteristics of VD in Morton, 52–92.
5. "Venereal Prophylaxis Among the Troops," *CMAJ*, 5(March 1915): 216–19.

6. See Janice Dickin McGinnis, "From Health to Welfare. Federal Government Policies Regarding Standards of Public Health for Canadians, 1919–45," Ph.D. thesis, (University of Alberta, 1980), Ch. 1.

7. Gordon Bates, "The Venereal Disease Problem in Canada," *Canadian Public Health Journal* (hereafter *CPHJ*), 28(October 1937): 487.

8. J. G. Fitzgerald, "Ehrlich-Hata Remedy for Syphilis," *CMAJ*, 1(January 1911): 38–46.

9. For a short assessment of the place of Ehrlich in the history of chemotherapy, see J. C. Krantz, Jr., *Historical Medical Classics Involving New Drugs* (Baltimore, 1974), 51–57.

10. "The New Treatment of Syphilis," *CMAJ*, 1(January 1911): 78.

11. G. S. Strathy and G. Bates, "The Results of Treatment of Syphilis as Shown by the Wassermann Reaction," *CMAJ*, 3(January 1913): 34.

12. J. G. Adami, R. D. Campbell, and F. S. Patch, "Experiences with '606': A Preliminary Report," *CMAJ*, 1(March 1911): 221.

13. H. K. Detweiler, "The Treatment of Syphilis," *CMAJ*, 7(March 1917): 216.

14. L. W. Harrison, "The Modern Treatment of Syphilis," *CMAJ*, 7(January 1917): 32.

15. Gordon S. Mundie and R. J. Erickson, "Cerebro-Spinal Syphilis," *CMAJ*, 8(September 1918): 839; "Salvarsan in Syphilis," *CMAJ*, 10(April 1920): 374–76.

16. J. E. R. McDonagh, "Syphilis: Its Cause and Treatment," *CMAJ*, 6(October 1916): 901–909.

17. Strathy and Bates, 33.

18. Adami, Campbell, and Patch, 222; R. P. Campbell and F. A. Patch, "Salvarsan: A Year's Experience," *CMAJ*, 2(April 1912): 285; and D. E. H. Cleveland, "The Skin Manifestations of Syphilis," *CMAJ*, 22(January 1930): 58.

19. S. C. Peterson, "Latent Syphilis," *CMAJ*, 32(June 1935): 658–59.

20. J. J. Mackenzie, "Notes on the New Pathology of Syphilis," *CMAJ*, 12(May 1922): 300–302.

21. R. G. Armour, "Salvarsan in the Treatment of Syphilitic Diseases of the Central Nervous System," *CMAJ*, 3(May 1913): 366.

22. He did, however, admit to being a little out of breath. Campbell and Patch, 282.

23. G. Bates, G. S. Strathy, and G. S. McVicar, "The Treatment of Tabes Dorsalis and General Paresis with Salvarsan," *CMAJ*, 4(March 1914): 197.

24. Mundie and Erickson, 824.

25. Adami, Campbell, and Patch, 217 and "The New Treatment of Syphilis," 76.

26. "The Administration of Arsphenamine," *CMAJ*, 11(June 1921): 462.

27. G. Bates, "Venereal Diseases from the Preventive Aspects," *CMAJ*, 9(April 1919): 313.

28. "Recent Investigations on the Clinical Use of Arsenic," *CMAJ*, 13(March 1923): 192.

29. F. Kalz, "Treatment Centres in the Control of Syphilis," *CMAJ*, 47(October 1942): 355.

30. See, for example, the series of articles by Pearl Stiver collected under the

general title "Public Health Nursing in the Control of Syphilis and Gonor-rhea," *CPHJ*, 37(April 1946): 143–45, (May 1946): 205–206, (June 1946): 249–50, (July 1946): 292–93, and (August 1946): 332–33.

31. See Suzann Buckley and Janice Dickin McGinnis, "Venereal Disease and Public Health Reform in Canada," *Canadian Historical Review*, 63 (September 1982): 337–54 and Dickin McGinnis, "From Health to Welfare," Ch. 3.

32. See G. O. Scott and G. H. J. Pearson, "A Course of Treatment for Early Syphilis," *CMAJ*, 10(October 1921): 916–23; and F. Green, "Bismuth in Syphilis," *CMAJ*, 15(February 1935): 163–70 for typical courses of treatment.

33. G. S. Fenton, "The Simplicity of the Treatment of Syphilis," *CPHJ*, 29(March 1938): 110. The series outlined by Fenton for Ontario was typical for the rest of Canada. For corroboration, see Alberta, *Annual Report of the Department of Public Health* (1929–30): 48.

34. Harrison, 38.

35. J. J. Heagerty, "Venereal Disease Control During Wartime," *CPHJ*, 30(December 1939): 567.

36. See S. H. McKee and H. D. Courtenay, "Some Cases of Syphilis of the Eye Following Treatment by Salvarsan," *CMAJ*, 6(November 1916): 996–97; G. O. Scott, "Advantages of the Early Diagnosis and Treatment of Syphilis," *CMAJ*, 8(November 1918): 1016–1017; G. S. Strathy, C. H. V. Smith, and B. Hannah, "Report of Fifty-Eight Cases of Delayed Arsenical Poisoning Following the Administration of '606' Preparations," *CMAJ*, 10(April 1920): 337.

37. Bates, "Venereal Diseases from the Preventive Aspects," 310–11.

38. Jennie E. Smillie, *Special Report on Control of Venereal Diseases* (Ottawa 1917), 4, Public Archives of Canada (hereafter PAC), Records of the National Council of Women of Canada, MG28, 125, Vol. 67.

39. W. Wilson, "Aortic Dilatation and Aneurism," *CMAJ*, 12(May 1922): 285.

40. Using an assembly-line method, two officers and two orderlies could give fifty to seventy injections of 606 in less than one hour. W. T. Lockhart and J. R. Atkinson, "Administration of Arsenic in Syphilis," *CMAJ*, 9(February 1919): 131–32. For a discussion of how effective First World War treatment was in the long term, see the disagreement expressed between F. S. Burke and M. Parks, "A Trial Study of 1,800 Cases of Syphilis Infected Twenty Years Ago," *CMAJ*, 39(August 1938): 154–58 and F. E. Cormia in a letter to the editor under the same title, *CMAJ*, 40(March 1939): 301–302.

41. H. C. Merserau, "The Modern Therapy of Syphilis," *CMAJ*, 14(June 1924): 492.

42. See PAC, Minutes of the Dominion Council of Health (hereafter DCH Minutes), MG28, 163, October 1919, 1; "The Venereal Disease Problem," *CMAJ*, 7(August 1917): 740–45; and E. J. Trow, "Report of the Special Clinic for the Treatment of Syphilis, Toronto General Hospital," *CMAJ*, 8(July 1918): 622.

43. See Janice Dickin McGinnis, "Whose Responsibility? Public Health in Canada, 1919–1945," in M. S. Staum and D. C. Larsen (eds.), *Doctors, Patients*

and Society. Power and Authority in Medical Care (Waterloo, 1981), 205–209.

44. Council of the College of Physicians and Surgeons of the Province of Alberta, *Code of Medical Ethics Approved by Alberta Medical Association and Schedule of Medical Fees* (Edmonton, 17 January 1917), 4.

45. R. R. McClenahan, "Syphilis and Gonorrhea from the Public Health Point of View," *The Canadian Medical Monthly*, 4(May 1920): 514.

46. According to W. C. Laidlaw, Alberta's representative to the Dominion Council of Health. PAC, DCH Minutes, December 1923, 17.

47. Harrison, 31.

48. Norman Viner, "Tryparsamide in Late Neurosyphilis," *CMAJ*, 14(October 1924): 978.

49. O. Wilson, "Venereal Diseases: Their Treatment and Cure," *CMAJ*, 9(February 1919): 136.

50. Detweiler (read before the Peterborough Medical Society), 213, and Scott and Pearson, "A Course of Treatment for Early Syphilis" (read before the Harvey Club, London, Ont.), 916, stated this as their objective.

51. Kells in D. R. Fletcher, C. Moorehouse, and G. W. Kells, "A Symposium on the Treatment of Neuro-syphilis with Special Reference to Malarial Therapy," *CMAJ*, 29(October 1933): 391.

52. E. C. Menzies, "The Treatment of Cerebro-Spinal Syphilis at the Verdun Protestant Hospital," *CMAJ*, 21(November 1929): 538.

53. F. E. Cormia, "Syphilophobia and Allied Anxiety States," *CMAJ*, 39(October 1938): 363.

54. PAC, DCH Minutes, June 1938 to November 1942, *passim*. Also PAC, Records of the Department of National Health and Welfare, RG29, Vols. 502–505 for the supply of arsenicals to the provinces, 1921–47.

55. See the various descriptions given in Fitzgerald, 39–41, Lockhart and Atkinson, 129–35, and A. Marin, "The Treatment of Early Syphilis," *CMAJ*, 46(April 1942): 336.

56. Among numerous references are "The Effect on the Kidney of the Modern Treatment for Syphilis," *CMAJ*, 14(June 1924): 527–28; W. Roland Kennedy, "On the Occurrence of Blood Dyscrasias Following the Administration of Neoarsphenamine," *CMAJ*, 19(October 1928): 439–42; H. Orr, "The Reactions Attending the Intravenous Use of the Arsphenamines," *CMAJ*, 32(January 1935): 19–23; H. A. Dixon, W. R. Campbell, and M. I. Hanna, "The Control of Arsphenamine Treatment by Liver Function Tests," *CMAJ*, 16(May 1926): 551–54.

57. See descriptions in Fitzgerald, 42, and W. T. Williams, "Treatment of Syphilis. Report of Special Clinic for Syphilis, Toronto General Hospital," *CMAJ*, 8(July 1918): 630–31.

58. F. E. Cormia, "Over-Treatment in Syphilis," *CMAJ*, 40(May 1939): 44.

59. See list of conditions where treatment was contra-indicated, Fitzgerald, 41–43.

60. Impression garnered from numerous articles in *CMAJ*, references in DCH Minutes and in annual health reports.

61. Fitzgerald, 45; Orr, 19.

62. N. Black, "An Unusual Reaction Following Arsenical Treatment of Syphilis," *CMAJ*, 22(May 1930): 673–74.

63. "The Administration of Arsphenamine," 462; Note from Public Health Service, Washington, D.C., *CMAJ*, 8(July 1918): 631.

64. Fitzgerald, 41.

65. See Adami, Campbell, and Patch, 220–21 for description.

66. Campbell and Patch, 278.

67. Lockhart and Atkinson, 130.

68. Fitzgerald, 40; Campbell and Patch, 278–79; Adami, Campbell, and Patch, 216.

69. Campbell and Patch, 278.

70. Lockhart and Atkinson, 130.

71. E. C. Menzies, "A Review of the Progress and Results in Forty-One Cases of Paresis and Tabo-Paresis with Tryparsamide," *CMAJ*, 20(March 1929): 243–44; G. E. Smith, "The Treatment and Management of Congenital Syphilis," *CMAJ*, 7(January 1917): 29.

72. Mersereau, 492.

73. For example, see J. W. S. McCullough, "Synopsis of the Venereal Diseases Prevention Act of Ontario," *CMAJ*, 8(September 1918): 840–41.

74. For early laments, see Campbell and Patch, 283; Detweiler, 215; Scott and Pearson, "A Course of Treatment for Early Syphilis," 917–18; and E. J. Trow, "Syphilis – Three Years' Observation," *CMAJ*, 12(July 1922): 455–58.

75. For example, Kalz, 356–57

76. For example, two sufferers of cerebro-spinal syphilis who quit because they felt so well and another two, already insane, whose friends stopped the treatments. R. W. Mann, "The Early Diagnosis and Treatments of Neuro-Syphilis," *CMAJ*, 13(August 1923): 585–86.

77. PAC, DCH Minutes, June 1923, 19.

78. Dixon, Campbell, and Hanna, 551.

79. See G. O. Scott and G. H. J. Pearson, "The use of the Wassermann Reaction in the Diagnosis of Syphilis," *CMAJ*, 13(July 1923): 501–504.

80. E. C. Menzies, "The Value of Tryparsamide as a Provocative Agent in the Diagnosis of Neurosyphilis," *CMAJ*, 19(October 1928): 427–30; G. N. Paterson-Smyth, "The Treatment of Syphilis of the Nervous System," *CMAJ*, 31(July 1934): 73.

81. W. S. Lindsay, "The Laboratory Diagnosis of Syphilis," *CMAJ*, 10(November 1920): 1011–20.

82. Trow, "Syphilis – Three Years' Observation," 456.

83. J. J. Heagerty, "Latency in Syphilis," *CMAJ*, 11(July 1921): 548–49.

84. For example, see W. E. Weeks, "Hospital Clinic on Syphilis of the Nervous System with a Case of Tabes Dorsalis," *CMAJ*, 11(January 1921): 56; J. C. Meakins, "Notes on Two Cases of Peculiar Medical Interest," *CMAJ*, 10(February 1920): 179–80; J. J. Robertson and R. C. Adams, "A Report of the Treatment of Twelve Cases of Psoriasis with Neo-Salvarsan," *CMAJ*, 27(August 1932): 177; E. A. Morgan and M. A. Cox, "Congenital Syphilis," *CMAJ*, 13(March 1923): 171; E. J. Trow, "The Management of a Clinic for

Syphilis," *The Canadian Medical Monthly*, 5(September 1920): 382.

85. For example, "The Cutaneous Manifestations of Syphilis," *CMAJ*, 8(May 1918): 417–23; A. R. Robertson, "Syphilis of the Central Nervous System: Its Early Recognition and Treatment," *CMAJ*, 10(October 1920): 924–29; H. A. Dixon, "The Clinical Diagnosis of Syphilis," *CMAJ*, 12(July 1922): 470–74.

86. Cleveland, 55.

87. Mundie and Erickson, 824.

88. Trow, "The Management of a Clinic for Syphilis," 383. Cleveland, 53.

89. Mundie and Erickson, 825; John H. Stokes and Harold A. DesBrisay, "Certain Factors in the Diagnosis of Syphilis Unrecognized in the Earlier Years of Infection," *CMAJ*, 14(August 1924): 716.

90. See, for example. D. H. Williams, "Venereal Disease Control," *CMAJ*, 49(September 1943): 211.

91. There was much discussion on this topic. See representative editorial, "Certificates of Health before Marriage," *CMAJ*, 16(August 1926): 970–71.

92. For example, see J. W. Tice, A. H. Sellars, R. H. Anderson, and W. Nichols, "Some Observations on Venereal-Disease Control in the Royal Canadian Air Force," *CPHJ*, 37(February 1946): 43–56; "Venereal Disease," *CMAJ*, 13(October 1923): 679–80.

93. See, for example, A. S. Kennedy and J. H. Lee, "The Treatment of Syphilis in the Presence of Pulmonary Tuberculosis," *CMAJ*, 30(April 1934): 403–405; E. J. Trow, "The Prevention of Congenital Syphilis," *CMAJ*, 23(July 1930): 49–50.

94. See E. C. Menzies, "Specific Treatment in Syphilis," *CMAJ*, 20(March 1929): 289–90; W. T. Williams, "Intravenous Injection of a New Mercurial in Treatment of Syphilis," *CMAJ*, 12(June 1922): 401–402.

95. C. J. Gross, "The New Bismuth Therapy of Syphilis," *CMAJ*, 13(April 1923): 265–68.

96. See G. O. Scott and G. H. J. Pearson, "The Management of the Neurosyphilitic," *CMAJ*, 14(August 1924): 724.

97. E. C. Menzies, "The Rationale of Malarial Therapy in Cerebrospinal Syphilis," *CMAJ*, 33(November 1935): 504.

98. For example, see N. Viner, "Tryparsamide in General Paresis and Other Forms of Neurosyphilis," *CMAJ*, 14(August 1924): 719–20; G. H. Stevenson, "Tryparsamide in the Treatment of General Paresis," *CMAJ*, 17(July 1927): 788–89.

99. See H. E. MacDermot, "New Knowledge of Malaria from Its Use in General Paresis," *CMAJ*, 16(August 1926): 962–63; "The Value of Malarial Therapy in Dementia Paralytica," *CMAJ*, 16(December 1926): 1520; A. D. B., "Malarial Therapy in General Paresis," *CMAJ*, 21(November 1929): 586.

100. Menzies, "The Rationale of Malarial Therapy in Cerebrospinal Syphilis," 506.

101. C. A. Porteous and E. C. Menzies, "The Therapeutic Value of Malaria Inoculation in Cerebrospinal Syphilis and General Paresis, with Some Observation upon the Use of Tryparsamide in Alliance Therewith," *CMAJ*, 18(May 1928): 536–42.

102. PAC, DCH Minutes, June 1924, five-page report.
103. W. H. Avery, "Treatment of Gonorrhea by Hyperpyrexia in General Practice," *CMAJ*, 37(November 1937): 482–85.
104. Curiously nothing appears on this subject in the *CMAJ*. The interested reader should consult Krantz, 76, or Edward Mellanby, *Recent Advances in Medical Science* (Cambridge 1939), 41–43. Evidence of Canadian use of sulfa drugs exists in Alberta, *Annual Report of the Department of Public Health* (1937), 68–69.
105. I. Weisstub, "Back to the Old Treatment of Gonorrhea," *CMAJ*, 40(April 1939): 389.
106. E. N. East and S. A. McFetridge, "Gonorrhea in the Female," *CMAJ*, 45(September 1941): 150–54.
107. "Penicillin and Gonorrhea," *CMAJ*, 53(August 1945): 184–85.
108. "Penicillin," *CMAJ*, 36(March 1945): 119–20.
109. See, for example, discussion in PAC, DCH Minutes, October 1939, Appendix A.
110. Rev. C. E. Silcox, "The Moral and Social Factors in Venereal-Disease Control," *CPHJ*, 36(December 1945): 472.
111. See Katherine McCuaig, "Tuberculosis. The Changing Concepts of Disease in Canada, 1900–1950" in C. G. Roland (ed.), *Health, Disease and Medicine. Essays in Canadian History*, (Toronto, 1982), 296–307.

The Search for the Decline of Maternal Mortality: The Place of Hospital Records

I wish to acknowledge Mrs. Ellen Kubisewsky of the Medical Audit and Research Department of the Ottawa Civic Hospital for her many courtesies. Thanks also to the directors of the hospital for their permission to use its records and to Toby Gelfand for his aid in getting that permission. I am indebted to the Hannah Institute for selecting me to be the Hannah Visiting Professor of the History of Medicine at the University of Ottawa for spring term 1981. The arrangement afforded me the opportunity to research this article. The Faculty and Institutional Research Programme of the Canadian Embassy graciously provided financial support to do the research on the Ottawa Maternity Hospital. C. Lesley Biggs allowed me to read her very helpful unpublished master's thesis, "The Response to Maternal Mortality in Ontario, 1920–1940" (University of Toronto, 1983). Finally a nod to Branwen who all too frequently provided a welcome distraction to the grim tale of maternal mortality.

1. Only Jo Oppenheimer has raised the issue for Canada. In "Childbirth In Ontario: The Transition from Home to Hospital in the Early Twentieth Century," *Ontario History*, 75(1983): 36, she speculates that the initial reduction of maternal deaths in Canada was "related to the general well-being of the individual and the community through a better understanding of 'health' and by the practice of healthful living."
2. Edward Shorter, *A History of Women's Bodies*, (New York: 1982), 100.
3. Joyce Antler and Daniel Fox, "The Movement Toward A Safe Maternity:

Physician Accountability in New York City, 1915–1940," *Bulletin of the History of Medicine*, 50(1976): 569–93.

4. *Annual Report*, Ottawa Maternity Hospital 1895. These materials are in the City of Ottawa Archives.

5. *Annual Report*, 1911.

6. *Annual Report*, 1920, 14.

7. Patient Registers, Ottawa Civic Hospital. The following material is taken from the registers and the annual reports.

8. *Annual Report*, 1921, 11–12.

9. For background about MacMurchy, see Kathleen McConnachie, "Methodology in the Study of Women in History: A Case Study of Helen Mac-Murchy, M.D.," *Ontario History*, 75(1983): 16–70.

10. Unless cited otherwise, the references in the following pages are drawn from Helen MacMurchy, "Maternal Mortality in Canada," *Canadian Medical Association Journal* (hereafter, *CMAJ*), 19(1928): 1434–37.

11. Grant Fleming, "The Future of Maternal Welfare," *CMAJ*, 29(1933): 162.

12. Dr. John Puddicombe's comments on maternal mortality statistics to Dr. H. B. Atlee, February 1935. Public Archives of Canada (hereafter, PAC), MG28, 110 (Council on Child Welfare), 53:466.

13. Fleming, "The Future," 162; Anne Wells, "Attacking Maternal and Infant Mortality in Rural Districts," *Social Welfare*, 5(1922): 32–33. Some people may also have questioned the efficacy of prenatal care.

14. "Report of the Committee on Maternal Welfare." *CMAJ*, 24(1934): 713–14.

15. Editorial, "The Tragedy of Motherhood," *Canada Lancet and Practitioner*, 77(1931): 161. MacMurchy was a member of the editorial board.

16. Canada, Department of Pensions and National Health, *Annual Report*. 1928–29, 125.

17. Eunice Dyke of the Council on Child and Family Welfare to Dame Janet Campbell, 13 August 1934, PAC, MG28, 110, 5:17.

18. Newspaper clipping (*Evening Review*) of Plumptre's report, PAC, MG, 125 (National Council of Women of Canada), 119.

19. Dr. Atlee to Puddicombe, MG28, 110, 53:466.

20. Editorial, "A Job for Supernurses," *Canadian Lancet and Practitioner*, 81(1933): 131–32.

21. Minutes of the Dominion Council of Health, Eleventh Meeting, 15–17 December 1924, PAC.

22. Newspaper clipping (*Victoria Daily Times*) "Tells Status of Midwives," Dame Janet Campbell addresses graduate nurses.

23. A. D. B. (A. D. Blackader), "On Maternity Teaching and the Obstetric Nurse," *CMAJ*, 20(1929): 648.

24. R. E. Wodehouse, "Maternal Deaths," *CMAJ*, 34(1934): 526. Wodehouse, Deputy Minister of Pensions and National Health, suggested that the high rate for maternal mortality was due in part to the use of forceps. He wanted the public to be made aware of the need for deliveries without forceps and for the profession to take action against "a few practising brothers" whose intervention at labour or before the fetus was viable was responsible for more than one-third of maternal deaths.

25. F. W. Jackson, R. D. Defries, and A. H. Sellers, "A Five-Year Survey of Maternal Mortality in Manitoba, 1928–1932," *Canadian Public Health Journal* (hereafter, *CPHJ*), 25(1934): 103–19; J. T. Phair and A. H. Sellers, "A Study of Maternal Deaths in the Province of Ontario," *CPHJ*, 23(1934): 563–79.

26. J. T. Phair, "Maternal Mortality – A General Survey," *CPHJ*, 23(1932): 179–81.

27. The statistics for national and provincial are compiled from annual reports of vital statistics, materials in files in the Council on Child Welfare, PAC, and M. C. Urquhart and K. A. H. Buckley (eds.) *Historical Statistics of Canada* (Toronto, 1965). See C. Lesley Biggs, "Class, Gender and Medical Dominance," a paper presented at the annual meeting of the Canadian Sociology and Anthropology Association, June 2, 1983, for the figures on home and hospital births in Ontario.

28. Ottawa Civic Hospital, Patient Records, Box 233/Case 2088.

29. Ibid., Box 218/Case 99873.

30. Ibid., Box 167/Case 88534; 184/91808; 223/101449; 231/1532 and 360/1351; 195/94285; 218/99728; 258/8329; 249/6021 and 338/7386; 297/7904; 277/2592; 320/2987 and 325/4706; 326/4561; 409/12894; and 404/11566.

31. Ibid., 150/82624.

32. Ibid., 241/9300.

33. Ibid., 168/86885; 187/92478; 147/81919 and 239/3518; 234/2259, 210/9716; 259/8714; 259/8726; 240/3817; 228/815; 291/6076; 352/10889; 375/4653; 391/8467; and 394/9145.

34. J. H. Ebbs, F. F. Tisdall, and W. A. Scott, "The Influence of Prenatal Diet on the Mother and Child," *Journal of Nutrition*, 22(1941): 515–26.

35. W. Peter Ward and Patricia C. Ward, "Infant Birth Weight and Nutrition In Industrializing Montreal," *American Historical Review*, 89(1984): 324–45.

36. For conjecture along these lines see W. J. Cosbie, "Maternal Mortality," *CMAJ*, 43(1940): 40.

Selected Bibliography

The following is a guide to further reading in the history of Canadian medicine. It is by no means an exhaustive list but is designed with a view to assisting those readers who are just developing their interest in this field. It reflects recent historiography and that which is accessible in non-specialized (non-medical) libraries. We have divided the items into ten thematic groupings which reflect the major areas of research concentration. *General and Reference* includes literature on source materials, historiography, collected essays, and general overviews of Canadian medical history. *Research, Professional Development, and Education* focuses on the evolution of medicine both as a science and as a profession. Of course, physicians did not and do not work in an isolated environment and the section *Medical Institutions* lists literature on the growth and history of hospitals. This is a very abbreviated list, for a wealth of literature exists on the various institutions, much of it written by those who worked for them. Abbreviated, too, is the section on *Biography* which reflects only a portion of the enormous literature on the lives of individual practitioners. We have included a cross-section of what is available to illustrate the lives not only of the famous but also of the ordinary practitioner. *Allied Health Services* was included to emphasize that the history of medicine is much wider in scope than a study of physicians and hospitals. It includes a study of various support agencies and groups such as the Red Cross and above all acknowledges the important role played by nurses in the health care system. *Disease and Health* focuses on the actual health history of Canadians and the specific diseases which have threatened them. At various times, governments, at every level, became concerned about some of the health threats and as a result developed different strategies for dealing with them. Histories of these have been included under *Public Health* which also encompasses studies of the medicare system in Canada. *Medical Specialties and Interest Groups* reflects the reality of medical specialization, a consequence of both the interests of the profession and the demands of the patients. One specialty about which historians have written a good deal is *Mental Health and Psychiatry*. This may reflect historians' beliefs that for much of our history, the care and treatment of the mentally ill and handicapped was custodial, not curative in nature, and consequently accessible to investigation by historians without expertise in medical science and technology. This latter point may also be the reason that the health of *Native Peoples* has attracted study, along with an examination of their medical lore.

General and Reference

Abbott, Maude E. *History of Medicine in the Province of Quebec*. Montreal, 1931.

"Archives and Medicine." *Archivaria*, 10 (Summer 1980): special issue.

Baldwin, Mary, ed. Compiled by M. Dunn. *A Directory of Medical Archives in Ontario*. Toronto, 1983.

Berlant, Jeffrey. *Professions and Monopoly: A Study of Medicine in the United States and Canada*. Berkeley, 1975.

Bonenfant, Yolande, *et al. Trois siècles de médecine québécoise*. Quebec City, 1970.

Bull, William Perkins. *From Medicine Man to Medical Man: A Record of a Century and a Half of Progress in Health and Sanitation as Exemplified by Developments in Peel*. Toronto, 1934.

Canniff, William. *The Medical Profession in Upper Canada, 1783-1850*. Reprinted, Toronto, 1980.

Coburn, David, Carl D'Arcy, George M. Torrance, and Peter New, eds. *Health and Canadian Society: Sociological Perspectives*. 2nd edition. Markham, 1987.

Craig, Barbara Lazenby. "The Canadian Hospital History and Archives," *Archivaria*, 21(Winter, 1985–86).

Godfrey, Charles M. *Medicine for Ontario: A History*. Belleville, Ontario, 1979.

Hamowy, Ronald. *Canadian Medicine: A Study in Restricted Entry*. Vancouver, 1984.

Heagerty, John J. *Four Centuries of Medical History in Canada: And a Sketch of the Medical History of Newfoundland*. Toronto, 1928.

_____. *The Romance of Medicine in Canada*. Toronto, 1940.

Jack, Donald, *Rogues, Rebels and Geniuses: The Story of Canadian Medicine*. Toronto, 1981.

Kerr, Robert. *History of the Medical Council of Canada*. Ottawa, 1979.

Koudelka, J. B. "Bibliography of the History of Medicine of the United States and Canada," *Bulletin of the History of Medicine*, 39, 6(1965) and 40, 1(1966).

Large, R. G. *Drums and Scalpel: From Native Healers to Physicians on the North Pacific Coast*. Vancouver, 1968.

Leblond, Sylvio. "A propos de quelques historiens de la médecine canadienne," *Canadian Bulletin of Medical History*, 3, 2(Winter 1986).

Lea, R. Gordon. *History of the Practice of Medicine in Prince Edward Island*. Charlottetown, 1964.

Lewis, D. Sclater. *The Royal College of Physicians and Surgeons of Canada*. Montreal, 1962.

MacDermot, H. E. *A Bibliography of Canadian Medical Periodicals, with Annotations*. Montreal, 1934.

———. *One Hundred Years of Medicine in Canada, 1867-1967*. Toronto, 1967.

McKechnie, R. E. *Strong Medicine: History of Healing on the Northwest Coast*. Vancouver, 1972.

McNab, Elizabeth. *A Legal History of the Health Professions in Ontario: A Study for the Committee on the Healing Arts*. Toronto, 1970.

Miller, G. *Bibliography of the History of Medicine of the United States and Canada, 1939-1960*. Baltimore, 1964.

———. "The Teaching of Medical History in the United States and Canada: Report of a Field Survey," *Bulletin of the History of Medicine*, 43, 3(1969).

———. "Bibliography of the History of Medicine of the United States and Canada," *Bulletin of the History of Medicine*, 35, 6(1961) and annually to 38, 6(1964).

Mitchell, Rosslyn Brough. *Medicine in Manitoba: The Story of Its Beginnings*. Winnipeg, 1955.

Mitchinson, W. "Canadian Medical History: Diagnosis and Prognosis," *Acadiensis*, 12, 1(Autumn 1982).

Murray, D. W. G. *Medicine in the Making*. Toronto, 1960.

Roland, Charles G., ed. *Health, Disease and Medicine: Essays in Canadian History*. Toronto, 1984.

———. *Secondary Sources on the History of Canadian Medicine: A Bibliography*. Waterloo, 1984.

———. "Ontario Medical Periodicals as Mirrors of Change," *Ontario History*, LXXII, 1(March 1980).

Roland, Charles G. and Paul Potter. *An Annotated Bibliography of Canadian Medical Periodicals*. Toronto, 1979.

Rose, T. F. *From Shaman to Modern Medicine: A Century of the Healing Arts in British Columbia*. Victoria, 1972.

Seaborn, Edwin. *The March of Medicine in Western Ontario*. Toronto, 1944.

Shortt, S. E. D., ed. *Medicine in Canadian Society: Historical Perspectives*. Montreal, 1981.

———. "The New Social History of Medicine: Some Implications for Research," *Archivaria* 10(Summer 1980).

———. "Medical Professionalization: Pitfalls and Promise in the Historiography," *History of Science and Technology of Canada Bulletin*, 5, 3(September 1981).

Staum, Martin and Donald E. Larsen, eds. *Doctors, Patients and Society: Power and Authority in Medical Care*. Waterloo, 1981.

Stewart, W. B. *Medicine in New Brunswick*. Moncton, 1974.

Sturgeon, Linda-Ann *et al. Health Care in New Brunswick, 1784-1984*. Fredericton, 1984.

Swan, Robert. "The History of Medicine in Canada," *Medical History*, 12, 1(1968).

"Trois siècles de médecine québécoise." *La Société historique de Québec: Cahiers d'histoire*, No. 22 (1970).

Research, Professional Development, and Education

Beck, Boyde. "Imperialism and Professionalization: Dominion Registration and Canadian Physicians During the Boer War," *Scientia Canadensis*, VIII, 1(June 1984).

Bernier, Jacques. "L'intégration du corps médical québécois à la fin du XIXᵉ siècle," *Historical Reflections*, 10, 1(1983).

_____. "Vers un nouvel ordre médical: Les Origines de la corporation des médecins et chirurgiens du Québec," *Recherches Sociographiques*, 22, 3(1981).

_____. "La Standardisation des études médicales et la consolidation de la profession dans la deuxième moitié du XIXᵉ siècle," *Revue d'histoire de l'Amérique française*, 37, 1(1983).

_____. "Les practiciens de la sante à Québec, 1871-1921: Quelques données statistiques," *Recherches Sociographiques*, 20, 1(1979).

_____. "Francois Blanchet et le mouvement reformiste en médecine au debut du XIXᵉ siècle," *Revue d'histoire de l'Amérique française*, 34, 2(1980).

Bliss, M. *The Discovery of Insulin*. Toronto, 1982.

_____. "Banting's, Best's and Collip's Accounts of the Discovery of Insulin," *Bulletin of the History of Medicine*, 56, 4(1982).

_____. "The Discovery of Insulin: How It Really Happened." In *Insulin, Its Receptor and Diabetes*, edited by Morley Hollenberg. New York, 1984.

_____. *Banting: A Biography*. Toronto, 1984.

Bois, Pierre. "Les débuts de l'enseignement de la médecine en français à Montréal: L'Ecole de médecine Victoria," *Canadian Bulletin of Medical History*, 2, 1(Summer 1985).

Boissonnault, Charles-Marie. *Histoire de la faculté de médecine de Laval: Contribution à l'histoire de la médecine au Canada français*. Quebec

City, 1954.

Clute, Kenneth F. *The General Practitioner*. Toronto, 1963.

Coburn, David, George Torrance, and Joseph Kaufeit. "Medical Dominance in Canada in Historical Perspective: The Rise and Fall of Medicine?" *International Journal of Health Services*, 13, 3(1983).

Connor, J. T. H. "Medical Technology in Victorian Canada," *Canadian Bulletin of Medical History*, 3, 1(Summer 1986).

———. "The Adoption and Effects of X-Rays in Ontario," *Ontario History*, LXXIV, 1(March 1987).

de la Cour, Lykke, and Rose Sheinin. "The Ontario Medical College for Women, 1883 to 1906: Lessons from Gender-Separation in Medical Education," *Canadian Woman Studies*, 7, 3(Fall 1986).

Dembski, Peter. "Jenny Kidd Trout and the Founding of the Women's Medical Colleges at Kingston and Toronto," *Ontario History*, LXXVII, 3(September 1985).

Douglas, John, introduction by Charles G. Roland. *Medical Topography of Upper Canada*. Canton, Mass., 1985.

Dupont, Jean-Claude, "Le forgeron-soigner au Canada français," *Canadian Bulletin of Medical History*, 1, 2(Winter 1984).

Emery, George. "Ontario's Civil Registration of Vital Statistics, 1869–1926: the Evolution of an Administrative System," *Canadian Historical Review*, 64, 4(1983).

Feather, Joan, and Vincent Matthews. "Early Medical Care in Saskatchewan," *Saskatchewan History*, 37, 2(Spring 1984).

Ferguson, John. *History of the Ontario Medical Association 1880–1930*. Toronto, 1930.

Gibson, W. C. "Frank Fairchild Westbrook (1868–1918): A Pioneer Medical Educator in Minnesota and British Columbia," *Journal of the History of Medicine*, 22, 4(1967).

Godfrey, Charles M. "The Origins of Medical Education of Women in Ontario," *Medical History*, 17, 1(January 1973).

Harris, Seale. *Banting's Miracle: The Story of the Discovery of Insulin*. Toronto, 1946.

Howell, Colin. "Reform and the Monopolistic Impulse: the Professionalization of Medicine in the Maritimes," *Acadiensis*, 11, 1(Autumn 1981).

Jarrell, Richard A. "Science Education at the University of New Brunswick in the Nineteenth Century," *Acadiensis*, 2, 2(Spring 1973).

Judek, S. "Medical Manpower in Canada," *A Study Prepared for the Royal Commission on Health Services*. Ottawa, 1964.

Kutcher, S. P. "Toronto's Metaphysicians: The Social Gospel and Medical Professionalization in Victorian Toronto," *History of Science and Technology of Canada Bulletin*, 5, 1(January 1981).

Lawrence, D. G. "Resurrection and Legislation, or Body-snatching in Relation to the Anatomy Act in the Province of Quebec," *Bulletin of the History of Medicine*, 32, 5(1958).

MacDermot, H. E. *History of the Canadian Medical Association, 1867–1921*. Toronto, 1935.

MacFarlane, J. A., *et al.* "Medical Education in Canada." *Report Prepared for the Royal Commission on Health Services*. Ottawa, 1965.

Masse, Claude. "Regard médical sur l'histoire des anciens Acadiens," *Les Cahiers de la Sociéte Historique Acadienne*, 16, 2(April/June 1985).

Naylor, C. D. "The CMA's First Code of Ethics: Medical Morality or Borrowed Ideology," *Journal of Canadian Studies*, 17, 4(Winter 1982–83).

_____. "Rural Protest and Medical Professionalism in Turn-of-the-Century Ontario," *Journal of Canadian Studies*, 21, 1(Spring 1986).

Riddell, W. R. "Popular Medicine in Upper Canada a Century Ago," *Ontario History*, xxv (1929).

Sawyer, Glen. *The First 100 Years: A History of the Ontario Medical Association*. Toronto, 1980.

Scott, John William. *The History of the Faculty of Medicine of the University of Alberta, 1913–1963*. Edmonton, 1963.

Seagull, H. N. "Introduction of the Stethoscope and Clinical Auscultation in Canada," *Journal of the History of Medicine*, 22(October 1967).

Sequin, Robert-Lionel. *La Sorcellerie au Canada français du xviiᵉ siècle*. Montreal, 1961.

Shephard, David A. E. *The Royal College of Physicians and Surgeons of Canada 1960–1980: The Pursuit of Unity*. Ottawa, 1985.

Shortt, Samuel. "Banting, Insulin and the Question of Simultaneous Discovery," *Queen's Quarterly*, 99, 2(1982).

Spragge, George W. "The Trinity Medical College," *Ontario History*, lviii, 2(June 1966).

Travill, A. A. "Early Medical Co-education and Women's Medical College Kingston, Ontario 1888–1984," *Historic Kingston*, 30(January 1982).

Turnbridge, J. E. "Separation of (the Doctor's) Residence from Workplace: A Kingston Example," *Urban History Review*, 7, 3(1979).

Medical Institutions

Allaire, M. *L'hôpital-général de Québec 1692–1764*. Montreal, 1971.

_____. "Origine sociale des religieuses de l'hôpital-général de Québec," *Revue d'histoire de l'Amérique française*, 23, 4(mars 1970).

Agnew, G. H. *Canadian Hospitals 1920–1970: A Dramatic Half-Century*. Toronto, 1974.

Angus, Margaret. *Kingston General Hospital: A Social and Institutional History*. Montreal, 1973.

Calgary General Hospital. *Calgary General Hospital, 1890-1955; Sixty-Five Years of Community Service*. Calgary, 1955.

En collaboration. *L'Hôtel-Dieu de Montréal 1642-1973*. Montreal, 1973.

Cosbie, W. G. *The Toronto General Hospital, 1919-1965: A Chronicle*. Toronto, 1975.

Craig, Barbara Lazenby, and Ronald K. MacLeod. *A Separate and Special Place - The Queen Elizabeth Hospital*. Toronto, 1984.

Doyle, M. G. *The Story of the Catholic Hospitals of Ontario*. Ottawa, 1968.

Guay, Marcel. "Les médecins dans un monde clérical : L'Hôtel-Dieu de Québec au XIXe siècle," *Canadian Bulletin of Medical History*, 1, 2 (Winter 1984).

Lewis, D. S. *Royal Victoria Hospital, 1887-1947*. Montreal, 1969.

MacDermot, H. E. *A History of Montreal General Hospital*. Montreal, 1950.

Medovy, H. *A Vision Fulfilled: The Story of the Children's Hospital of Winnipeg, 1909-73*. Winnipeg, 1979.

Montreuil, Anna B. *Three Came with Gifts: The Story of the First Hospital, the First School and the First Cloister in Canada and Their Heroic Founders*. Toronto, 1955.

Perron, Normand. *Un Siècle de vie hospitalière au Québec: Les Augustines et l'Hôtel-Dieu de Chicoutimi, 1884-1984*. Sillery, 1984.

Rousseau, François. "Hôpital et société en Nouvelle-France: l'Hôtel-Dieu de Québec à la fin du XXIIe siècle," *Revue d'histoire de l'Amérique française*, 30, 1(1977).

———. *L'oeuvre de chère en Nouvelle-France. le régime des malades à l'Hôtel-Dieu de Québec*, Quebec City, 1983.

Runnalls, John. *A Century with the St. Catharines General Hospital*. St. Catharines, 1974.

Scriver, Jessie Boyd. *The Montreal Children's Hospital: Years of Growth*. Montreal, 1979.

Shortt, S. E. D. "The Canadian Hospital in the Nineteenth Century: An Historiographic Lament," *Journal of Canadian Studies*, 18, 4(Winter 1983-84).

Sullivan, John R., and Norman R. Ball. *Growing to Serve . . . A History of Victoria Hospital, London, Ontario*. London, 1985.

Biography

Allan, Ted, and Sydney Gordon. *The Scalpel, the Sword: The Story of Dr.*

Norman Bethune. Toronto, 1971.

Angel, Barbara: *Charlotte Whitehead Ross*. Winnipeg, 1982.

Atherton, William H. *The Saintly Life of Jeanne Mance, the First Lay Nurse in North America*. St. Louis, 1945.

Benoit, Pierre. *La Vie inspirée de Jeanne Mance*. Montreal, 1945.

Bett, W. R. *Osler: The Man and the Legend*. London, 1951.

Bigelow, Wilfred. *Forceps, Fin and Feather*. Altona, Manitoba, 1969.

Buck, Ruth M. *The Doctor Rode Side-Saddle*. Toronto, 1974.

Campbell, Marjorie Freeman. *Holbrook of the San*. Toronto, 1953.

Collins, W. E. "Sir James Alexander Grant, 1831–1920: Physician and Politician," *Canadian Bulletin of Medical History*, 2, 1(Summer 1985).

Comber, W. M. *Wilfred Grenfell: The Labrador Doctor*. London, 1950.

Copland, Allan Dudley. *Livingston of the Arctic*. Ottawa, 1967.

Cormack, Barbara Villy. *The Red Cross Lady. (Mary H. Conquest, MBE)*. Edmonton, 1960.

Cushing, Harvey. *The Life of Sir William Osler*. Oxford, 1925.

Gibson, Morris. *A Doctor in the West*. Don Mills, 1983.

———. *A Doctor's Calling*. Vancouver, 1986.

Groves, Abraham. *All in a Day's Work: Leaves From a Doctor's Casebook*. Toronto, 1934.

Hacker, Carlotta. *The Indomitable Lady Doctors*. Toronto, 1974.

Hoople, Elizabeth. *Medicine Maid: The Life Story of a Canadian Pioneer*. Belleville, 1977.

Howard, R. Palmer. *The Chief: Doctor William Osler*. Canton, Mass., 1983.

Houston, C. J. and C. S. Houston. *Pioneer of Vision: The Reminiscences of T. A. Patrick, MD*. Saskatoon, 1980.

———. *Arctic Ordeal: The Journal of John Richardson, Surgeon-Naturalist with Franklin*. Montreal and Kingston, 1985.

Hunt, Frazier. *The Little Doc: The Story of Allan Roy Dafoe, Physician to the Quintuplets*. New York: 1939.

Johnston, William Victor. *Before the Age of Miracles: Memoirs of a Country Family Doctor*. Toronto, 1972.

Kelley, Thomas P. *The Fabulous Kelley: He Was King of the Medicine Men*. Toronto, 1968.

Kerr, J. Lennox. *Wilfred Grenfell: His Life and Works*. Toronto, 1959.

Lafleur-Hétu, Ruth. *Le conte de Jeanne Mance*. Montreal, 1947.

Lewis, Jefferson. *Something Hidden: A Biography of Wilder Penfield*. Toronto, 1981.

MacLeod, Wendell, *et al. Bethune, the Montreal Years: An Informal Portrait*. Toronto, 1978.

MacDermot, Hugh E. *Maude Abbott: A Memoir*. Toronto, 1941.

Oxorn, Henry. *H. B. Atlee, MD: A Biography*. Hantsport, Nova Scotia, 1983.

Penfield, Wilder. *No Man Alone: A Neurosurgeon's Life*. Boston, 1977.

Quinn, Kevin. "Banting and his Biographies," *Queen's Quarterly*, 99, 2(1982).

Ray, Arthur. "William Todd: Doctor and Trader for the Hudson's Bay Company, 1816–1851," *Prairie Forum*, 9, 1(1984).

Reimer, Mavis. *Cornelius W. Wiebe: A Beloved Physician*. Winnipeg, 1983.

Richards, R. L. "Rae of the Arctic," *Medical History*, 19, 2(1975).

Roland, Charles G. "Diary of a Canadian Country Physician: Jonathon Woolverton (1811–1883)," *Medical History*, 15, 2(1971).

Royce, Marion. *Eunice Dyke: Health Care Pioneer*. Toronto, 1983.

Shaw, Margaret Mason. *He Conquered Death: The Story of Frederick Grant Banting*. Toronto, 1946.

Shute, Evan. *Two Steps Forward: The Memoirs of Dr. Evan Shute*. Burlington, Ontario, 1984.

Shephard, David, and Andrée Lévesque, eds. *Norman Bethune: His Times and His Legacy*. Ottawa, 1982.

Smith, Dorothy B., ed. *The Reminiscences of Doctor John Sebastien Helmcken*. Vancouver, 1976.

Stevenson, Lloyd. *Sir Frederick Banting*. Toronto, 1946.

Stewart, Roderick. *Bethune*. Toronto, 1973.

Street, Margaret. *Watch-fires on the Mountain: The Life and Writings of Ethel Johns*. Toronto, 1973.

Strong-Boag, Veronica. *A Woman with a Purpose: The Diaries of Elizabeth Smith, 1872–1884*. Toronto, 1980.

Teigen, Philip. "William Osler's Historiography: A Rhetorical Analysis, *Canadian Bulletin of Medical History*, 3, 1(Summer 1986).

Thompson, Joanne Emily. "The Influence of Dr. Emily Howard Stowe on the Woman Suffrage Movement in Canada," *Ontario History*, LIV, 4(December 1962).

Tolmie, William F. *The Journals of William Fraser Tolmie, Physician and Fur Trader*. Vancouver, 1963.

Tyrem, R. *Saddle-bag Surgeon: The Story of Murrough O'Brien, MD*. Toronto, 1954.

Vipond, Mary. "A Canadian Hero of the 1920s: Dr. Frederick G. Banting," *Canadian Historical Review*, 63, 4(December 1982).

Wild, Marjorie. *Elizabeth Bagshaw*. Markham, 1985.

Willinsky, A. I. *A Doctor's Memoirs*. Toronto, 1960.

Allied Health Services

Alberta Association of Registered Nurses. *Facts for a History of Nursing in Alberta, 1864-1942*. Edmonton, 1943.

Beamish, Rahno M. *Fifty Years a Canadian Nurse*. New York, 1970.

Campbell, Marjorie Freeman. *The Hamilton General Hospital: School of Nursing, 1890-1955*. Toronto, n.d.

Copeland, Donalda McKellop. *Remember Nurse*. Toronto, 1960.

Desjardins, Edouard, *et al. History of the Nursing Profession in the Province of Quebec*. Montreal, 1971.

Gibbon, John Murray. *The Victorian Order of Nurses for Canada, 1897-1947*. Montreal, 1947.

_____. *The Leaf and the Lamp*. Ottawa, 1968.

Gibbon, John Murray, and Mary S. Mathewson. *Three Centuries of Canadian Nursing*. Toronto, 1947.

Gordon, P. H. *Fifty Years in the Canadian Red Cross*. No place name, 1969.

Gullett, D. W. *A History of Dentistry in Canada*. Toronto, 1971.

Hanna, James. *A Century of Red Blankets: History of Ontario's Ambulance Services*. Erin, Ontario, 1983.

Jackson, Harold. *The Story of the Royal Canadian Dental Corps*. Ottawa, 1956.

Keddy, Barbara A. "Private Duty Nursing Days of the 1920s and 1930s in Canada," *Canadian Woman Studies*, 7, 3(Fall 1986).

Knowles, V. *Leaving with a Red Rose. A History of the Ottawa Civic Hospital School of Nursing*. Ottawa, 1981.

Lent, D. G. *Alberta Red Cross in Peace and War, 1917-1947*. Calgary, 1947.

MacDermot, H. E. *History of the School for Nurses of the Montreal General Hospital*. Montreal, 1940.

Nesbitt, Joyce. *White Caps and Black Bands: Nursing in Newfoundland to 1934*. St. John's, 1978.

Nicholson, G. W. L. *Seventy Years of Service: A History of the Royal Canadian Army Medical Corps*. Ottawa, 1977.

_____. *The White Cross in Canada. A History of St. John Ambulance*. Montreal, 1967.

_____. *Canada's Nursing Sisters*. Toronto, 1975.

Porter, McKenzie. *To All Men: The Story of the Canadian Red Cross*. Toronto, 1960.

Raison, A. V., ed. *A Brief History of Pharmacy in Canada*. Toronto, 1967.

Spalding, Jean. *Sunrise to Sunset: The History of the Toronto East General Hospital School of Nursing*. Scarborough, 1979.

Watson, E. H. A. *History: Ontario Red Cross, 1914-1946*. Toronto, 1946.

Disease and Health

Andrews, Margaret. "Epidemic and Public Health: Influenza in Vancouver, 1918-1919," *British Columbia Studies*, 34(Summer 1977).

Baldwin, Douglas. "Smallpox Management on Prince Edward Island, 1820-1940: From Neglect to Fulfilment," *Canadian Bulletin of Medical History*, 2, 2(Winter 1985).

Bilson, Geoffrey. *A Darkened House: Cholera in 19th Century Canada*. Toronto, 1980.

_____ . "Cholera in Upper Canada 1832," *Ontario History*, LXX, 1(March 1975).

_____ . "The First Epidemic of Asiatic Cholera in Lower Canada, 1832," *Medical History*, 21, 4(1977).

_____ . "Two Cholera Ships in Halifax," *Dalhousie Review*, LIII(Autumn 1973).

Buckley, Suzann, and Janice Dickin McGinnis. "Venereal Diseases and Public Health Reform in Canada," *Canadian Historical Review*, 63, 3(1982).

Cassel, Jay. *The Secret Plague: Venereal Disease in Canada, 1838-1939*. Toronto, 1987.

Canada. Department of National Health and Welfare. *Canadian Food and Nutrition Statistics, 1935 to 1956*. Ottawa, 1959.

Craig, Barbara Lazenby. "State Medicine in Transition: Battling Smallpox in Ontario, 1882-1885," *Ontario History*, LXXV, 4(December 1983).

Dechêne, Louise, and Jean-Claude Robert. "Le choléra de 1832 dans le Bas-Canada: mesure des inégalites devant la mort," in *The Great Mortalities: Methodological Studies of Demographic Crises in the Past*, edited by H. Charbonneau and A. Larose. Liège, 1979.

Fallis, A. Murray. "Malaria in the 18th and 19th Centuries in Ontario," *Canadian Bulletin of Medical History*, 1, 2(Winter 1984).

Feather, Joan, and Vincent Matthews. "Early Medical Care in Saskatchewan," *Saskatchewan History*, 37, 2(1984).

Gale, G. L. *The Changing Years: The Story of Toronto Hospital and the Fight Against Tuberculosis*. Toronto, 1979.

Gibson, James R. "Smallpox on the Northwest Coast, 1835-1838," *British Columbia Studies*, 56(Winter 1982-83).

Godfrey, Charles M. *The Cholera Epidemics in Upper Canada, 1832-1866*. Toronto, 1968.

Innis, Mary Quayle. "The Record of an Epidemic," *Dalhousie Review*, XVI(October 1936).

Kalisch, Philip A. "Tracadie and Penikese Leprosuria: A Comparative Analysis of Societal Response to Leprosy in New Brunswick, 1844–1880, and Massachusetts, 1904–1921," *Bulletin of the History of Medicine*, 47, 5(1973).

Kennedy, Estella. "Immigrants, Cholera and the Saint John Sisters of Charity 1854–1864," *Canadian Catholic History Association. Study Sessions*, XLIV(1977).

Krasnick, Cheryl, " 'Because There Is Pain': Alcoholism, Temperance and the Victorian Physician," *Canadian Bulletin of Medical History*, 2, 1(Summer 1985).

Lewis, Jane. "The Prevention of Diphtheria in Canada and Britain 1914–1945," *Journal of Social History*, 20, 1(Fall 1986).

Lloyd, S. "The Ottawa Typhoid Epidemics of 1911 and 1912: A Case Study of Disease as a Catalyst for Urban Reform," *Urban History Review*, 8, 1(1979).

McGinnis, J. D. "A City Faces an Epidemic," *Alberta History*, 24, 4(1976).

———. "The White Plague in Calgary: Sanatorium Care in Southern Alberta," *Alberta History*, 28, 4(1980).

Moore, Percy, H. D. Kruse, and F. F. Risdall. "Nutrition in the North," *The Beaver*, 273 (March 1943).

Pettigrew, Eileen. *The Silent Enemy: Canada and the Deadly Flu of 1918*. Saskatoon, 1983.

Ray, Arthur. "Smallpox: The Epidemic of 1837–38," *The Beaver*, 306 (Autumn 1975).

Rich, E. E. "The Fur Traders: Their Drugs and Diet," *The Beaver*, 367 (Summer 1976).

Roland, Charles G. "Saturnism at Hudson's Bay: The York Factory Complaint of 1833–1836," *Canadian Bulletin of Medical History*, 1, 1(1984).

Rowles, Edith. "Bannock, Beans and Bacon: An Investigation of Pioneer Diet," *Saskatchewan History*, 5, 1(1952).

Taylor, J. H. "Fire, Disease, and Water in Ottawa: An Introduction," *Urban History Review*, 8, 1(1979).

———. "Disease, Fire, and Water in the Nineteenth Century City: A Bibliography," *Urban History Review*, 8, 1(1979).

Weaver, S. M. "Smallpox or Chickenpox: An Iroquoian Community's Reaction to Crisis, 1901–1902," *Ethno-history*, XVIII(Fall 1971).

Wherrett, George. *The Miracle of Empty Beds: A History of Tuberculosis in Canada*. Toronto, 1977.

Wilkins, Russell. *Health Status in Canada 1926–1976*. Montreal, 1980.

Wrenshall, C. A., G. Hetenyi, and W. R. Feasby. *The Story of Insulin: Forty Years of Success Against Diabetes*. London, 1962.

Public Health

Andrews, Margaret. "The Best Advertisement a City Can Have: Public Health Services in Vancouver, 1886–1888," *Urban History Review*, 12, 3(1984).

———. "The Course of Medical Opinion on State Health Insurance in British Columbia, 1919–1939," *Histoire Sociale*, 16(mai 1983).

———. "The Emergence of Bureaucracy: The Vancouver Health Department 1886–1914," *Journal of Urban History*, 12, 2(February 1986).

Angus, Margaret. "Health, Emigration and Welfare in Kingston, 1820–1840" in *Oliver Mowat's Ontario*, edited by D. Swainson. Toronto, 1972.

Badgley, Robin F., and Samuel Wolfe. *Doctor's Strike: Medical Care and Conflict in Saskatchewan*. Toronto, 1967.

Baker, Melvin. "The Development of the Office of a Permanent Medical Health Officer for St. John's, Newfoundland, 1826–1905," *History of Science and Technology of Canada Bulletin*, 7, 2(May 1983).

———. "Disease and Public Health Measures in St. John's, Newfoundland, 1832–1855," *Newfoundland Quarterly*, 78, 4(Spring 1983).

———. "The Appointment of a Permanent Medical Health Officer for St. John's, 1905," *Newfoundland Quarterly*, 79, 3(Winter 1985).

Baldwin, Douglas. "Public Health Services and Limited Prospects: Epidemic and Conflagration in Cobalt," *Ontario History*, LXXV, 4(December 1983).

———. "The Campaign Against Odors: Sanitarians and the Genesis of Public Health in Charlottetown, Prince Edward Island (1855–1900)," *Scientia Canadensis*, X, 1(Spring-Summer 1986).

Bator, P. A. "The Struggle to Raise the Lower Classes: Public Health Reform and the Problem of Poverty in Toronto, 1910 to 1921," *Journal of Canadian Studies*, 14, 1(Spring 1979).

———. "The Health Reformers versus the Common Canadian: The Controversy Over Compulsory Vaccination Against Smallpox in Toronto and Ontario, 1900–1920," *Ontario History*, LXXV, 4(December 1983).

Bilson, Geoffrey. "Science, Technology and 100 Years of Canadian Quarantine," in *Cultural Issues in the History of Canadian Science, Technology and Medicine*, edited by R. Jarrell and A. Roos. Thornhill, 1983.

Blishen, Bernard. *Doctors and Doctrines*. Toronto, 1969.

Bothwell, Robert S. "The Health of the People," in *Mackenzie King: Widening the Debate*, edited by John English and John O. Stubbs. Toronto, 1978.

Bryden, Kenneth. "How Public Medicine Came to Ontario," in *Government and Politics in Ontario*, edited by Donald MacDonald. Toronto, 1975.

Canada. Department of National Health and Welfare. *Government Expenditures on Health and Social Welfare, Canada, 1927-1959*. Ottawa, 1961.

Connor, J. T. H. "Preservatives of Health: Mineral Water Spas of Nineteenth Century Ontario," *Ontario History*, LXXV, 2(June 1983).

Copp, Terry. *Anatomy of Poverty. The Conditions of the Working Class in Montreal, 1897-1929*. Toronto, 1974.

DeFries, R. D. *The Development of Public Health in Canada*. Toronto, 1940.

Farley, Michael, Othmar Keel, and Camille Limoges. "Les commencements de l'administration montréalaise de la santé publique (1865-1885)," *History of Science and Technology of Canada Bulletin*, 6 1(January 1982).

———. "Les commencements de l'administration montréalaise de la santé publique (1865-1885) (suite)," *History of Science and Technology of Canada Bulletin*, 6, 2(May 1982).

Feather, Joan. "Public Health at the Fair," *Canadian Bulletin of Medical History*, 1, 1(Summer 1984).

———. "Horse Trading and Health Insurance: Saskatchewan and Dominion Provincial Relations, 1937-1947," *Saskatchewan History*, 39, 3(Autumn 1986).

Gaucher, D. "La formation des hygienistes à l'Université de Montréal, 1910-1975: de la santé publique a la médecine preventative," *Recherches Sociographiques* 20, 1(1979).

Goffman, Irving J. "The Political History of National Health Insurance in Canada," *Journal of Commonwealth Political Studies*, 3(July 1965).

Heeney, B. "Opposition to State Medicine and State Education: An Historical Analogy," *Queens Quarterly*, 75, 1(1968).

Kelly, A. D. "Health Insurance in New France," *Bulletin of the History of Medicine*, 28, 6(1954).

Lesemann, F., L. Huston, and M. Heap. *Services and Circuses: The Reform of Health and Social Services in Quebec*. Montreal, 1983.

Lewis, Jane. "On the Medicare Crisis," *Canadian Bulletin of Medical History*, 1, 1(Summer 1984).

Lomas, Jonathan. *Alternative Health Service: A History of the Sault Ste. Marie and District Group Health Association*. Toronto, 1984.

_____. *First and Foremost in Community Health Centres. The Centre in Sault Ste. Marie and the CHC Alternative*. Toronto, Buffalo, London, 1985.

McCuaig, Katherine. "From Social Reform to Social Service. The Changing Role of Volunteers: The Anti-tuberculosis Campaign, 1900–1930," *Canadian Historical Review*, 61, 4(December 1980).

MacDougall, Heather. "Public Health in Toronto's Municipal Politics: The Canniff Years," *Bulletin of the History of Medicine*, 55, 2(1981).

_____. "Epidemics and the Environment: The Early Development of Public Health Activity in Toronto, 1832–1872," in *Cultural Issues in Canadian Science, Technology and Medicine*, edited by R. Jarrell and A. Roos. Thornhill, 1983.

_____. "The Genesis of Public Health Reform in Toronto, 1869–1890," *Urban History Review*, 10, 3(1982).

MacTaggart, K. *The First Decade: The Story of the Birth of Medicine in Saskatchewan*. Ottawa, 1973.

Matters, D. L. "A Report on Health Insurance: 1919," *British Columbia Studies*, 21(Spring 1974).

Meilicke, Carl A., and Janet Storch, eds. *Perspectives in Canadian Health and Social Services Policy: History and Emergency Trends*. Ann Arbor, Michigan, 1980.

Mishler, W. and D. B. Campbell. "The Healthy State. Legislative Responsiveness to Public Health Care Needs in Canada, 1920–1970," *Comparative Politics*, 10(July 1978).

Morton, Desmond. "Military Medicine During and After the First World War – Precursor of Universal Public Health Care in Canada," *Canadian Defence Quarterly*, XIII, 1(Summer 1983).

Naylor, C. D. "Canadian Doctors and State Health Insurance, 1911–1918," *History of Science and Technology of Canada Bulletin*, 6, 3(September 1982).

_____. *Private Practice, Public Payment: Canadian Medicine and the Politics of Health Insurance, 1911–1966*. Montreal, 1986.

_____. "Canada's First Doctors' Strike: Medical Relief in Winnipeg, 1932–34," *Canadian Historical Review*, 67, 2(1986).

Nesmith, Tom. "The Early Years of Public Health: The Department of Agriculture, 1867–1918," *The Archivist*, 12, 5(September/October 1985).

O'Gallagher, Marianna. *Grosse Ile: Gateway to Canada, 1832–1937*. St. Foy, 1984.

Paddon, Anthony. "Public Health in Sub-Arctic Labrador, 1912–1978," *Canadian Journal of Public Health*, 75(September/October 1984).

Pierre-Deschênes, Claudine. "Santé publique et organisation de la profession médicale au Québec, 1870–1918," *Revue d'histoire de l'Amérique française*, 35, 3(1981).

Piva, Michael J. "The Workman's Compensation Board in Ontario," *Ontario History*, LXVII, 1(March 1975).

Reid, John G. "Health, Education, Economy: Philanthropic Foundations in the Atlantic Region in the 1920s and 1930s," *Acadiensis*, 14, 1(Autumn 1984).

Richter, L. "The Effect of Health Insurance on the Demand for Health Services," *Canadian Journal of Economics and Political Science*, X (May 1944).

Shillington, C. Howard. *The Road to Medicare in Canada*. Toronto, 1972.

Splane, Richard. *Social Welfare in Ontario 1791–1893*. Toronto, 1965.

Taylor, Malcolm. *Health Insurance and Canadian Public Policy. The Seven Decisions that Created the Canadian Health Insurance System*. Montreal, 1978.

Tollefson, E. A. *Bitter Medicine; The Saskatchewan Medicare Feud*. Saskatoon, 1963.

Tunis, Barbara. "Public Vaccination in Lower Canada, 1815–1823: Controversy and a Dilemma," *Historical Reflections*, 9, 1-2(1982).

_____. "Dr. James Latham (*c.* 1734–1799): Pioneer Inoculator in Canada," *Canadian Bulletin of Medical History*, 1, 1(1984).

Medical Specialties and Interest Groups

Bailey, Thomas. *For the Public Good: A History of the Birth Control Clinic and the Planned Parenthood Society of Hamilton*. Hamilton, 1974.

Ball, Christine. "Female Sexual Ideologies in Mid to Later Nineteenth-Century Canada," *Canadian Journal of Women and the Law*, 1, 2(1986).

Becker, A. "Radiological Pioneers in Saskatoon," *Saskatchewan History*, 36, 1(1983).

Buckley, Suzann. "Ladies or Midwives? Efforts to Reduce Infant and Maternal Mortality," in *A Not Unreasonable Claim: Women and Reform in Canada, 1880–1920*, edited by Linda Kealey. Toronto, 1979.

_____. "Efforts to Reduce Infant and Maternity Mortality in Canada Between the Two World Wars," *Atlantis*, 4(Spring 1979).

Chapman, T. L. "Drug Use in Western Canada," *Alberta History*, 24, 4(1976).

_____. "Early Eugenics Movement in Western Canada," *Alberta History*,

25, 4(1977).

Dodd, Dianne. "The Canadian Birth Control Movement on Trial, 1936–1937," *Histoire Sociale*, 16(novembre 1983).

——. "The Canadian Birth Control Movement: Two Approaches to the Dissemination of Contraceptive Technology," *Scientia Canadensis*, 9, 1(June 1985).

Golder, Zlata. "Doctors and the New Immigrants," *Canadian Ethnic Studies*, 9, 1(1977).

Kennedy, J. E. "Jane Soley Hamilton, Midwife," *Nova Scotia Historical Review*, 2, 1(1982).

Laurendeau, France. "Le médicalisation de l'accouchement," *Recherches sociographiques*, 24, 2(mai/aôut 1983).

Lévesque, Andrée. "Mères ou Malades: Les Québécoises de l'entre-deux-guerres vues pas les médecins," *Révue d'histoire de l'Amerique française*, 38, 1(1984).

Lewis, N. "Reducing Maternal Mortality in British Columbia," in *Not Just Pin Money*, edited by B. K. Latham and R. J. Pazdro. Victoria, 1984.

McLaren, Angus. "Birth Control and Abortion in Canada, 1870–1920," *Canadian Historical Review*, 59, 3(1978).

——. "The First Campaigns for Birth Control Clinics in British Columbia," *Journal of Canadian Studies*, 19, 3(Fall 1984).

McLaren, Angus, and Arlene Tigar McLaren. "Discoveries and Dissimulations: The Impact of Abortion Deaths and Maternal Mortality in British Columbia," *B.C. Studies*, 64(Winter 1984/85).

——. *The Bedroom and the State: The Changing Practices and Politics of Contraception and Abortion in Canada, 1880–1980*. Toronto, 1986.

Ontario History, LXXV, 1(March 1983). Special issue on midwifery.

Mitchinson, Wendy. "Historical Attitudes Toward Women and Childbirth," *Atlantis*, 4(Part 2)(Spring 1979).

——. "A Medical Debate in Nineteenth-Century English Canada: Ovariotomies," *Histoire Sociale*, 17(mai 1984).

——. "Medical Perceptions of Female Sexuality: A Late-Nineteenth-Century Case," *Scientia Canadensis*, 9, 1(June 1985).

——. "The Medical View of Women: The Case of Late-Nineteenth-Century Canada," *Canadian Bulletin of the History of Medicine*, 3, 2(Winter 1986).

Partington, Michael. "Paediatric Admissions to Kingston General Hospital, Kingston, Ontario, 1889–1909," *Families*, 22, 1(1983).

Simkin, R. J. "The Inadequacy of Health Care of Women," *Atlantis*, 4(Spring 1979).

Snell, James. " 'The White Life For Two': The Defence of Marriage and

Sexual Morality in Canada, 1890–1914," *Histoire Sociale*, 16(mai 1983).

Strong-Boag, Veronica, and Kathryn McPherson. "The Confinement of Women: Childbirth and Hospitalization in Vancouver, 1919–1939," *BC Studies*, 69–70(Spring-Summer 1986).

Ward, Peter, ed. *Charlotte Führer: The Mysteries of Montreal: Memoirs of a Midwife*. Vancouver, 1984.

Ward, Peter, and Patricia Ward. "Infant Birth Weight and Nutrition in Industrializing Montreal," *American Historical Review*, 89, 2(1984).

Mental Health and Psychiatry

Anglin, Betty, and June Braater, *Twenty-five Years of Growing Together: A History of the Ontario Association for the Mentally Retarded*. Toronto 1978.

Baehre, Rainer. "Victorian Psychiatry and Canadian Motherhood," *Canadian Women's Studies*, 2, 1(1980).

Baker, Melvin. "Insanity and Politics: The Establishment of a Lunatic Asylum in St. John's, Newfoundland, 1836–1853." *Newfoundland Quarterly*, 77(Summer/Fall, 1981).

_____. "Henry Stuart Stubb and the Establishment of a Lunatic Asylum in St. John's, Newfoundland, 1836–1855," *Scientia Canadensis*, VIII, 1(June 1984).

Beaudet, Céline. *Evolution de la psychiatrie anglophone au Québec: 1880–1963: le cas de l'Hôpital de Verdun*. Quebec City, 1976.

Berry, E. G. "Whitman's Canadian Friend," *Dalhousie Review*, XXIV (April 1944).

Bliss, M. "Pure Books on Avoided Subjects: Pre-Freudian Sexual Ideas in Canada," Canadian Historical Association, *Historical Papers*, 1970.

Boudreau, F. "The Quebec Psychiatric System in Transition: A Case Study," *Canadian Review of Sociology and Anthropology*, 17, 2(1980).

Brown, Thomas E. "The Origins of the Asylum in Upper Canada, 1830–1839," *Canadian Bulletin of Medical History*, 1, 1(1984).

_____. "Foucault Plus Twenty: On Writing the History of Canadian Psychiatry in the 1980s," *Canadian Bulletin of Medical History*, 2, 1(Summer 1985).

Chapman, T. "The Early Eugenics Movement in Western Canada," *Alberta History*, 25, 4(1977).

Dubé, Viateur, *et al. Bibliographie sur le prehistorie de la psychiatrie canadienne au dix-neuvieme siècle*. Trois Rivières, 1976.

Frankenburg, Frances. "The 1978 Ontario Mental Health Act in Historical

Perspective," *Journal of Canadian Science, Technology and Medicine*, VI, 3(September 1982).

Greenland, Cyril. *Charles Kirk Clarke: A Pioneer of Canadian Psychiatry*. Toronto, 1966.

———. "Services for the Mentally Retarded in Ontario 1870–1930," *Ontario History*, LIV, 4(December 1962).

Griffin, J. D., and C. Greenland. "The Asylum at Lower Fort Garry, 1874–1886," *The Beaver*, 310 (Spring 1980).

Hector, R. Ian. *History of the Ontario Hospital, Queen Street*. Toronto, 1961.

Horne, James. "R. M. Bucke: Pioneer Psychiatrist and Practical Mystic," *Ontario History*, LIX, 3(September 1967).

Kaiser, H. Archibald. "Involuntary Psychiatry in Nova Scotia: The Review Board Proposals (1979–1983) and Recent Proposals for Legislative Change," *Dalhousie Law Review*, 10(June 1986).

Krasnick, Cheryl. " 'In Charge of the Loons': A Portrait of the London, Ontario, Asylum for the Insane in the Nineteenth Century," *Ontario History*, LXXIV, 3(September 1982).

———. "The Aristocratic Vice: The Medical Treatment of Drug Addiction at the Homewood Retreat, 1883–1900," *Ontario History*, LXXV 4(December 1983).

Lauder, Brian. "Two Radicals: Richard Maurice Bucke and Lawren Harris," *Dalhousie Review*, LVI (Summer 1976).

Lavell, Alfred E. "The Beginning of Ontario Mental Hospitals," *Queen's Quarterly*, 49, 1(1942).

Lozynsky, Arten, ed. *Richard Maurice Bucke, Medical Mystic*. Detroit, 1977.

MacLennan, David. "Beyond the Asylum: Professionalization and the Mental Hygiene Movement in Canada, 1914–1928," *Canadian Bulletin of Medical History*, 4, 1(Summer 1987).

Marshall, John. *Madness: An Indictment of the Mental Health Care System in Ontario*. Toronto, 1982.

McLaren, Angus. "The Creation of a Haven for 'Human Thoroughbreds': The Sterilization of the Feeble-Minded and the Mentally Ill in British Columbia, *Canadian Historical Review*, 67, 2(1986).

Mitchinson, Wendy. "R. M. Bucke: Asylum Superintendent," *Ontario History*, LXXIII, 4(December 1981).

———. "Gynecological Operations on Insane Women, London, Ontario, 1895–1901," *Journal of Social History*, 15, 3(1982).

———. "Hysteria and Insanity in Women: A Nineteenth-Century Canadian Perspective," *Journal of Canadian Studies*, 21, 3(Fall 1986).

Paradis, A. *Essai pour une pré histoire de la psychiatrie au Canada 1500–*

1885. Montreal, 1977.

Shortt, S. E. D. "The Myth of a Canadian Boswell: Dr. R. M. Bucke and Walt Whitman," *Canadian Bulletin of Medical History*, 1, 2(Winter 1984).

_____ . *Victorian Lunacy: Richard M. Bucke and the Practice of Late 19th-Century Psychiatry*. London, 1986.

Simmons, Harvey. *From Asylum to Welfare*. Downsview, 1982.

_____ . "The New Marxist Orthodoxy," *Canadian Bulletin of Medical History*, 2, 1(Summer 1985).

Native Peoples

Barbeau, Marius. *Medicine-men in the North Pacific Coast*. National Museum of Canada, Bulletin no. 152. Ottawa, 1958.

Blumensohn, Jules. "The Fast Among North American Indians," *American Anthropologist*, xxxv (July-September, 1933).

Dailey, Robert C. "The Midewiwin, Ontario's First Medical Society," *Ontario History*, L, 3(Summer 1958).

Davenport, C. B. "The Dietaries of Primitive Peoples," *American Anthropologist*, xlvii (January-March, 1945).

Duffy, J. "Smallpox and the Indians in the American Colonies," *Bulletin of the History of Medicine*, 25, 4(1951).

Fortuine, Robert. *The Health of the Eskimos; a Bibliography, 1857-1967*. Hanover, New Hampshire, 1968.

Keehn, Pauline. *The Effect of Epidemic Diseases on the Natives of North America: An Annotated Bibliography*. London, 1978.

MacLean, John. "Blackfoot Medical Priesthood," *Alberta Historical Review*, 9(Spring 1961).

Mao, Y., H. Morrison, R. M. Semenciw, and D. T. Wigle. "Mortality on Canadian Indian Reserves 1977-1982," *Canadian Journal of Public Health*, 74 (July/August 1986).

Marcoux, Yves. "Flore laurentienne et médecine iroquoise," *L'Archiviste*, 12, 2(mars/avril 1985).

Margetts, Edward. "Canada, Indian and Eskimo Medicine with Notes on the Early History of Psychiatry Among French and British Colonists," in *World History of Psychiatry*, edited by John G. Howells. New York, 1975.

Morrison, H. I., R. M. Senemciw, Y. Mao, and D. T. Wigle. "Infant Mortality on Canadian Indian Reserves 1978-1983," *Canadian Journal of Public Health*, 77 (July/August 1986).

Romaniuk, A. "Increase in Natural Fertility During the Early Stages of Modernization: Canadian Indians Case Study," *Demography*, 18,

2(May 1981).

Smith, Harlan. *Materia Medica of the Bella Coola and Neighbouring Tribes of British Columbia*. National Museum of Canada, Bulletin no. 56, Ottawa, 1929.

Vogel, V. J. *American Indian Medicine*. Norman, Oklahoma, 1970.

Wallace, A. F. C. "Dreams and Wishes of the Soul: A Type of Psychoanalytic Theory among the Seventeenth-Century Iroquois," *American Anthropologist*, LX, (April-June 1958).

Wallis, W. G. "Medicines Used by the Micmac Indians," *American Anthropologist*, 4, 1(1922).

Watkins, Donald. "The Practice of Medicine Among the Indians," *Ontario Historical Society Report*, XXXIV(1970).

Weaver, Sally. *Medicine and Politics Among the Grand River Iroquois*. Ottawa, 1974.